1213/32
519/41
323/42

The Car That Brought You Here Still Runs

The Car That Brought

You Here Still Runs

REVISITING *the* NORTHWEST TOWNS *of* RICHARD HUGO

Frances McCue

WITH PHOTOGRAPHS *by* MARY RANDLETT

A SAMUEL AND ALTHEA STROUM BOOK

UNIVERSITY *of* WASHINGTON PRESS   *Seattle & London*

This book is published with the assistance of a grant from
the Samuel and Althea Stroum Endowed Book Fund.

Copyright © 2010 by
University of Washington Press
Printed in the United States of America
18 17 16 15 14 13 12 11 10   10 9 8 7 6 5 4 3 2 1

All photographs © Mary Randlett.
Design by Thomas Eykemans

UNIVERSITY OF WASHINGTON PRESS
P.O. Box 50096, Seattle, WA 98145, U.S.A.
www.washington.edu/uwpress

The paper used in this publication is acid-free
and 90 percent recycled from at least 50 percent
post-consumer waste. It meets the minimum
requirements of American National Standard for
Information Sciences—Permanence of Paper for
Printed Library Materials, ANSI Z39.48–1984.

LIBRARY OF CONGRESS
CATALOGING-IN-PUBLICATION DATA
McCue, Frances.
The car that brought you here still runs : revisiting
the northwest towns of Richard Hugo / Frances
McCue with photographs by Mary Randlett.
    p. cm.
Includes bibliographical references and index.
ISBN 978-0-295-98964-8 (cl. : alk. paper)
1. Hugo, Richard, 1923–1982—Travel—Northwest-
ern States. 2. Literary journeys—Northwestern
States. 3. Hugo, Richard, 1923–1982—Criticism
and interpretation. 4. Northwestern States—In
literature. 5. Cities and towns in literature.
I. Randlett, Mary, 1924– II. Title.
PS3515.U3Z77 2010
811'.54—dc22   2009036279

For Ripley and Lois

And for Donna Gerstenberger

Contents

Illustrations

Acknowledgments

I N THESE TIMES, scholarly publishing and literary prose are unsupported by commercial markets. I am very grateful to the generous donors who have supported this work in particular and to those who support the University of Washington Press itself, the largest publisher of scholarly and artistic work in our region. Thank you to them and to everyone who helped me realize this book: Nancy Nordhoff, Ann Morris, Peggy Enderlein, The Prop Foundation, Elizabeth Wales, Pat Soden, Beth Fuget, June Lamson, Chuck Nordhoff, Grace Nordhoff, Lois Fein, Marie La Fond, Dana Standish, Kerrie Ann Maynes, Anne Stadler, Lucy Dougall, Matthew Stadler, Annick Smith, Ripley Schemm Hugo, the Undergraduate Honors Program at the University of Washington, Gene Edgar, the University of Washington Special Collections, the University of Montana Special Collections, Tracy Manning, Ginny Merriam, Fritz and Mary Wolff, and the finest readers in the West: Bill Kittredge, Dick Dunn, Bill Bevis, and Lois Welch. And, of course, Mary Randlett, the eye given to it all. Thank you.

To Gary and Madeleine Greaves, my dear family, thank you.

Hugo's Triggering Places

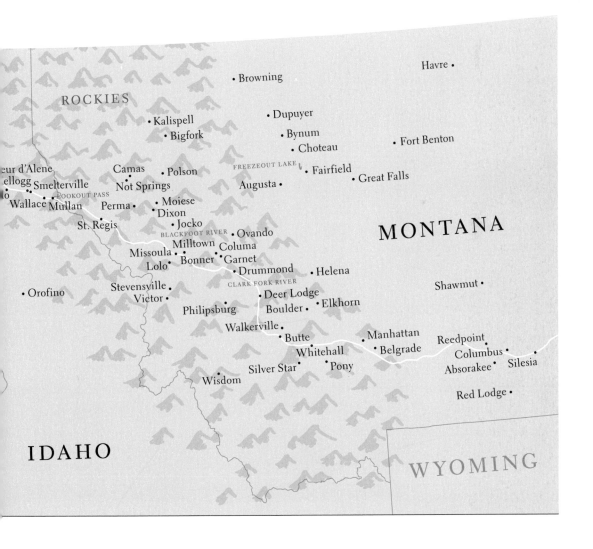

ROCKIES

• Browning

Havre •

• Kalispell
• Bigfork

• Dupuyer
• Bynum
• Choteau

• Fort Benton

eur d'Alene
ellogg Smelterville
o
Wallace Mullan
LOOKOUT PASS
St. Regis

Camas
Not Springs
Perma •
Dixon
• Jocko
BLACKFOOT RIVER
Milltown Columa
Bonner • Garnet
• Drummond

• Polson

FREEZEOUT LAKE
Augusta •

• Fairfield
Great Falls

• Moiese

MONTANA

• Ovando

Missoula •
Lolo •

Stevensville •
Victor •

• Orofino

CLARK FORK RIVER
Philipsburg
Walkerville •
• Butte
Whitehall •
Silver Star •

Wisdom •

• Helena

Deer Lodge •
Boulder • • Elkhorn

Shawmut •

• Pony

• Manhattan
• Belgrade

Reedpoint •
Columbus •
Absorakee •

Silesia

Red Lodge •

IDAHO

WYOMING

The Car That Brought You Here Still Runs

Setting Out

RICHARD HUGO VISITED places and wrote about them. He wrote about towns in Washington, Idaho, and Montana, and villages in Italy and Scotland. Often, his visits lasted little more than an afternoon, and his knowledge of the towns was confined to what he heard in bars and diners. From these snippets, he crafted poems. His attention to the actual places could be scant, but Hugo's poems resonate more deeply than travelogues or feature stories; they capture the torque between temperament and terrain that is so vital in any consideration of place. The poems bring alive some hidden aspect of each town and frequently play off of the traditional myths that an easterner might have of the West: that it is a place of restoration and healing, a spa where people from the East come to recover from ailments, that it is a place to reinvent oneself, a region of wide-open, unpolluted country still to settle. Hugo steers us, as readers, to eye level. How we settle into and take on qualities of the tracts of earth that we occupy—this is Hugo's inquiry. From this vantage, we'll see how much more complicated, and how much more impoverished, the actual places are. Before his death in 1982, in a writing career that spanned little more than twenty years, Hugo published a book of essays, a mystery novel, and nine books of poetry, and all of them immerse personas into particular, named places—most often towns.

The towns "triggered" the poems. Hugo shuffled these often remote, and always overlooked, places into his drafts of poems. They became part of his process, his nets for gathering images. Hugo describes this in *The Triggering Town*, his book of essays on writing and teaching. At first, the town is a "triggering subject which starts the poem or 'causes' the poem to be written," and then, he says, the poem develops "the real or generated subject, which the poem comes to say or mean." This is "discovered in the poem during the writing" of it. This deliberation, I realize, implies more than a haze of "inspiration" that artists are presumed to conjure up. For Hugo, taking a real town and using it as a springboard to create an imagined one is a process that unearths his other concerns as a writer and as a human being. Just as a stranger might come into a town and look around for a while, so Hugo suggests that a writer might fiddle with new material until he gets to know it, until it "tells him something." The visitor begins to see himself in the new place; the poet sees his subject within the images he's collected.

As I set out—first by reading Richard Hugo's poems and then by going to most of the Northwest towns that he wrote about—I got the sense that when you start to look at places, you carry with you one of two attitudes, though you may not be aware of them. One is that all places must conform to your own sense of nostalgia. The other is that all places have their own stories to tell, expanding your notions of what scenery, landscape, and home are. (Here, I'm actually imitating Hugo—leaning on his prose in *The Triggering Town* and using it as a scaffolding to describe how a poet, "you," might envision towns as muses for writing poems.) If you believe that towns must conform to your own sense of nostalgia, then you are making your job very difficult, and you are not only limiting your experiences to the realms you have known, you are weakening the justification for travel. Life is bewildering, and what's interesting, it seems to me, about coming to new places, as well as about coming to writing, is that you get to feel things that are altogether strange and unfamiliar to you. One mark of a novice traveler is his impulse to attribute qualities to places that then allow him to feel at home. By insisting that places conform to the truth he already knows, he is imposing upon them a whole series of expectations, untenable and invariable, that the locations cannot accommodate. A place may have a triggering subject, the thing you see when you stumble upon it. But that triggering image is not the real story. The real story lurks underneath—in history, in the environment itself, in the people living there now.

That's the way Hugo might have said it, anyway.

From Seattle, a place that poets come to (as I did more than twenty years ago) but where few are born (as Hugo was more than eighty years ago), I headed out to the Olympic Peninsula and to the rivers up north—the Skagit and the Stillaguamish, to the Snohomish and Skykomish. I went to Port Townsend, La Push, and the old forts on Whidbey Island. To the south, I journeyed to Carbonado and Kapowsin. Exploring this region came naturally to me, even before I had read Hugo's work with much attention. I was a poet myself and read plenty of other poets, but somehow I didn't get to Hugo until later. For ten years I roamed these towns in Washington State, and I even moved to one, Snohomish, because I was inspired by the feel of the streets: old Victorian houses lining the sidewalks and taverns and antique stores crowding along the river. Quaint and rustic at the same time, Snohomish's tacit promise to me was that I could fit in. It was a place, as so many western towns are, where a person's imagined life might coincide with her actual one. She'd see the hardware store where she'd buy lumber; she chose the bar where she'd play pool. She could see herself in the town.

In 1996, after I'd published a book of poems, after I had given up on the dream of living in a small town and had moved back into Seattle, I started a literary center with my friends and we named it Richard Hugo House. For years, I'd worked on my own as a writer and teacher, seeking camaraderie and learning opportunities. I'd wanted to create a community place, one centered on creative writing. It would be a hub where children, elderly people, students, teachers—writers all—hung out with accomplished poets, novelists, and playwrights. As the writers' house grew, so did my infatuation with Hugo and his poems. In the summers, I began driving to Missoula to visit his people— Hugo's wife, his neighbors and friends, and later his stepdaughter and stepgrandson. With these journeys, the possibility of seeing the towns that Hugo wrote about inspired me to exit I-90 and take smaller byways. Soon, my many trips to Missoula included visiting towns throughout Washington, Idaho, and Montana.

Over time, I grew more deliberate in my tours. I made lists of the towns, put them on spreadsheets, and lined them up and created routes. In some cases, such as when I found Wisdom, a remote town tucked into the southwestern corner of Montana, at the edge of the biggest open valley between mountain ranges that I've ever laid eyes on, I drove for hours to see barely a town at all. Hugo's poems about Wisdom didn't describe the place, so I didn't have much luck mapping the poetic lines onto the actual cross-roads. Still, I went back twice, both times to the same café, the one where Hugo ate.

As my trips intensified and my readings of the poems deepened, I proposed this book to the University of Washington Press. The director, Pat Soden, was thrilled. "We haven't published a book that looks at the Northwest through a poet's work," he said. "Hugo is important. And I want to assign Mary Randlett to the project."

"*The* Mary Randlett?" I asked. "The photographer? The famous one?"

"I think you'd be a good pair," Pat said. He laughed. "You will have a good time with Mary." There was mischief in his eyes. I admire that in a publisher.

Years earlier, back when I had been putting together Seattle's Rendezvous Room

Reading Series, with Jan Wallace and Matthew Stadler, Matthew had invited Mary to photograph the writer James Purdy. I remembered how she put one leg forward and leaned over the camera as she took photographs. She strode into her shots, and I recall how confident she looked, even from that distance. This time, I would actually work with her. She was eighty-three now.

She wore jeans, a button-down shirt, and running shoes. "Howdy," she said, and put out her hand. We were at the door of her split-level house. She waved me in.

"Wow," I said. "Is that a Morris Graves painting?" I pointed to a wall beyond stacks of papers and books.

"Oh, yes, it is. Morris gave that to me." Mary lifted a stack of envelopes and loose papers from the couch. "Here," she said. "Have a seat."

"And Clayton James? That pottery?"

She laughed. "Yes, you're right. He told me to take it with me one afternoon. He called it 'the pebble pot' and he saw that I liked it. Of course, Clayton is a superb painter too."

I couldn't help looking at everything. The walls in that house were filled with paintings by all the major artists that were working in our region forty, fifty, and sixty years ago—Mark Tobey, Kenneth Callahan, Graves, and little sketches by Wes Wehr, an elderly friend of mine who had died a few years back. Mary was at the center of a whole generation of actors, painters, and composers: George Tsutakawa, Ted D'Arms, Ambrose Patterson, Viola Patterson, and many others. She'd even taken the last photograph of the poet Theodore Roethke, in 1963, just before he died. Roethke, Hugo's former professor, was a National Book Award and Pulitzer Prizewinning master of the craft, and after accepting his position at the University of Washington in 1947, he became poetry's grand personality in the region. In *The Triggering Town*, Hugo devotes a chapter to Roethke's teaching style and to how that pedagogy influenced the younger poet. On the day he died, Ted Roethke had been swimming near Mary's mother's home on Bainbridge Island.

"All those people knew Mother," she said. "She ran the Henry Gallery. Most of the artists came and stayed with us." She paused. "Ted was staying in Mother's guest house out at Agate Point and had gone over to the Bloedels' to use the pool." The next day, Mary received calls from the *London Observer* and the *New York Times*. Since Mary's photo had been the last one taken of Roethke, the papers wanted to use it in their obituaries for the poet. Mary said, "The other photos of him were taken by Imogen Cunningham."

Mary Randlett, I realized, was a contemporary of Hugo. She was a year younger than he would have been.

"I wish I'd photographed Hugo," she said. "Never did. Got most of the others though."

It was true. When I'd gone to visit the University of Washington Press, the main corridor was lined with photographs of artists and writers, all by Mary Randlett. The hall was almost the length of a city block.

The day I visited her at home, Mary showed me her darkroom—a bedroom in the basement of her house on the fringes of Olympia. "Here's where I do all this," she said. She laughed. "Can't reach me before nine-thirty at night. I'm always in here."

A few months later, Mary and I ended up driving together through eastern Washington, into Idaho and Montana. The luck of that assignment, Mary taking photographs, shifted my perspective on the project. Not only would I hold the towns up to the poems, but I would also have photographs to see the places in the present, through the lens of another artist. So would my readers. Her "pictures," as she calls them, tell the region a story about itself, about its relationship to the natural world.

Mary transformed the project of creating a new dialogue between the towns and the poems into one that would be triangulated with photographs from one of the greatest living American photographers, a woman who grew up in the Northwest and knows the landscapes of Washington State better than anyone I've ever met. When we traveled together, I wrote and she clicked away with her Nikon, dashing across two-lane highways, climbing barbed wire fences, waving to people in trucks that sported gun racks. "Geez-us!" she would exclaim when we'd come around a bend in Montana, or when the sun would crawl across a ridge, "This landscape is unbelievable." Mary had only passed through Montana and never paused to take photographs. "Stop, pull over!" was the phrase I heard the most as we roared through, trying to reach so many towns in the two weeks we'd allotted. Mary took almost forty rolls of film, and we tucked them, cylinder by cylinder, into a cooler behind the driver's seat.

Arriving in the towns with Mary lifted those places from the sockets of landscape and then settled them back down. When she zoomed in on a particular sight, I could see how her frame worked the way a poem does, isolating an image then contextualizing others beyond it. Just as I'd originally been ratcheted up by Hugo's language, I was brought to the visual image by Mary's particular ways of seeing the landscape; she brought to visibility parts of the towns that I wouldn't have even noticed.

Looking back, I'm convinced that I went all the way to the towns because I was so wound up on the adrenaline of absorbing Hugo's language. His is a diction and syntax like none I'd ever seen; in all of my academic training and absolute fall-down-and-worship feelings for Yeats and Auden, for Adrienne Rich and Sylvia Plath, for Elizabeth Bishop, Robert Lowell, and William Stafford, for Donald Justice, James Tate, Lucille Clifton, Sharon Olds, Thylias Moss, Seamus Heaney, Charles Simic, Mark Strand, Amy Gerstler, Dara Wier, Lynn Emanuel, and Frank O'Hara—for all of these and so many more, none inspires me to actually travel somewhere the way Hugo does. His poems form language out of salal and slough, from river rock and bar stool—chunked rhythms, more percussion than strings—and the lonely narrators (or "speakers" in poetry's technical glossary) are caught in the flotsam washing through these land-scapes. The syntax alone turns me upside down inside.

I was attracted to him. Not the round-bellied Hugo, compact and bald, but the out-sider in those poems, the one you don't quite see up close but who you know is clumsy and sad. Sensing Hugo in a poem was like seeing a glimpse of an uncle or neighbor with a big sense of humor, the one you might listen to because his stories were so funny and wise. He was the man who could toss his head back and exhale those laughs that made you giggle. Mentors come in strange shapes and ages, I realize, and certainly poetry is an interest that tethered me to Hugo, but typically, a mentor is someone who is alive. Hugo, conversely, would exercise his influence from the great beyond. He'd died in 1982, when I was twenty and living in the East. I wouldn't see him in these towns or be able to ask him about the best taverns or the best fishing spots. Instead, I set out on my own, driving through Washington State, starting from Seattle, where I lived, and then on to Montana and Idaho, mapping the towns back onto the poems.

Most of the time, Hugo ended up in these places because he was going fishing. "Dick discovered the beauty of trout at the same time he discovered the beauty of poetry," scholar Donna Gerstenberger told me in a 2003 interview.[1] "It was an interesting conjunction. He was, I believe, in third grade when his teacher read Tennyson's 'The Brook' to the class, and for Dick it was like a light going off. He pursued poetry and he pursued trout with a kind of equal affection."[2] As a reader, you could trace Hugo's actual migrations by push-pinning the fishing spots he describes in poems onto maps of the Pacific Northwest, Italy, and the Isle of Skye. Once you marked these waterways that Hugo visited, you'd find the towns.

"I've got a lot of river poems," he once said in an interview. "I grew up on rivers and creeks."[3] Out looking for the best stream or lake flush with trout, Hugo, after serving five years in the Army Air Corps during World War II, drove around Puget Sound with his wife, Barbara Williams, to whom he was married for almost fourteen years. Together, they traveled to the islands and the coast to fish; they often drove to Lake Kapowsin, the Stillaguamish and the Skagit rivers, the ocean surf at La Push, and the towns nearby. Later, the poet traversed all of western Montana in his yellow Buick. The cooler he kept in the trunk probably held beer and schnapps and a sandwich or two. Sometimes, he'd drive between Seattle and Missoula, his home for the last nineteen years of his life, and pause at towns along the way. But he was always on the lookout for a spot to unwind a cast. Think of a man in a yellow car, roof pushed back, driving alongside his fishing rod. It's a comic frame, rich in color and contrast—that sleek, cartoon-colored Buick, and in the front seat, a big, bald man in a polyester shirt, heading out to fish.

Hugo believed in fish and small towns the way Yeats carved poetry from political events and the longing sprung from a broken heart. Fishing, as an enterprise, pulled Hugo along:

> I will swim
> a week to be a witness to the spawning,
> be a trout, eat the eggs of salmon—
> anything to live until the trout and rain
> are running in the river in my ear.

The fisherman swimming after the trout is like a poet chasing the invitation for the next poem, wondering how he can both keep it on the line and reel it in and pin it to the page. The speaker here, in "Skykomish River Running," like so many of the "I's" and "you's" that populate Hugo's poems, wants to blend into what surrounds him, whether that medium is a river or a town. The immersion echoes Yeats's "Coole Park and Ballylee, 1931," a poem about the Irish poet's own home turf, a locale fringed with water:

Under my window-ledge the waters race
Otters below and moor-hens on the top,
Run for a mile undimmed in Heaven's face
Then darkening through 'dark' Raftery's 'cellar' drop,
Run underground, rise in a rocky place
In Coole demesne, and there to finish up
Spread to a lake and drop into a hole.
What's water but the generated soul?

While Yeats forges pentameter, Hugo too hovers around the iambs of an unrhymed ten-syllable line and, as in his speaker's attempt to be a part of the scene, it's not a predictable or pure fit. Hugo's poem, instead, slants its way along with partial rhymes: *week* and *eat*, *anything* and *running*. Both the prosody and the subject underscore the notion that it is a difficult enterprise, finding one's way. "Art and fishing," as Hugo's friend, the poet Dave Smith, writes, "require a willingness to endure everything."[4] A fisherman, after all, needs to be patient. He needs to find the right place for a catch and avoid snags. Afterward, he'll return to civilization, and that journey into the company of others is rarely an easy transition. "If on the banks of clear rivers the fisherman has the perfect worlds of action and reflection, he must also return to the less perfect worlds of towns," Smith says.[5] "In cities, towns, and all social gatherings Hugo's fisherman is never comfortable and is always crushed by what he sees," and unlike Yeats's verse, Hugo's poem isn't recounted from a tower; he's in the water.[6]

Fishing tethered Hugo to particular places at the same time that it set up his poetic dilemma, again and again: How could he "angle" his way into a river? Or, better yet, "How will an outsider like him ever fit in?" In this distillation, Hugo identifies the great question of American poetry over the last fifty years; he finds it tucked into his afternoons along the banks of streams. Though it began as a deeply personal question, it turns out to be universal. "How will any outsider fit in?" is the small-scale version of "How will an immigrant belong?" and "Are we all immigrants?"

Hugo was, in other words, looking for a place. Unlike Baudelaire, another poet who wandered in search of poems to write, Hugo was a *flâneur* not of cities but of the American West. He didn't wear effete clothing or adopt any other trappings of the poseur or artist. He was a fisherman, and a fisherman roams until he finds a place where the trout are running. And so, Hugo filled his cooler, tucked his rod over the seat, and drove. He passed through towns that became sets onto which he would project his own dark visions and his persona, the one he used in his poems.

Towns bloomed as settlements from which he could confirm his status as an outsider. Hugo used the bars, a few locals, and some scenery as sites of projection for his own discomforts and aspirations to belong, but other than his own roots in poverty and his working-class history, he didn't really have too much in common with the people he met in these towns. They were laborers, ranchers, and miners. Some were out of work and spent their days in bars. Hugo, on the other hand, was employed at a major university: the University of Montana. He held advanced degrees. He was becoming a well-known poet. Though he looked like one of the men hunkered over a beer, he wasn't. Even if he wasn't a rich tourist attired in an L. L. Bean duck-hunting jacket, he hardly belonged in these places, except as a man on his way to a trout stream.

The beginning of "Degrees of Gray in Philipsburg," Hugo's greatest poem (in his opinion and mine), sounds like an invitation to write or to fish: "You might come here Sunday on a whim. / Say your life broke down. The last good kiss / you had was years ago." You're not quite alone in a Hugo poem, but you feel as if you were standing in some foundation of a house blown down long ago, and you're looking around. And you could find yourself packing one bag and moving into a town where the degrees of gray feel somehow more alive than your regular life. Richard Howard once wrote of Hugo, "Here is a poet concerned not to console or even sanctify, but merely—merely—to make privation credible and therefore rich."[7] His loneliness, the speaker's, is an invitation into companionship in the face of loss and despair, though your companionship will be only the solace of a poem. What, after all, is a poem if not a synthetic space where the poet might finally fit in?

On my tours of the towns and the poems triggered by them, I realized that Hugo's first town, the one he named his 1980 collection of poems after (one of his two last books), the one just off of the south end of Seattle, was his most important one. Everything, his personal history, his attraction to small towns, and his poems—all of it begins in White Center, Washington. Just over the border of Seattle's city limits, on the western edge of the environs where the city runs between Puget Sound and the Duwamish Waterway, Hugo grew up with his grandparents in a small house. Nearby, the Nisei truck farmers sold their goods, Boeing unrolled its airstrip at the base of the hill, and in the shadow of the Cascade and Olympic mountains, Hugo played baseball and ran through empty lots looking for lost balls.

White Center, named for George White, an early real estate developer in the area, was a run-down lean-to of a town off the backside of Seattle, a city that was far from any historical Eastern metropolis or the glamorous San Francisco, barely an urban space at all, where, after a Boeing downturn in the 1970's, someone posted the billboard: "Will the last one leaving Seattle please turn out the lights?" Here, Hugo saw plenty that wasn't glittery or shiny, but rather dimly lit and shaggy in daylight. Poor immigrants, Greeks and Slavs, lived near the Duwamish, where debris from the outflow pipes clogged the river with "dredge that heaps a hundred tons / of crud on barges for the dumping ground."

Despite this poverty and gray mist that pressed down over White Center, Hugo witnessed the natural beauty of his environs. Mount Rainier's enormous dome filled the horizon on sunny days; the Olympic Mountains rose with snowy jags through the clouds beyond Puget Sound; and, to the east, the Cascades ran the full length of his vision. Instead of writing these spectacles into romantic poems about the natural world, Hugo focused on the scenery closer to the ground, the sights within his own neighborhood: the drunk neighbor "bleeding from the corners of his grin" and the tugboat hauling "an afternoon of logs upriver." Hugo chooses the downtrodden characters and the shacks and gravel pits, the shingle mills and brickyards along the polluted Duwamish River, instead of writing about Mount Baker or Snoqualmie Pass. As he traveled to other towns that triggered his poems, he would find places that felt lacking in some way, finite and worn, sometimes tawdry. For a lifetime, Hugo would sidestep the magnificent in favor of magnifying the overlooked.

All other towns would come under that first lens, the one from which he never really took his gaze. Byron, whom Hugo adored, captured the sentiment in "When I Roved a Young Highlander": "As I felt, when a boy, on the crag-cover'd wild / One image, alone, on my bosom impress'd, / I lov'd my bleak regions. . . . " White Center, the bleakest of regional places, was Hugo's indigenous place. He looked into its worn storefronts and at the poor inhabitants, and, like Byron's verse, his own would also pine for lost women.

In Hugo's case, his first longing was for his mother, the woman who left him to be raised by his grandparents from the age of eighteen months. Later, the women whom Hugo locates in the towns (or whom he plants in his imagined versions of the towns) are idealized—lost maidens or matrons—blurring into mixed-up versions of mother/

lovers. His personas, the stand-ins for him in the poems, try to create places where the poet's created selves will belong with the women he's invented. He's always hoping that they will finally be together. Such romantic temptations, finding the ideal woman and growing up in a land of overwhelming natural beauty, led Hugo to project his own sadness and impaired childhood through his speakers and onto the physical scenery. It also led him to invent versions of his mother. Sometimes, he needed whole towns to contain her.

Esther Monk Hogan gave birth to Richard Franklin Hogan (the boy changed his name to his stepfather's—Hugo—when he was in eighth grade), when she was only seventeen and left him, before he was two, with her parents. Hugo's grandparents were quiet people with simple, structured lives, strict in their religious beliefs and cold in demeanor. Immigrant German farmers who had moved out from the Midwest, the Monks had elementary school educations and a parenting style that swung radically between abuse and neglect. Enduring the gamut of emotions in the household and subjected to frequent "gratuitous beatings," Hugo grew up without much stimulation, warmth, or security. Abandonment, and the longing for a place, became the deeper subject of the town poems; his speakers craved attachment. The towns of his poems externalize this longing and, on the outside, all towns strangely resemble White Center.

As Hugo wrote in a draft of an essay about William Stafford, whom he describes as a "landscape poet": "For such a poet, there are two landscapes: internal and external."[8] In Hugo's own work, the collision of internal and external triggers shows up in an elegant clumsiness, what poet Dave Smith calls "Hugo's pell-mell cadences."[9] They arise through the thumps of hard consonants and long vowels bumping along almost in the complete absence of ornament—articles and conjunctions—like a large person making his way down a dark hallway. Then, you realize, it's a dance. There's music in it. Some of his poems remind me of Roethke's "My Papa's Waltz," only Hugo forges a different, less predictable music out of sad situations. He doesn't create waltzing rhythms. It's as if he is saying, as a nonpoet might, "I felt lonely without a father and the world seemed empty." He would funnel those emotions into attempts at musical language and let the music conjure up the context, as he does in "What the Brand New Freeway Won't Go By":

To live here you should be a friend of rain
and fifty with a bad job on the freights,
knowing the freeway soon will siphon
the remaining world away . . .

Inside this music, there's a damaged character running the show, and that speaker doesn't really change until the poems grow and move away from White Center. When he finally reaches *The Right Madness on Skye*, a collection of poems set in Scotland, the "land of slow recovery," he truly comes to terms with his mortality. Physically leaving his hometown did not mean that Hugo ever departed the place emotionally. He carried it with him, even as he swam upstream to live in Missoula.

Because the invitations that Hugo takes from the muse are humble ones—not grandiose sweeps of Mount Rainier and Puget Sound—the poems instigate emotional reactions from surprisingly small realms, as in "Dwelling": "They won't go away, the sea perch / circling piles, the searun cutthroat / hammering home upriver in the rain," he writes. Then, "I try to ignore them, to focus on women, / on the news. They swim between the lines." The intentional blur, in hammer-blow iambs, between the women, the news and the trout, urges the poem out of the landscape and into animation. The speaker stands, suspended over the stream, trying to figure things out. He's trying to order things. The iambic thumps of "they swim between the lines," with emphasis on *swim* and *between* and *lines*, echo that.

By appropriating locale in what critic Donna Gerstenberger described as "not only a psychological mapping of limitations . . . but an aspect of western American consciousness, of belonging to a land not fully possessed," Hugo's poems trigger a particular kind of longing in his readers.[10] Trapped in his isolation as a poet (Hugo worked at Boeing until he was almost forty, and he lived in Seattle, the far edge of a "land not fully possessed"), he leans on you, as a reader, to keep him company. Here is a writer from an unlikely place (not James Dickey's South, not Robert Lowell's northeast or Lawrence Ferlinghetti's California) who takes on outsider status by mere geography. Hugo's voice bore the tones and diction of a westerner who knew a lot more about working in an airplane factory than he did about avant-garde literary theories. More importantly, Hugo introduced western towns fading from prosperity and urban industrial rubble that were far from the plush divans and anxiety-ridden concordances made public by Brahmin poets such as Robert Lowell and Anne Sexton. Instead of viewing the landscapes of Montana, Washington, and Idaho with his face pressed against a train window, as Lowell did, seeing "life changed to landscape," Hugo went into towns to sit at the bars.[11] The pleasures of Hugo's poems don't startle a reader as a purely confessional voice might; instead they pulse with emotional recognition in places that most wouldn't regard as potential sites of poems. Hugo craved the merger of voice with the warps of landscape and the serrations of poetic form. In many of his poems, he favored the bulky, large stanzas that strained for the margins as if compacted into warehouse crates, ready to be hauled over the mountains.

The westerner's art, according to Hugo, is to deny the expanse of the West itself. Though he's considered a Northwest poet, a particular "school" of verse designated by historians and critics, Hugo is less interested in describing the natural terrain than his contemporaries David Wagoner, Carolyn Kizer, William Stafford, and Kenneth Hanson are. Hugo carries a tough-minded antiromanticism that the others don't have. "Out west, survival is enough," he writes in "Overlooking Yale," a title playing on his view from atop a Yale-New Haven hotel, about the notion of discarding the importance of the university. The poetry establishment, after all, hummed along, far from Seattle and Missoula. Only later in his life did Hugo become a part of it by becoming the editor of the Yale Younger Poets prize and by publishing in the *New Yorker* and the *Atlantic Monthly*. Critic and scholar Michael Allen writes, "For Hugo, the west is a dream that does not belong to those who would—and do—exploit the land; the dreams of the West are those failed hopes of the poor and the greedy and the wishful who come there to find a better life. To Hugo, the American dream is not in the unlimited possibilities of expansion but in the ache of need."[12] Those needs are basic—to pat the hood of the Buick and murmur, "Old hero—two hundred thousand miles and only / five changes of oil and one valve grind." In contrast, the poet closes "Overlooking Yale" with:

> The limousine leaves soon
> for New York and the plane, the plane for points west . . .
> For the first time the east is not the east
> dreamed from a hill on the edge of Seattle.

So many of Hugo's poems begin with an abandoned scene that, over the course of a Hugo collection, a reader aches from loneliness and kicks through the rubble of these places, in search of companionship. In the poem "Kapowsin," named after a lake where Hugo fishes, he traces a town that "died in 1908." Only ghosts remain: "a woman who gets pregnant from a song" and a "tavern always filled but never loud." In "No Bells to Believe," the speaker wonders "Who rings bells in the abandoned chapel, / once a school, once a shed where hide / was stored?" And in "Back of Gino's Place," the place is also haunted: "Most neglect this road. . . . " These lines from early poems presage later scenes where Hugo will manufacture desolation as if creating a stage set: "I wanted it depressed, one dusty road / and two cafés both with 'help wanted' signs." In these scenes, Hugo insists that you can see the whole lineage of a place peeking through.

This is why Hugo is not a poet of nostalgia. As Allen writes, "There is less a romance of landscape than there is an education in the realities of space."[13] Nostalgia, after all, is the desire for a past that never really happened, while Hugo is interested in giving a steely, unflinching look at a place. His hero arrives in town, stops at a bar or diner, and sees how the sadness of the world is reflected there. Then he leaves, his outsider status confirmed, and goes fishing. "Even in despair and loneliness their persona . . . seemed to state . . . the world could be kinder, fairer and more just," critic David Axelrod notes in his description of Hugo's and James Wright's speakers.[14]

Hugo's poems aren't searching for the mementos of working-class lives but instead yearn for some connection to the people who live in these places. The search extends to the reader, who begins to ache for some living people to hang out with, people to join her in riffling through the relics. Frederick Garber calls it "stereoscopic vision" that "sees the past and the present and the point of change all together and at once."[15]

Within these almost-vacant places, the speaker sees himself—one lonely character. "I write about unpeopled worlds," Hugo told interviewer Susan Zwinger:

> Very seldom does a person in my poems have a relationship with anybody else. If he does, it's nearly always someone who's dead. I see the world as a sad place without any people in it. Decaying shacks, abandoned ranches, desolation, endless spaces, plains, mountains, ghost towns. They are right for my sensibilities.[16]

In these imagined crossroads vacant of people and activity, Hugo finds his tones as a poet. Donna Gerstenberger notes that the site of a Hugo poem is "usually abandoned or in decay" and it "touches off in him the need to fill out an imagined life in that place, which he does best, he says, when he knows little or nothing about the place."[17] Longing emanates from the speaker's desire to inhabit the vacancies he uncovers. In the midst of the abandoned towns, he imagines the men he might have become. As a reader, one feels the narration from a guide who projects and receives back from the landscape, simultaneously: "Hugo's is not the camera's eye, though, capturing the scene as it exists, his is the poet's eye, catching the scene as it inhabits him so that he discovers its meaning. The relationship is entirely reciprocal."[18]

This give-and-take, I hoped, would also show up in the relationship between the towns and the poems. That each poem would enhance the town that inspired it, and that the town would deepen the associations within the poem—I wished for these small dialogues. I imagined myself standing on the street in Dixon, Montana reading "The Only Bar in Dixon," or along the ocean at Taholah, Washington, reciting "Road Ends in Tahola." My going to the headwaters of Hugo's poems came from the same impulse that causes one to drive by an old school and think of attending the class reunion. Or, more gritty than that, it reminded me of the compulsion that gets kids from garage bands to drive out to Aberdeen, Washington, a sad place, to see where Kurt Cobain lived underneath the bridge and wrote his pre-Nirvana songs. My desire, I realized, was a primal wish. I wanted to know where the poems began, where Hugo began, and, by implication, perhaps, where I began. What triggered the poem to become something *from* the town that wasn't *of* the town? What gave poets their starts? What tethered us to particular places?

While the philosopher Jerome Bruner says that we *act* our way into knowing, out here in the West, we *drive* to find things out. In my little capsule, sometimes with Mary Randlett, sometimes with my little dog, Ida, sometimes with my daughter, Maddy, or my husband, Gary, I drove and drove in search of these poems and towns. I found out that the car was literally a physical transport into an artistic realm. It was a metaphoric vehicle, accelerated. As travelers or artists, we drift, headlong, over the roads that stretch to the hinterlands. Driving is romantic, the contemporary version of taking horse and buggy down a country lane and being, as Hugo wrote in "Driving Montana," "lost / in miles of land without people." Hours from cities, along highways populated mostly with trucks—I'd arrive in places I'd thought were the hinterlands, and the stores would have exactly the same provisions as the places where I'd stopped before. Even the faraway is not far away anymore. It's just a long drive.

The light from my car's headlamps brushed long, empty Montana roads. Once, in a coffee shop, when I pulled off to rest and find a place to stay, I read "Letter to Oberg from Pony." I was sleepy, and the poem rattled me awake. It animated that sense of being between places: "you'd love to pack your things and move here. / This is lovely. This is too great for a poem. The only / way here is by dream." As I sat at the Formica table and tapped the fork on the paper place mat, I realized that I'd have to imagine my own way into seeing these towns. Sure, I'd go to them. I'd drive in and get out and walk around. I'd admire the storefronts, the signs, the one feed mill, the gas pumps and hardware store. I'd be secretly smitten with the sense of civilization in miniature—like a train set—but I'd imagine the lives grown complicated with things hidden behind the facades: mortgages, illnesses, love gone crossways. The microeconomies in these places would have pulled income from some natural resource: agriculture, mining, ranching, or logging. As a result, I'd aspire to being, as Hugo was, "not interested in quaintness or sadness for its own sake. It's not an exercise of the painterly eye, but an interest in inhabiting the place . . . to recreate the human dimensions of loss."[19] I'd try to imagine beyond the snow globe image of each town, and the sealed biosphere of the imagination that pulls us toward it, to see it for what it was—a place.

I was early into one of the first of many trips around the region. I remember that the lights in the diner were harsh, and I read through that letter from Pony maybe ten times. I ordered a grilled cheese sandwich and sat looking at the pages, open to the poem. Thinking about the towns as actual places beyond my romanticized impressions brought me to another poem set in Montana, a harsh one called "Late Summer, Drummond." In this poem, Hugo drops the bottom out of any fantasy notions of small towns, and, by choosing Drummond, a site that locals claimed was full of "world famous bull shippers," lays out the real stuff. "Real chance to make it: none. . . . Life becomes a hobby seen like this from hills," he writes. As a visitor, and a writer tracking down the work of another writer, I'd risk seeing life in these towns from an elite vantage point. The distance I'd have, standing on one of the sandpaper hills outside Drummond, looking to the town, where meat is the prime industry, would be nothing like looking from Mount Monadnock, the legendary hillock in New Hampshire, over to Thornton Wilder's gracious, sentimental and sanitized descriptions of "Our Town."

In Drummond, Montana, the stench of rendering ponds would clamp the throat, I'd find out, and the "Rocky Mountain oysters" would sound nothing like the calf testicles they are.

I'd be the outsider to the towns I visited. They were isolated. Trains barely came through anymore, and schools were closing as people moved on to cities. As Hugo said in "Letter to Oberg from Pony," our "nation . . . is no longer one but only an / amorphous collection of failed dreams, where we have been told / too often . . . that our lives don't matter." I'd be stitching the failed dreams of Hugo's poems back onto places that might not be able to bear them. I could see myself as the outsider narrator (or speaker) in those poems because I was the outsider narrator in the actual towns.

Back on the road, the lights of the diner fading under the arc of the highway's ramp, I thought of the difference between what I read in books and what exists outside of them. Right then, I knew that mapping these towns, following the poems, would be like living out that most basic, and radical, of literary theories, reader-response theory, and using it in three dimensions instead of two. I'd merge the actual text of the poems with my own responses to them, trying to bring scholarship closer to the roads where pavement gave out and people lived in trailers. Poems, after all, are not histories.

I thought of this as I came past Coeur d'Alene, Idaho, where signs for tourist attractions crowd miles of highway. Poems aren't even philosophies about how to live a good life; they aren't self-help broadsides, and they aren't swaths of wisdom formatted to a page. A poem can't hold a whole place, or even a memory, intact. Its floors are lined with half-heard sayings and old tin cans, so that when the speaker finally enters, she's a singer of sorts, someone who picks these things up and improvises until they fit together.

When encountered by an outsider, any village reads like a fiction. Everyone living inside it lives in a role: the undertaker, the cook, the shopkeeper, the teacher, the schoolchild—disassembling into parody and caricature—and these flattened characters belie a whole other set of genealogies and intentions. Hugo, that wise man, knew all of this. A town was an incubator for a fledgling set of impressions that could become mature enough to grow up and move on. Like a high-school kid aching for the big city, the poem could take little pieces of the town with it "until the town you came from dies inside" and become something utterly different.

For more than twenty-two years, I've journeyed to towns throughout the Northwest. At first, I drove around as a traveler, curious about my new home, and then, in the last twelve years, I concentrated on going to places that served as the origins of Hugo's poems. I drove from Seattle out to the seacoast, up and down to the rivers along the Cascade foothills, and along the Olympic Peninsula. Each summer, and sometimes in the fall and spring, I set out from the city and headed east, into western Montana, where I came to know Hugo's friends and family. Images from the poems accumulated inside me as did flashes from the landscapes and people I encountered. The overlapping richness of reading and traveling, of seeing these places and connecting poems to them—this was something I craved to simulate. In my written tour, I wanted to bring Hugo, that faint character behind the lamp of the poems, into visibility. I aspired to illuminate his stage sets—the towns.

My tour of Hugo's Northwest towns, the one presented here, follows the barest chronology of Hugo's own life: he was born near Seattle, headed out into the world, and landed, ultimately, in Montana. At the end of his fifty-eight years, he returned to Seattle for medical care and died. The poems that I've chosen do not always line up on this biographical arc, but instead shadow the towns that inspired the stanzas, creating a traceable loop that simulates Hugo's own life as well as his development as a poet. Some early poems, "La Push," and "Tahola," for example, are presented later in this book, while some poems that Hugo wrote at the end of his life, poems such as "White Center," appear earlier. The journey is meant to be psychological as well as poetic; it aspires to engage readers who are, as I am, smitten with pilgrimages. What follows is a reproducible road trip for those who want to travel as literary tourists, collected poems in hand, to some of the most interesting towns in the Northwest, seeing how the poems connect to these ever-changing places. These essays trace Hugo's poems along a route, progressing toward a poetic and biographical crescendo of Hugo's own artistic concerns and his concerns as a man, one who finally comes into a family—creating a journey that ends not far from where he began.

I never met Richard Hugo. I was twenty when he died, living in a different world in the crowded, worn-out East, and I was oblivious, until years later, to the loss the West (and American letters) had suffered. The great burly poet of overlooked towns and industrial sloughs, Hugo never cut a poetic figure, but his impulse to follow what happened in these places came from an aesthetic sense of following a line, and a deep humanity and humility in tracing the lives of other people. His friend Annick Smith says that Hugo was "unrivalled in expressing what it was to be of those places. He understood that really deeply."[20] And another close friend and colleague, Bill Kittredge, says that Hugo had an "absolute understanding that what he was interested in and what he thought was real about the world—how people feel, interact with each other, treat each other, use power over each other, how people respond to that power—all of that, there was a continual focus on that rather than on ideologies, abstract concepts, conceits."[21]

Our work as human beings, I gathered from Richard Hugo, is to travel far from where we began—not necessarily physically, but emotionally and spiritually, so that we can know an arc of our own development and live within some kind of ongoing sense of bewilderment and challenge. You need only look to Hugo and his launch from that White Center cabin with his grandparents, into the service as a bombardier over Eastern Europe and Italy for thirty-five missions, then back to his grandparents' place, on through a bachelor's and master's degree in poetry writing and English literature, into the life of a college professor—to see the movement away from his origins. His obsession with returning to where he started off, using towns that reminded him of his beginnings, fueled his poems and displayed the magnificence of his journey away from them.

"Towns arrive ahead of imagined schedule," Hugo writes in "Driving Montana," and he envisions himself within the landscapes that he's passing. "Where did you stop along the road / and have fun?" And, "Did you park at that house, the one / alone in a void of grain, white with green / trim and red fence, where you know you lived / once?" In *The Triggering Town*, more manifesto than guidebook, Hugo instructs a budding poet to imagine a town that he's only "passed through," and then "take emotional possession of it." What follows are my attempts to follow Hugo's advice, to arrive in the towns as I'd arrived in the poetry, and to try to imagine myself there.

Pathway to the Duwamish, 2008.

White Center, Riverside, and the Duwamish

DUWAMISH

Midwestern in the heat, this river's
curves are slow and sick. Water knocks
at mills and concrete plants, and crud
compounds the gray. On the out-tide,
water, half salt water from the sea,
rambles by a barrel of molded nails,
gray lumber piles, moss on ovens
in the brickyard no one owns.
Boys are snapping tom cod spines
and jeering at the Greek who bribes
the river with his sailing coins.

Because the name is Indian, Indians
ignore the river as it cruises
past the tavern. Gulls are diving crazy
where boys nail porgies to the pile.
No Indian would interrupt his beer
to tell the story of the snipe
who dove to steal the nailed girl
late one autumn, with the final salmon in.

This river colors day. On bright days
here, the sun is always setting or obscured
by one cloud. Or the shade extended
to the far bank just before you came.
And what should flare, the Chinese red
of a searun's-fin, the futile roses,
unkept cherry trees in spring, is muted.
For the river, there is late November
only, and the color of a slow winter.

On the short days, looking for a word,

knowing the smoke from the small homes
turns me colder than wind from
the cold river, knowing this poverty
is not a lack of money but of friends,
I come here to be cold. Not silver cold
like ice, for ice has glitter. Gray
cold like the river. Cold like 4 P.M.
on Sunday. Cold like a decaying porgy.

But cold is a word. There is no word along
this river I can understand or say.
Not Greek threats to a fishless moon
nor Slavic chants. All words are Indian.
Love is Indian for water, and madness
means, to Redmen, I am going home.

WEST MARGINAL WAY

One tug pounds to haul an afternoon
of logs up river. The shade
of Pigeon Hill across the bulges
in the concrete crawls on reeds
in a short field, cools a pier
and the violence of young men
after cod. The crackpot chapel,
with a sign erased by rain, returned
before calm and a mossed roof.

A dim wind blows the roses
growing where they please. Lawns
are wild and lots are undefined
as if the payment made in cash
were counted then and there.

These names on boxes will return
with salmon money in the fall,
come drunk down the cinder arrow
of a trail, past the store of Popich,
sawdust piles and the saw mill
bombing air with optimistic sparks,
blinding gravel pits and the brickyard
baking, to wives who taught themselves
the casual thirst of many summers
wet in heat and taken by the sea.

Some places are forever afternoon.
Across the road and a short field
there is the river, split and yellow
and this far down affected by the tide.

DUWAMISH HEAD

1.
That girl upstream was diced by scaling knives—
scattered in the shack I licked her knees in
where she tossed me meat and called me dog
and I would dive a dog at her from stars,
wind around my ears—violins and shot.

With salmon gone and industry moved in
birds don't bite the water. Once this river
brought a cascade color to the sea.
Now the clouds are cod, crossing on the prowl
beneath the dredge that heaps a hundred tons
of crud on barges for the dumping ground.

My vision started at this river mouth,
on a slack tide, trying to catch bullheads
in a hopeless mud. The pier was caving
from the weight of gulls. Wail of tug
and trawl, a town not growing up
across the bay, rotten pay for kings—
these went by me like the secret dawns
the sea brought in. I saw the seaperch
turn and briefly flare around a pile
and disappear. I heard bent men
beg a sole to look less like a stone.

Beyond the squatters and the better homes
stars were good to dive from. Scattered
in the shack I licked her knees in.
Diced, the paper said, by scaling knives.

2.
River, I have loved, loved badly on your bank.
On your out-tide drain I ride toward the sea
so deep the blue cries out in pain from weight.
Loved badly you and years of misery
in shacks along your bank—cruel women
and their nervous children—fishhooks filed
for easy penetration—cod with cracked necks
reaching with their gills for one more day.
Last year's birds are scouting for the kill,
hysterical as always when the smelt run thin.

Jacks don't run. Mills go on polluting
and the river hot with sewage steams.
In bourbon sleep, old men hummed salmon
home to mountains and the river jammed
with blackmouth, boiled in moonlight while the mills

boomed honest sparks. October rolled
with dorsal fins and no man ruled the runs.

When I see a stream, I like to say: exactly.
Where else could it run? Trace it back to ice.
Try to find a photo of your cradle.
Rivers jump their beds and don't look back
regretting they have lost such lovely rides.

I could name those birds, see people
in the clouds. Sight can be polluted
like a river. When this river asks me:
where were you when Slavs gave up their names
to find good homes on paved streets west of here?
I talk back. What are you, river?
Only water, taking any bed you find.
All you have is current, doubled back
on in-tide, screaming out on out.
I am on your bank, blinded and alive.

3.
Where cod and boys had war, a bolt plant roars.
Sparks are stars. Next Sunday, when I die
no drunk will groan my name in spasms
as he vomits last night from the dock.
I have memories of heat upstream.
Her arms and eyes had power like the river
and she imitated salmon with a naked roll.

My vision started at this river mouth
and stuck here (bullhead in the mud)
a third of what could be a lifetime.
The city blares and fishermen are rich.

Tugs and trawls repainted slide to ports
and perch found better color in the sea.

My fins are hands. The river, once
so verbal drifts with such indifference
by me I am forced to shout my name:
backing up on in-tide, screaming out on out—
river, I have loved, loved badly on your bank.

Scattered in the shack I licked her knees in—
beyond her, nothing, just the Indian
I use so often infantile in dreams
of easy winters, five-day runs of silvers,
festive bakes, the passing of the jacks
to sand pools promised by the rain.

To know is to be alien to rivers.
This river helped me play an easy role—
to be alone, to drink, to fail.
The world goes on with money. A tough cat
dove here from a shingle mill on meat
that glittered as it swam. The mill is gone.
The cat is ground. If I say love
was here, along the river, show me bones
of cod, scales and blood, faces in the clouds
so thick they jam the sky with laughter.

DUWAMISH NO. 2

Mudhens, cormorants and teals take
legal sanctuary in the reeds,
birds and reeds one grey. The river

when the backed-up tide lets go
flows the only north the birds believe.
North is easy. North is never love.

On the west hill, rich with a million
alders and five hundred modern homes,
birds, deep in black, insist the wind
will find the sea. The river points
the wrong way on the in-tide
and the alders lean to the arid south.

Take away all water. Men are oiling
guns beside ripped cows. Wrens have claws
and clouds cascade with poison down
a cliff mapped badly by an Indian.
Tumbleweeds are plotting to stampede.
Where there is no river, pregnant
twice a day with tide, and twice each day
released by a stroking moon,
animals are dangerous as men.

When the world hurts, I come back alone
along the river, certain the salt
of vague eyes makes me ready for the sea.
And the river says: you're not unique—
learn now there is one direction only—
north, and, though terror to believe,
quickly found by river and never love.

WHITE CENTER

Town or poem, I don't care how it looks. Old woman
take my hand and we'll walk one more time these streets

I believed marked me weak beneath catcalling clouds.
Long ago, the swamp behind the single row of stores
was filled and seeded. Roses today where Toughy Hassin
slapped my face to the grinning delight of his gang.
I didn't cry or run. Had I fought him
I'd have been beaten and come home bloody in tears
and you'd have told me I shouldn't be fighting.

Wasn't it all degrading, mean Mr. Kyte sweeping
the streets for no pay, believing what he'd learned
as a boy in England: 'This is your community'?
I taunted him to rage, then ran. Is this the day
we call bad mothers out of the taverns and point them
sobbing for home, or issue costumes to posturing clowns
in the streets, make fun of drunk barbers, and hope
someone who left and made it returns, vowed
to buy more neon and give these people some class?

The Dugans aren't worth a dime, dirty Irish, nor days
you offered a penny for every fly I killed.
You were blind to my cheating. I saw my future certain—
that drunk who lived across the street and fell
in our garden reaching for the hoe you dropped.
All he got was our laughter. I helped him often home
when you weren't looking. I loved some terrible way
he lived in his mind and tried to be decent to others.
I loved the way we loved him behind our disdain.

Clouds. What glorious floating. They always move on
like I should have early. But your odd love and a war
taught me the world's gone evil past the first check point
and that's First Avenue South. I fell asleep each night
safe in love with my murder. The neighbor girl
plotted to tease every tomorrow and watch me turn

again to the woods and games too young for my age.
We never could account for the python cousin Warren
found half starved in the basement of Safeway.

It all comes back but in bites. I am the man
you beat to perversion. That was the drugstore MacCameron
flipped out in early one morning, waltzing
on his soda fountain. The siren married his shrieking.
His wife said, "We'll try again, in Des Moines."
You drove a better man into himself where he found tunes
he had no need to share. It's all beginning to blur
as it forms. Men cracking up or retreating.
Resolute women deep in hard prayer.

And it isn't the same this time. I hoped forty years
I'd write and would not write this poem. This town would die
and your grave never reopen. Or mine. Because I'm married
and happy, and across the street a foster child
from a cruel past is safe and need no longer crawl
for his meals, I walk this past with you, ghost in any field
of good crops, certain I remember everything wrong.
If not, why is this road lined thick with fern
and why do I feel no shame kicking the loose gravel home?

Along the Duwamish

T o begin where Richard Hugo began, I drive from Capitol Hill, where I
live, in the middle of Seattle, to White Center, a town just off the city's southern edge. The journey takes about a half an hour, longer if the First Avenue
drawbridge opens. I'm traveling south, toward the white, rounded scoop of Mount
Rainier, through downtown, then on to an industrial area south of the city, where
railroad tracks crisscross the streets. My little dog Ida sits, alert in the passenger seat,
sniffing at the windshield.

After the downhill ride, toward the bay and piers downtown, I turn south into
Pioneer Square, past Elliott Bay Books (*I'll stop later*), down beyond Safeco Field, the
only Japanese-styled stadium in America, past building supply stores, Sears, and the
Starbucks headquarters. Once over the drawbridge, a few miles later, I am adjacent
to the greenbelt along the ridge of West Seattle. I turn up the hill, heading west, at
Highland Park Way.

Long considered by many Seattleites to be a tough neighborhood of white red-
necks, more poor than working-class, White Center is now where artists are moving.
Rents are cheaper, thanks to the low-flying aircraft coming into Sea-Tac, and things
are livelier than when immigrant Germans, farmers such as Hugo's own grandparents
(with whom he lived), resided there; now Africans, Samoans, Eastern Europeans, Viet-
namese, and Latinos gather in the Salvadorian Bakery and the taco shops, places where
I sometimes have lunch with my family.

Set into a divot, a dent in the rise of the ridge between Puget Sound and the
Duwamish River, White Center has no views of the sound or the river. Only the
main drag of Sixteenth Avenue Southwest, a string of run-down storefronts and bars,
attracts pedestrians, and these folks aren't tourists; they're people who live within a half

mile of the strip of shops. In the 1930s, the village was much the same, though some vacant blocks are filled in now with houses and apartments. Back then, White Center sprawled through smatterings of wooded areas and small houses, almost identical in layout. Today, not much has changed except the people and the goods peddled at the shops.

North of Southwest Roxbury Street, on the Seattle side of the street, the houses are larger; vacant areas are groomed into parks; and, as Hugo would say, "churches are kept up." In White Center, on the south side of the boundary, many of the chapels don't have steeples—instead the gathering places are set in storefronts. As in much of impoverished America, these are the venues in which churches take root now—many are congregations of immigrants who, once divided into separate strains of Christianity, are merging their religious views into these new faith houses. Like the stores they've replaced, the small churches are accessible to passersby; there are no lawns to cross or anterooms to linger in. Once you step inside the door, you are in the midst of services.

Back in the 1920s and '30s, when Hugo was a boy, St. James Lutheran Church, not a storefront church but a brick edifice with a steeple, centered the activities of his household. For his grandparents, the church offered a rigid moral dogma and limited opportunities for socializing—a fine combination for people who preferred to remain silent and mostly invisible to others. The church, still standing, is to the west of where Hugo's house stood.

At Fifteenth Southwest and Henderson, Hugo spent his boyhood in a neighborhood of small houses, vacant lots, and pockets of woods. He describes the area in *The Real West Marginal Way*, his autobiography:

> Our house was on the edge of Seattle, less than two blocks inside the city limits, in a district that was then a town, isolated from the parent city by miles of woods and undeveloped land, and whose reputation for violence and wild behaviour seemed to put it on the edge of civilization. Seattle itself is practically on the edge of the nation.[1]

It was a place outside urban life. "From the time I can remember, I was living with my grandparents, silent people who communicated little, and who left me to my own devices for hours. For long periods I seemed barely a part of their lives."[2] From that vantage point, Hugo says, "I was at the edge of their existence. And our house was at the edge too, for my entire boyhood the only house on our side of the block, thick rich woods all around it, willows, cedars, dogwoods, alders, hazel nut trees (filberts), red hawthorn, ferns, moss, grass salal."[3] And so he headed into those woods, and the ones north of his house, where there were "three rain ponds." There he practiced "fishing" with twigs.

In the midst of lush, mossy forests on the fringe of settlements, Hugo played with sticks, gathered berries (a rarity near sea level—huckleberries!), and sailed ships in puddles, using thorns and ferns as masts and sails —the whole array of flora there. Despite this rich ecology, Hugo doesn't set the majority of his early poems in those woods. Instead, it was "several miles south of the Riverside area where [his] early poems locate themselves."[4] He settles them into the area to the east, along the Duwamish, where West Marginal Way ran parallel to the river, more than a mile from White Center.

For all my years reading Hugo, I've taken in his passion for the Duwamish and his knowledge and experience there and turned it over many times in my imaginings of him. It was an important place, I knew, especially since so much of his prose hovered around West Marginal Way (he named his collection *The Real West Marginal Way*, pleased with the distinction between life and art that "Real" implied) and the dark road lined with mills and boat launches, reiterating its hard, cold shadowing of the river's western banks: "In many of my early poems, the speaker is, I am, somewhere along West Marginal Way, the slow lower reaches of the Duwamish River, the last two or three miles before the river ends in Elliot Bay, Puget Sound. I was only partially familiar with the landscape. Reading these poems, one might think I had spent much time in that area and had an intimate knowledge of the place, but that's not true."[5] Here, Hugo admits something important. He "was only partially familiar with the landscape." While the poems might indicate that he "had spent much time in that area and had an intimate knowledge of the place," Hugo insists, "that's not true." He *didn't* know the nooks and crannies of the river and the settlements along it. His porgies "nailed to the pile" may not have been caught there, but instead in Lake Meridian, a recreational fishing spot he sometimes went to with his grandfather and cousin Warren, his Aunt Sarah, and, "before her divorce, Uncle Carleton."[6] Any reader would assume, and most do, that he knew the place by heart, but Hugo didn't really know the Duwamish very well. What he knew was White Center—those few blocks around his house.

What of a writer's early places? I'm wondering as I pull out of my parking spot in White Center and head east, toward the river. I'm aiming for that area Hugo wrote about, the one that seemed just murky enough to be rich in images for poems. Did a writer's childhood home, or even his hometown, seal firmly onto his psyche, filtering through all the poems and prose he would write? Did the act of passing through, of riding the trolley along the river or bumping along in his grandfather's Model A, give Hugo glimpses of the river that would trigger his imagination?

Partly knowing and partly not knowing the area, it seemed, was what rendered it perfect terrain for Hugo's poems: "Often, a place that starts a poem for me is one I have only glimpsed while passing through." For him, the Duwamish was glimpsed again and again, until it became what he describes in *The Triggering Town* as a "base of operations for the poem . . . a stage setting." The river remained a mystery too, a stretch of waterway and taverns where down-and-out people fished and tossed their dead pets in gunny sacks during the Depression, where boys fished through outhouse holes, and old machinery floated up in the brackish tides. The poems describe the docks and smoke-enshrouded steel and shingle mills, the rotten pilings along the piers, the fish landed by the boys, tossed upon the dock planks, sputtering grit and blood. Murders happened down there. People out of work pulled up salmon from the depths, poisoned with chemical runoff, and took them to their shacks. The valley's darkness spread all the way to Tacoma from that northern section huddled up against Delridge Way, the spine of West Seattle.

Oddly, not having "intimate knowledge of the place" gives Hugo more credibility than he might have had if he'd written purely about his home turf in White Center. In the same way a method actor fashions a realistic concoction of self by pinching details from reality and then crafting imagined events around those, Hugo took his glimpses of the Duwamish and created narratives that feel personally witnessed. If he had known every stone and bush and rotten barge, his poems might be documentaries, bloodless and dogmatic. Letting "the truth conform to music," Hugo created poems in which the rhythm of the lines overrode an adherence to actual locations and events. For Hugo, this was the crux of his aesthetic about writing—the "triggering town" was a place imagined from remnants, and the Duwamish—that tired, old river, bookended by White Center and Riverside—was the richest possible source of those remnants. Hugo appropriates this place of broken weirs, submerged hulls, and decaying porgies, and it opens a world of rain and failure to him.

"I am a regionalist," Hugo said to his friend Donna Gerstenberger, a professor at the University of Washington and chair of the English Department there. "Though of course there are several ways of defining region," he continued. "When I write a poem, I lay emotional claim to the setting."[7] Gerstenberger describes Hugo's attraction: "The poet places himself in relationship to a particular place and lets the poem explore the spaces that the relationship makes possible."[8] Perhaps because of the dark, unknowable nature of the place, something gripped the boy Hugo, and he wrote about that stretch of river again and again.

As I make the drive down the hill from White Center, passing a new development of townhouses painted in reds, oranges, and blues, I'm realizing that the area Hugo actually wrote about was just out of reach, almost two miles from the small house where he lived with his grandparents. It would have been a long walk for a boy. Instead, he'd stayed in his yard, and in the woods nearby, sailing twigs through stumps of rainwater and pinching slugs from the paths and pulling rocks from Longfellow Creek. The river was too far off to actually experience.

Just as Hugo had, I lived just far enough from a river that I could never actually get to it. On the southeastern edge of Cincinnati, our home was near the Ohio, a clay-milk river of sludge and barges. That waterway, a "slow and sick" river, also "Midwestern in the heat," pushed its way into the "mighty Mississippi," as my grandparents often called it. The Duwamish, on the other hand, finds salt water to the north. It turns into the bay.

While Hugo's house was almost two miles from the Duwamish River, my childhood home was even closer to the Ohio. Had I traveled the mile to my own nearby river on foot, I too would have crossed a ridge, descended through a spray of deciduous trees where deer roamed, and I also would have come upon a major byway, a four-lane road with fast-moving traffic. My West Marginal Way was Columbia Parkway, a secondary highway that followed the Ohio River through Cincinnati. Crossing that, as Hugo would have had to cross West Marginal Way, I then would have slid down to the riverbank. For me, it would be a steep descent from the fringe of rocks and clay into the water. There, like Hugo, I would have seen barges huffing past. Mine would have been carrying coal, and Hugo's would have been hauling lumber.

Many times, I'd heard my grandfather say that he'd swum in the Ohio as a boy. It seemed so brave to me, slipping into all that mud with those twirling currents and no rocks or outcroppings to hang onto, that I imagined him clutching for a raft, one he'd fashioned out of logs. My grandfather told me that he remembered a church steeple poking up from the water during the river's worst flood, the one that happened when he was small. He said that whirlpools were almost invisible at eye level; you could see them only from above. Boys drowned back then, just after the turn of the century. According to my grandfather, canoes of Little Miami Indians regularly came down the Little Miami River from small settlements and journeyed into the open water of the Ohio.

Do I remember this as part of the folklore that I've pinned to the triggering place near my childhood home? From that house, the one tucked behind the hill from the waterway, I might have walked up the path all the way to the top so that I could have a view of the magnificent river. But I didn't. Instead, the little trail disappeared into a wrinkle of clay and rocks between two hillsides. I never ventured that far. I kept to the low-lying trails, climbed trees, and built little shelters out of branches and leaves.

To be sure, my landscape wasn't like Hugo's at all. Instead of looking across the river to estuaries and evergreens, we had oaks, maples, and elms and the bluegrass hills. In my place, the heat of summer baked the giant leaves into the clay, and snakes—garters—crawled through the woods, and if the creek had been deeper, water moccasins. But I felt that pull of the river—ominous in its attraction. Because I was supposed to stay away, I was drawn toward it. Over that hill, right on the Mason-Dixon Line, I imagined that muddy river floating the coal and limestone barges along its winding shit-colored passage to the Mississippi. And my whole imagination about my childhood home, what I call upon in dreams and in crafting language, rests on the other side of that hill from the river. My reality was away from the water, nestled in the gentle little valley where my family's house sat on Grandin Road. In that world, on my side of the slope, mercury-quick salamanders sunned themselves on creek rocks and our dogs barked at strangers. I remember a box turtle, maybe ten inches long, that lived in those woods. Standing above him and then squatting to see his little reptilian face, I'd talk to him. Since eastern box turtles can live to be a hundred, he might still be pawing his way along the creek's drying trickle. I still dream of him.

Even now, just before sleep, I return to those trails I'd run thirty-five, even forty years ago. There, I walk the loops and dead ends through those woods, seeking always the hard, hollow sound of my feet across the worn dry paths of summer, or the cluck of knee-deep mud in April, the wild overgrowths of late spring. My mother, who grew up in the same house, tells me that sheep pastures once rolled across the hills next to our property and across the road. Our trees, fat-trunked elms and oaks, might never have been cut for fields, and since my grandparents had built the house in 1935–39, there had been nothing else on the land for at least thirty years. Before that? Yankee camps to guard the river? I imagine the Little Miami walking those same trails where my little spotted dog ran, where I ran, shirtless in the heat, whipping against nettles and seedlings, sharp switches that tingled my skin as I tore through the woods. One path ran from a small opening in the yard, through a swath of maple and oak starts, deep into the cover of the larger trees, and down to the creek.

What, I always wonder, if I had lived there until now? If I had seen the property's subtle shifts over the years? On a trip back a few years ago, I'd toured those woods with my daughter Maddy, who was nine then, and the landscape seemed like a set of familiar props, things I'd touched before, and they had been imported into a place that didn't quite feel like the one I'd known. It felt like a simulation. The hills had worn down, either from erosion of weather or memory; the creek dried up and the little seam where it ran had folded in upon itself.

I grew up and moved away and these places and people turned away from me. But when I write, I can't help going back there. I am with that rotted elm, that maple with limbs just beyond reach, the oak from which I hung, up high, over the hillside. Behind that ridge, the river moves along, barely an acquaintance, still a stranger to me.

Going back to these early places is a historical act, but more of an imaginary one. As Hugo often said, the poet's job is to misremember things until they feel true. The brain is wired to allow the pastiche of actual facts to blur into something more meaningful, something that betters reality by making it feel more authentic. Magic resides in the places you barely know. Those are the ones you can make up.

That's what Hugo did with the area around Riverside, the old neighborhood just south of the river's mouth. The two miles of mills and barges were not in any town, they were just a tossed-aside part of Seattle. To him, the place must have felt exotic. It was on the east side of Delridge and Pigeon Hill, inclines that ran between the river and Youngstown, a rough-and-tumble neighborhood near the steel mill. Riverside, a few miles north of White Center, rested against the hill—three rows of frame houses stacked up against the slant that rises into the trees. Little roads, shedding crusts of pavement more and more each year, dead-end into those structures.

At one time, during Hugo's boyhood, Riverside's isolation from West Seattle made it into a village of its own, with a restaurant that sold hardware and lunch, and one hotel. In this little three-block strip, Greeks and Slavs—families with a knack for fishing and storytelling—lived in small cabins along the streetcar tracks. Others managed to haul boards up the hill and build frame houses. Otherwise, Riverside's tiny section of houses had little to resemble a full-scale town—it was more a hamlet locked into the industrial world along the river. South of the designated poetry-generating area was White Center, a place with schools, churches, and stores.

When I drive into Riverside, I can see the outline of the old hotel—that western frame storefront once so prevalent in old western places—within a building now used for storage. Sixteenth Avenue Southwest and Seventeenth Avenue Southwest, streets that reappear a block or two from Hugo's house down in White Center, converge in a triangle at the base of the hill. A few of the old buildings shadow the footprint of a town, but there's no real commerce, not now—only broken-down yards with car and boat parts. West Marginal Way, the busy road that carries me under the West Seattle Bridge, carves the line between Riverside and the loading yards fenced in along the water. I turn into a side street because I catch a glimpse of two tiny and very old cottages standing at a forty-five-degree angle to the street. They remind me of places Hugo wrote about; both would be quaint if they were in good repair. Instead, the porches would fall under the weight of a small child, and the shingles are drying into powder. Resembling the cottages that suffered through Hurricane Katrina in New Orleans, they have entrances several feet above ground level, with little rickety steps. The tiny yards hold old boat parts. I wonder what the residents are like—the folks who have kept the original flavor of Riverside intact. No one is visible.

The wisp of a town gone by reverberates with possibilities for poems. The cottages are structures Hugo would have written about. I hear a whoosh of time roaring through that space off the river, up the street of Riverside, tugging at the clapboard of these tiny cabins. Above me, larger houses are tethered to the hill with long wooden stairs and the crumbling dead-end streets gone to pathways. I have the feeling of being watched, a sensation that comes to me in towns that are on the verge of passing out of existence.

Hugo captures the haunted stirrings of Riverside in his poem "Duwamish Head." Re-imagining a woman who was actually killed in the little settlement along the river, Hugo says that she was "diced by scaling knives" and "scattered in the shack." She was a "girl" whom the speaker of the poem claims to know. "I licked her knees," Hugo writes, lifting a true-to-life story of a girl who turned up dead along the

Riverside cabins, 2008.

Duwamish and bringing it into his own experience, transforming it into an imagined encounter. "If I once subjected girls to cruelty in fantasies, of vengeance for the pain and rejection I had suffered at the hands of women, I could also turn myself into a snipe and dive heroically out of the sky to rescue them."[9] It was a fictional leap, the kind a mystery novelist might set up for his main character after reading enough newspaper stories. Along a dark pier, in the fishing shack, the hero would fall into a tumble with a girl who lived nearby. "She tossed me meat and called me dog," he writes in the poem. In my car, parked at the little ramshackle cottage, I can almost see the dead girl along the floorboards inside the shack. It's that kind of personal suction into the poem that Hugo creates, and the tone of "Duwamish Head" pulls readers into Hugo's self-denigration, expressed through his speaker's murky desperation, confusing sex with violence until the poem tugs us into Hugo's imagined tryst and

Riverside house, 2008.

the horrid murder that ensued. Then, just as quickly, Hugo leans into the landscape, letting the "wind around [his] ears" ring of "violins and shot." Like a Romantic Era poet, he's letting the physical world blurt out his, the poet's, state of mind. Caught between the rough beauty of the place and the destroyed people who live there, Hugo describes the tension in this crossfire of music and gunpowder. It's what establishes the music in his verse: "violins and shot."

Organic things have disappeared from the spillway—no violins here. The Duwamish no longer bears "a cascade color to the sea": "With salmon gone and industry moved in / birds don't bite the water." The river is an environmentalist's "shot" or wake-up call; the waterway is mostly dead. However, more than being a poem for nature advocates, "Duwamish Head" is a poem for armchair psychologists. Hugo trolls the Duwamish for images to furnish the speaker's misery: "River, I have loved, loved badly on your bank," he writes, and "Loved badly you and years of misery / in shacks along your bank." He's becoming the fish, the flailing creature in poor health: "My fins are hands."

He captures the essence of that place and becomes entwined in it: "This river helped me play an easy role— / to be alone, to drink, to fail." At the end, the poem turns almost to incantation: " . . . show me bones / of cod, scales and blood, faces in the clouds / so thick they jam the sky with laughter." The poem is open on my lap, and I put it on the floor of the passenger side. The dog leans over and licks my hand. Here, I'm thinking, is where Hugo once stood. Only he didn't fail, his persona did. The poem is what's left. I turn on the car and pull around, toward the river. The metal siding of the buildings across West Marginal Way blocks my view of the water. I can't help thinking that not long from now what remains of Riverside will be torn down and replaced by condominiums. The city is already planning "live-work spaces," dog parks, and even a gondola up to Delridge Way.

Of course, for that to happen, the Duwamish would have to be cleaned up. The river, once an estuary of tidal flats that brought together the Black, Cedar, White, and Sammamish rivers, knotting through black cottonwoods until the Duwamish emerged, looped like a half-coiled rope on a floor. That was until 1906, when a group of white settlers decided to connect Seattle's two freshwater lakes, Lake Washington and Lake Union, and dug a canal between the two bodies of water. This lowered the water level of Lake Washington. Water drained into Lake Union to the north, and at the southern end of Lake Washington the water dropped, drying out the Duwamish valley. The Black River completely disappeared, and people told stories about seeing the fish flopping around on dry riverbeds.

Then the plan emerged to straighten the river. In "Plans for Altering the River," Hugo describes a contemporary version of the same impulse, one that grew out of the same sort of hunger for commerce and growth that inspired the white settlers of the early 1900s. He gives a sarcastic soliloquy on altering the flow "just when the water was settled and at home." Seattle's pioneers wanted to shape the Duwamish into a straight canal. Dirt from Beacon Hill and the Denny Regrade, a project that razed a Cascade foothill from an area near downtown, absorbed the curves and sponge islands of eelgrass, straightening the river. By 1920 the refurbished waterway became two straight lines connecting in a "V" around Harbor Island, a new construct hailed as the largest man-made island in the world. The passages were fifty feet deep and would allow

Duwamish barges, 2008.

barges and seaworthy vessels to dock or turn around. Some came in through the West Waterway, around the island, and left via the East Waterway.

The wide swath of tidelands disappeared. The original river, where the Duwamish people had lived and fished, was erased. To the city limits, several miles south, the river now ran as straight as water through a tube. It sliced through the landscape like the lines in a cubist painting. Where there had been eelgrass, clamming beds, herring, and salmon, now there were pilings and dirt. The curves in the water's path, once sheltering little peninsulas for water birds, drained into the large canal. Only Kellogg Island, a muddy-banked mass of scrub, remains—an oddity in the shaft of waterway where barges travel in and out with scrap metal.

On West Marginal Way, I pass the Gray Line bus lot and the river appears—looking pressed down under a graphite sky. It flows north, the region of the compass that frightened Hugo. In "Duwamish #2," he describes how "the river points / the wrong way on the in-tide / and the alders lean to the arid south." Then, "learn now there is one direction only— / north, and, though terror to believe, / quickly found by river and never love." It's cold here, and the clouds fill up. By the time I get out of the car, I'm reaching for my rain slicker. In some strange superstition, I believe that it always rains at the Duwamish—even if it rains nowhere else in the city.

I'm in an urban park that was once was the setting for two shipping terminals. T105 and T107 were docks to offload barges and fishing boats; now they are grassy fronts along the banks of the river. Ragged laurels and salal fill in the view, and I walk along some little paths over to the water. There, the rain comes, at first making a sound like shuffling paper across the leaves. Drops here form larger rings than rain elsewhere. At the edge of the path, where it drops over to the sludge that some might call a beach, I'm looking out at Kellogg Island. A collection of cottonwoods, the island fills in the view to Boeing. Nearby, the old Plant #2 is being taken down; the demolition cranes are pulling out the boards.

"This river's curves are slow and sick," Hugo wrote in "Duwamish." "The river, split and yellow / and this far down affected by the tide," lines from "West Marginal Way," traced his boyhood waterway through the silt caught underneath the Boeing Plant #2 where he would later work—the guck seeping in the brackish tides, backwashing into the flats. More than forty years later, things haven't changed much. The most current EPA report on the area says that Boeing Plant #2, built in 1936, "has manufactured airplane parts . . . using a wide range of hazardous chemicals, including heavy metals (chrome, zinc, copper, cadmium, silver), cyanide, mineral acids and bases, petroleum products, polychlorinated biphenyls (PCBs), and chlorinated solvents, such as trichloroethylene. . . . The facility has contaminated soil and groundwater, and sediment in the Duwamish Waterway. The site poses potential risk to the health of people, fish, wildlife, and the environment."[10]

I want to let my dog swim here, but I don't. Ida stays in the car, her face poking through the half-rolled window. I've read that the toxins that would burrow into her fur could be enough to kill her. And she'd shake her wet coat all over the inside of the car so that I'd breathe the stuff for weeks. Many animals living in South Park, a community another mile south along the Duwamish, die after moving to the area. The high incidence of cancer for these doomed creatures—most die of liver cancer—pervades South Park, a neighborhood like White Center in its rich ethnic populations and its poverty, where life expectancy is seven years shorter than that of other Seattleites.

Ida tosses her head and yelps. She wants me to let her out. She looks at me and gives a whimper, then curls onto the seat.

The history of this place before the arrival of the "changers," as the Duwamish people call those who transform their landscapes, is one of settlements, sophisticated harvest techniques, and complex, robust connections to family and community. Basketry Hat, a collection of shelters that was more of a community than Riverside ever managed, was located right where I'm standing. Long before the Denny party (the "first white settlers," according to popular historical legends) landed at Alki, the beach along West Seattle, white trappers and traders had been passing through the area, some arriving as early as the 1700s. The native peoples were not isolated.

However, white settlers and indigenous people shared "no common vision of the river."[11] Where the Indians saw spirits in the physical places where they rested their nets, the clutch of invading settlers saw the land around Elliott Bay as something to seize and exploit for material gain.[12] Whites considered the native symbols to be ornaments and had no trouble destroying the tribal icons. Historian Coll Thrush notes how those "numinous places along the river and its delta: a boulder carved with shamanic power spirits, the home of a malevolent spirit that took the form of a fingerless hand rising from the water, the ruins of an ancient fish weir" were impossible to explain to the recently arriving white settlers.[13] Consequently, "people of the inside place," as the Duwamish tribe was known, moved up to Suquamish or further south with the Muckleshoot tribe. With them went the "salmon-drying frames, duck nets stretched between tall poles," and the curing wood that the Duwamish people had set up all along the river's banks.[14] Their spiritual references remained throughout the estuary, but the physical ones disappeared.

In 1866, a petition drafted by natives and settlers garnered support, but not enough to create a reservation along these lands. The Duwamish, denied their place, watched it become submerged by the bilge water of ships and the outflow pipes of mills. To discover what happened along the Duwamish, you'd have to acknowledge that the river isn't there anymore. In its place, a waterway has been installed. Even archeology couldn't pull up the past, not here. Natives and whites have interwoven their cultures so much that what's submerged rises into the air. The past, I come to believe while looking at the river's muddy out tide, actually hovers above the spaces where people once gathered, where dugout canoes once passed and fishing lines caught on Depression era pilings. Over time, flashes of what happened collect and sift into a location and that makes a place. We come into it and the shapes are constantly shifting.

By the 1930s, a time when Hugo sets some of his poems, urban Indians were relegated to the bottom of the cultural heap. West Seattle "towered over the sources of felt debasement, the filthy, loud, belching steel mill, the oily slow river, the immigrants hanging on to their odd ways, Indians getting drunk in the unswept taverns, the commercial fishermen, tugboat workers, and mill workers with their coarse manners."[15] Thrush says, "For Hugo, Indian people were simultaneously neighbors and metaphors, members of the urban lower classes as well as symbols of urban poverty."[16] Thrush underscores two different versions of a "place-story." Those were: "this city is Indian land" and "this city is no place for Indians."[17]

The contradiction sounds as though it were pulled directly from one of Hugo's verses: same flatness, same directness. Hugo too had laid a hand on both narratives about the city's past. Both were true. Each one was polarizing. Remarkably, Hugo managed to look into the ravaged land that was once tidal flats and homeland for the Duwamish natives and into the decline of many Duwamish themselves, still living in the city. Hugo nails this with a stereotype of his own, calling the Duwamish people by the old slur: "Madness means, to redmen, I am going home."

Hugo describes the Indians as being in taverns instead of longhouses. In this realm, he writes that "no Indian will interrupt his beer" to "tell the story" of a murdered girl on the nearby dock. For the Indian, the madness of "going home" is untenable. He can't go home. Someone else is occupying his land, a place his people had known for 1900 years. To claim even the devastated, polluted place where they'd once lived was impossible. It had become Seattle's dumping ground. Indians were no longer in possession of it. They could visit the bar, a public place, but not fish the river—a site that would garner a Superfund rating from the Environmental Protection Agency.

In 1971, Duwamish tribal members each received just sixty-four dollars for lands that had become the city of Seattle, land worth billions of dollars. In 1975, the port of Seattle destroyed what archeological remnants there were of the old Duwamish village of Basketry Hat, the place where I stand now. Bulldozers thundered in and tore down five old houses on the bank. Once again, the spirit of the place went further underwater, along with the mussels, octopuses, clams, eelgrass, and herring that had once lived there. By 1979, the Duwamish were denied fishing rights that had been guaranteed by treaty.

Today, the Duwamish tribe has secured land across from Terminal 107 Park, once the home of two villages: Ha-Ah'-poos ("Where There are Horse Clams") and Tohl-ahl-too ("Herring House"). The tribe, numbering about 600 enrolled members, is raising money to build a longhouse there, keeping their presence in West Seattle and along that destroyed river.

Eventually, thirty-five years after leaving White Center, Hugo will bring his poems back to where they began—along the Duwamish near Riverside. In his first book, *A Run of Jacks* (1961), he writes about the river, West Marginal Way, and Alki Beach while homing in on other towns and rivers in western Washington—places where he fished as a boy and as a young man: the Skykomish, Stilliguamish, and Snoqualmie. From there, the poems in his next five books roll out to Italy, where Hugo was a bombardier during World War II; to the Isle of Skye, where he lived for a winter; and to Montana, where he lived for the last nineteen years of his life: quite a lot of territory for a "regionalist." In 1980, two more books of Hugo's came out—the last two before his death: *White Center* and *The Right Madness on Skye*. The first was a return home, and the second, a return to the far off.

Beginning from that area along the Duwamish River and zooming outward to Europe and back, is to see the palindrome of Hugo's life and his poems. He ends up dying at Seattle's Virginia Mason hospital in a room several floors up, in the middle of Seattle, not far from White Center. The poems, too, return to their familiar themes of broken people and places, alongside rivers and bays—places where "this water started it all, this sullen / arm of gray wound loose about the islands / whipped in patches by the north wind white." Hugo is consumed more by the river than by the town. Along its slow, flat current he encounters the edge of the country, of the psyche, the palm at the end of the mind, the final weave of his life.

Going back there, at the end of his days, brings Hugo directly to his past. "Town or poem, I don't care how it looks," he writes in "White Center," the title poem of one of these last books. Behind the old stores, the swamp was "filled and seeded." "Wasn't it all degrading?" he asks, remembering an old man whom he had baited "to rage." It's as if he is looking in a mirror.

Hugo sees himself in men who pull in the day's final catch, who sit in taverns, who pass out in the yard. They all represent what he might grow into being. One of the great moments in all of Hugo's work is the slowing down, the pause between his description of the drunk who fell, so often, into the salal while Hugo was growing up across the street. " . . . I loved some terrible way / He lived in his mind and tried to be decent to others. / I loved the way we loved him behind our disdain." And then, the move to the next stanza:

> Clouds. What glorious floating. They always move on
> like I should have left early. But your odd love and a war
> taught me the world's gone evil past the first check point
> and that's First Avenue South.

That distance between "the way we loved him behind our disdain" and "clouds" is remarkable. You can feel the poet pausing and then looking up. Skyward, away from the pain of the situation, Hugo travels and the verse follows. The breath between stanzas, the open space of the page, is a peek through urban clutter into a white river.

To pull away from Riverside is to think of that gap in the poem—how remarkable the distance between the present and the past. "It's all beginning to blur / as it forms. Men cracking up or retreating." The "blur" closes the gap between the poems and the actual river. Unlike me, in my position as a reader, Hugo had hoped that "this town would die / and your grave never reopen. Or mine." He's "kicking the loose gravel home." I, on the other hand, am seeing the whole place reopened. In our conversation, the one that a poet undertakes with his reader, Hugo is "certain I remember everything wrong," as if he is remembering incorrectly, or as if he is remembering the "wrong" things that happened there. The pun stings.

Hugo's poems present him as "a wrong thing in a right world," his version of a poet's job description. But he knew that one's persona could dissolve here. He couldn't live up to being that man who forever lived in despair and isolation. He would find a woman with two children, marry her, and give up drinking. He wouldn't live his life in this place. Still, the poems couldn't shake it off. "Water knocks / at mills and concrete plants, and crud / compounds the gray." No one had described the airplane-metal color of the mist with such bluntness. Music resonates in these stocky lines, even in the despairing descriptions of Depression-era Seattle, when gunnysacks of cats and dogs washed up on the shores, or when boys fished for porgies and "nailed them" to the pilings, when Duwamish fishermen still hunkered down by that river, hoping for salmon.

Hugo's poems begin in towns; he sets the compass within settlements and then the poems steer away, following a trajectory outward to a trout stream. Some never leave the places where the poems start but bear a longing to go further, to reach the stream. The lifeblood of the poems counts on that tension between village and water rapids, between settled and indigenous. Rivers haunt. Towns too.

Third Generation Restaurant in Cataldo, 2007.

Cataldo, Idaho

CATALDO MISSION
for Jim and Lois Welch

We come here tourist on a bad sky day,
warm milk at 15,000 and the swamp across
the freeway blinding white. No theory
to explain the lack of saint, torn tapestry.
Pews seem built for pygmies, and a drunk
once damned mosquitoes from the pulpit,
raging red with Bible and imagined plague.
Their spirits buoyed, pioneers left running
for the nothing certain nowhere west.
Somewhere, say where Ritzville is, they would
remember these crass pillars lovely
and a moving sermon they had never heard.

More's bad here than just the sky. The valley
we came in on: Mullan. Wallace. Jokes
about the whores. Kellogg and, without salvation,
Smelterville. A stream so slate with crap
the name pollutes the world. Man will die again
to do this to his soul. And over the next hill
he never crosses, promises: love, grass,
a white cathedral, glandular revival
and a new trout, three tall dorsal fins.

We exit from the mission, blind. The haze
still hangs amplifying glare until
two centuries of immigrants in tears
seem natural as rain. The hex is on.
The freeway covers arrows, and the swamp
a spear with feathers meaning stop.
This dry pale day, cars below crawl thirsty,
500 miles to go before the nation quits.

Overlooking the Mission

COMING INTO A TOWN that inspired a Hugo poem is like opening a trapdoor between the lines of verse and stepping into a storeroom. Inside, the present and past sift together—the historical town, the imagined town, and the real town converging into some splintered masterpiece of flotsam and woe. That's one reason I go on the road. One minute I'm at home reading the poem, and the next minute some kind of longing and excitement takes over and I'm packing the car and putting Hugo's book on the passenger seat. Later, I look up, leaning over the steering wheel, and the town is upright in my line of vision like a page in a pop-up book. Forms emerge into real churches, real school houses, real general stores, poking through my former imaginings in the same way a poem comes off the page and goes three-dimensional in the mind.

First, from the highway, you see the old mission church of Cataldo on the hill, a yellow flat-fronted structure, clear of ornament, standing over the sweep of trees and grasses. It looks like it's painted on a screen hung against the backdrop of the hills, beckoning the amateur historian and landmark seeker or the lapsed churchgoer.

This place is a National Park site now, nestled along Interstate 90, less than forty miles into Idaho from the Washington State border. Generic preservation replaces the once-Catholic markings: plaques detailing the history of the original mission (moved in the mid-1800s to De Smet, Idaho, a town named for the mission's Jesuit founder), and crisp bureaucratic signs directing you to the parking lot. All that's left here is this chapel and an outbuilding.

The church reminds me of Wallace Stevens's little poem, "Anecdote of the Jar," three simple quatrains with short lines, beginning with: "I placed a jar in Tennessee, / And round it was, upon a hill." The vessel "took dominion everywhere." Every time

I read that poem, I think of a chapel set deep in the woods. That jar is an imposition that alters the surrounding territory because people project whatever sacred or profane notions they desire to onto it. It orders the slovenly wilderness around it.

The church is closed so I don't even get to look at the "tapestry," or the pews "built for pygmies," as Hugo described them. I can't see in the windows.

"I think it was closed when we went there too," says Lois Welch when I later tell her about my little trip. "We just walked around and left."

Hugo went to Cataldo specifically to write a poem and dedicate it to his friends, Jim and Lois Welch. He was close to them; he'd taught Jim, worked with Lois as a colleague, and spent years fishing and partying with both of them. Toward the end of his life, long after he wrote the poem, he became their neighbor. Hugo and his second wife, Ripley, lived three doors down from the Welchs on Wylie Street, in Missoula.

On the way to and from Seattle, Hugo had always passed the yellow mission church at Cataldo and had wanted to get off the highway to take a look. It was almost a four-hour drive from Missoula, but one day, at Hugo's prompting, Jim and Lois agreed to go there with him. In Hugo's Buick, the three of them drove west and toured the mission site.

Jim Welch always recoiled a bit from the Jesuit missions; he was a Blackfeet and Gros Ventre who grew up under the tutelage of strict nuns who pulled him by the ear and sat him in the back row, even though his vision was terrible. (He'd assumed that only "smart" kids could see the board.) Also, Jim had heard horror stories from his dad. At the Indian boarding schools, the Jesuit fathers washed out the boys' mouths with soap when the Jesuits heard them speaking in their native language. The priests cut off the children's long dark hair until they had the same white-boy haircuts that the Jesuits did. Jim's father ran away twice. The programs instilled by the priests, Jim always felt, were intended to pull families from their tribes, disconnect them from their native language, and "educate" their children in the ways of white people by erasing their culture.

Jim, however, was a good sport, especially when it came to Hugo, and went along for the ride. Hugo had been his teacher and grew into being his friend. Between them, they had a love of poetry and of a good trout stream. Lois's wry humor and spirit of fun made them both laugh. "Let's go!" she had said.

Even a day with his friends, an outing of fun and laughter, and a poem in honor of their afternoon together doesn't cheer up Cataldo. "The freeway covers arrows," Hugo writes, and the verse leaks a sour history that spans the entire Silver Valley, a place where "more's bad . . . than just the sky," and where leftovers from mining include "two centuries of immigrants in tears." Inside the church, Hugo imagines, "a drunk / once damned mosquitoes from the pulpit" and "pioneers left running / for the nothing certain nowhere west."

These were once the Coeur d'Alene's grounds, self-defined and governed, stretching from southeastern Washington through the Idaho panhandle and down into the flesh of the state. The tribe spoke an inland Salish, a language decipherable by Flatheads and Kootenays, and was tagged with the French name "Heart of the Awl." A hard-trading chief, intimidating French traders, inspired the moniker, which translates to "Coeur d'Alene." He'd refused some offers from the Frenchmen, and, in defying their overtures, he was forever labeled as a brutal, tough-hearted leader, and "Coeur d'Alene" became the name of his entire tribe.

Naming a kinship group after one trapper's slur to the chief (Heart of the Awl), that one simple act, spins out through time into contemporary Coeur d'Alene—the hotels and tinny restaurants, the plastic siding, artificial trees, Best Buys and Wal-Marts, sidewalks without pedestrians, yachts motoring with giant toilet-flushing sounds and Jet Skis, the land of "fun, American style," and there's nothing of these natives in it at all. No solitude or reflection, no contemplation or exertion without engines or oils or smoke, just the paved, tree-stripped hills named for a shrewd chief who wouldn't hand over a pelt to an insolent French woodsman.

Outside that chapel, I can imagine the steamboat that came up the river, now a trickle behind the church, carrying passengers to Sunday Mass at this place, then called the Sacred Heart Mission. Views along the river must have been spectacular: deepening mountains and dark evergreens against the water shimmering and splashing as the paddle wheel tugged through it, the sound of a set of knives on velvet, pulling up alongside the hill behind the church.

Women must have lifted their dresses as they stepped from the planks, and the men might have taken the women's elbows and led them up the path. The riverbank was marshy, and the water seeped to mud near the building. Once they reached the crest of the hill, the churchgoers might have raise their palms over their brows and squinted into the Bitterroots. It was a peaceful place, land tilting into mountains. Inside, they

Chapel at Cataldo, once the Chapel of the Sacred Heart, 2007.

heard the gospel in Latin and admired the way that Father Ravalli converted the Indians to the language of the Mass, though they attended separate services.

The church that Jim and Lois came to with Dick Hugo was one built by local natives who cut and milled the wood on the site. Constructed between 1848 and 1853 under direction of Fr. Ravalli, the structure is a plain-fronted primitive design, inspired by peasant churches in the Italian countryside. According to promotional Parks Department material, "wattle and daub construction [was] used to make the walls both durable and light. The decorations of the interior illustrate both the piety of the workers and their ingenuity. Chandeliers were constructed from old tin cans, the altar was faux-painted to resemble marble, etc."[1] The altar timbers were larch, five feet in diameter, raised into place by pulleys. It was hard work for the laboring Indians—readying the place for white-gloved ladies who appeared on Sundays and holy days of obligation.

I climb back into my little car, turn out gates, and travel over the highway, to see if there's a spot to get a glass of iced tea. Down the hill, around the wild rice paddy that is cover for the Environmental Protection Agency's Superfund status of the site, I come upon an intersection—two dirt streets, a bike path, and one paved road converging into a ragged asterisk. It looks like a town drawn in pencil, not filled in.

Hugo never made it here with Lois and Jim. They'd gone only to the mission. And I can see how they missed it; Cataldo seems like a town without a village—one of those places named on highway signs but that turns out to be some bad excuse for an on-and-off-ramp to the super road. Ahead of me, at the corner, is a brown wooden building. It doesn't appear to ever have been painted. Brown clapboard like you might find in a historic New England village covers the visible three sides, and the back pushes out addition after addition, plywood with fading white paint, rooms skittering along like a train off its rails. "Third Generation Restaurant" it says in faded lettering across the front. Closed now, the former eatery is overtaken with brush.

Down the street, a big pile of logs and two enormous Douglas firs stand in front of an old cottage. A big silver leaf maple shades the gravel. It's dusk, so the crickets are fiddling, and alongside the road is a sign that reads "Cataldo Mennonite Church." The hum of the freeways stuffs itself into the hollow. Further along is a dead end and in the other direction; if I'd kept driving, I'd have crossed an old bridge.

Alongside the road is a brand-new bicycle path atop an old railroad bed, pressed smooth as polished onyx. There's a chain fence through a row of small beams off to either side, like velvet ropes guiding you through a museum. This trail, according to the Environmental Protection Agency, is on the site of the old railway that was con-structed with "readily available materials including mine tailings and waste rock that contained low levels of heavy metals." On the heels of this description, the report takes on a cheerful tone: "The reuse of the railway was a cost effective, safe solution that eliminated the need to remove low level contamination." Today's path retains these waste products: "The asphalt barrier poured on top of the tailings and waste rock protects riders from interacting with the contamination and limits contamination migration," says the EPA report. "For the area of the trail near Chatcolet Lake on the Coeur d'Alene Tribe Reservation, it was determined that waste materials should be removed and replaced with non-contaminated materials." And then, things turn sinis-ter: "To ensure public safety, a trail guide offers common sense suggestions for limiting exposure including remaining on the trail, washing hands and face before eating, and removing dirt from clothing, shoes, children's toys, equipment and pets."[2]

To be out in the wilds of Idaho and have to be cautious when riding a bike along a scenic trail seems an irony that Hugo would have written about. Looking at the town and thinking of all that was buried in the wetlands behind it and underneath the bike trail was like imagining bobbing skulls in some kind of rusty pool of slaughterhouse runoff. Indeed, the sediments from mining have washed down from the Silver Valley, and though you couldn't tell upon first glance, this wetland south of town isn't a healthy place at all. In 2003, 100 migrating tundra swans landed to feed from the swampy grasses at Cataldo and died from consuming lead that had been carried into the wetland from mining runoff.

East Mission Flats, the Superfund cleanup storage site, is two miles west of Cataldo, north of Interstate 90 and across from the mission. It is a repository for waste from the mining in Silver Valley. The site is adjacent to wetlands—though the EPA says it isn't wetlands.[3] This area contains the largest load of mine tailings in the Coeur D'Alene basin, and the EPA is almost poetic in its description: "In the heart of the Silver Valley, down below heights with such old West names as Grizzly Ridge and Cougar Peak, lies a twenty one-square mile Superfund site, the nation's second largest."[4] Cataldo is well within the box—it's eight miles from the epicenter, the Bunker Hill Mine.

While I'm in Cataldo, I don't feel squeezed between these two tortured geographies: the Bunker Hill Mine and East Mission Flats. However, if I were to cut through the woods and hike along some pastureland and through several valleys, I'd come across an open, muddy area where a river would run through an S-curve of blue tarp walls propped up with sticks. It's the Coeur d'Alene River, rerouted. Near the mining ruins, which have been torn down in the last ten years, no vegetation grows. The land is stripped. That would be the Bunker Hill site.

I don't take that route. Instead, I look at the town. Across from the crooked crossroads where the "third generation" occupies one corner, crouches a little market, 3 Bridges Deli, with a seating area—plastic chairs and tables. Down the road, less than a full block away, is the Mission Inn Restaurant. There's no post office or library. In a town with a population of twenty or so houses down one dead end street, to have two eateries, neither of which is a fast-food franchise, is inspiring. I look into both before I decide on the one with more seating and table service. Over a Caesar salad, I prop up the Hugo book and read the poem "Cataldo Mission" again. To give equity in spending my dollars locally, I stop at the 3 Bridges Deli on the way out of town. There, I buy a pack of gum and some chips.

"Want a beer to go with that?" the man at the counter asks.

"Too early," I say. "But thanks."

Richard Hugo would have taken the beer. He and his friends, had they known about it, would have come to the Third-Generation Restaurant. But I'm not Hugo, and sometimes I don't aspire to live out his choreographed assemblies of poems. I want to go to interesting places, but I don't want to stage everything so that it fits into verse. The poem "Cataldo Mission" is not a typical road-trip poem or even a warm reverie on friendship. Instead, it begins: "We come here tourist on a bad sky day," a line I've always thought had a typo—"We come here *tourists* on a bad sky day," accounting for himself and his friends who accompany him. To Hugo, his companions, Jim and Lois Welch, are folks with whom he drinks and fishes, people who, he insists, share his hard look at the world. Lois Welch has told me that "with Hugo there was no division between poetry and real life." He brought his friends along, through the poems and through the actual towns. The poem reads as his kind of intimacy—authentic and direct.

On the other hand, I could read the singular "tourist on a bad sky day" as Hugo himself steering his way through the mission, and subliminally forgetting that his friends were with him at all. "Tourist" could be an adjective. The "we" in the rest of the poem could be read as another version of "you," the oft-used perspective in Hugo's portrait of a town.

The poem rolls underneath clouds that are like "warm milk at 15,000," depositing us into the Cataldo Mission chapel. Inside, Hugo's resistance of religious trappings takes hold. He's picking away at the rotting things in the place—the "torn tapestry" and "pews [that] seem built for pygmies." Then he imagines the priest, a "drunk . . . raging red with Bible and imagined plague." The parishioners, "their spirits buoyed," were nonetheless "pioneers left running / for the nothing certain nowhere west." The service, as Hugo imagines it, is a collage of icons worn beyond use and people left without things they can accomplish. Interestingly, he's painting the West as the land of the unexpected ("nothing certain") and the barren and empty ("nowhere west"), confounding the myths that have been taking hold for almost two hundred years of the land west of the Mississippi as a place where people go to recover from ill health, get on their feet, or reinvent themselves. Hugo doesn't perpetuate the "land of opportunity" fairy tale or the notion that sanctuary is guaranteed in the mountains and prairies spreading to the Pacific. He's from the other side of the American dream.

The language of "Cataldo Mission" is sodden with despair, but it's funny too. "More's bad here than just the sky," he writes, then adding "The valley we came in on." Like the horse he might have come in on, (a comic, John Wayne sort of idiom like "the car that brought you here still runs"), the freeway passes through the Silver Valley, and Hugo and his companions are traveling west through Mullan, Kellogg, and, "without salvation," Smelterville. (Later, Hugo would say to his fellow poet Madeline DeFrees, as they drove from Missoula to Spokane, "How would you like to be the poet in residence in Smelterville?"⁵) With the northern end of the Bitterroot Mountains, deep green and steep, and the tributaries of the Coeur d'Alene River, the place should read as glorious, breathtaking. Hugo sees it as just the opposite: "A stream so slate with crap / the name pollutes the world."

For poets, the act of naming is the art's core practice. Pinning an identity to something—a place, a river, a person—marks it in the world. It grants a verse maker the source of songs, even the saddest ones in which "the name pollutes the world," or where "Man will die again / to do this to his soul." As the opposite image from that of Christ rising from the dead so that his followers could live eternally, Hugo's depiction of "a stream so slate with crap" marks the death of the land, a way for "man" to "die again." It's a gesture toward original sin, the disobedience of Adam in the garden that, according to Catholicism, leads to the loss of eternal life unless the sin is washed away in baptism. Imitating that hope of recapturing the lost garden, Hugo also plants an image of paradise "over the next hill / he never crosses," with "love, grass / a white cathedral," and, most iconic of all to Hugo, "glandular revival / and a new trout, three tall dorsal fins."

It's a place "man" can't reach because he doesn't aspire to it, or is simply too weak to get there. Since the glands (as in "glandular revival")—pancreas, salivary glands, liver, and gallbladder—are filters for human systems, the poem has me considering how a revival rings as Baptist in tone, aimed at cleansing the toxins of disbelief and sin, and how a "glandular revival" might be some kind of cancer-aborting phenomenon in the human body. Since the slag and tailings from the mining pollution have washed into the rivers of the valley, people have been getting sick with cancer for generations, and Hugo recognized this. Even the "new trout, three tall dorsal fins" reads as a dual take on paradise: the mighty fish, disfigured by a steroid-like infusion of two extra dorsal fins, is both godlike and maimed.

Hugo elevates the poem to the power of incantation, as if calling something by the wrong name would cause the alteration of the physical properties of what surrounds him: "The hex is on." (To this day, people believe that a curse was placed on the chapel.) In a place where trout and religion intermingle and outside the mission, "the freeway covers arrows." Even "the swamp" is a warning: "a spear with feathers meaning stop." The wetlands is now a wild rice paddy, disguising some of the country's most toxic sludge, a Superfund site containing the tailings from 150 years of mining, and the highway is a lid on the relics of the Coeur d'Alenes' tribal life.

In the last stanza, Hugo, Jim and Lois "exit from the mission, blind." It's a hazy, "dry pale day," the same kind as it is on this day, while I'm walking around the church, getting a glimpse of the wizened valley where the south fork of the Coeur d'Alene runs shallow. I imagine the three of them, Hugo and his friends, looking across the mountains toward Seattle. "500 miles to go before the nation quits," he writes. As the poem's closure, it reads as a two-sided reference. On one side, "the nation quits" under the weight of its own economic engines (mining, logging, or fishing). And on the other side, he means that the coast, the edge of the sea, is the point of exhaustion where "cars below crawl thirsty" to get there. The land gives way. I imagine that craving for water as I look down to where the river used to be.

Wallace—looking up the Silver Valley, 2007.

Wallace, Idaho

LETTER TO GILDNER FROM WALLACE

Dear Gary: The houses in Wallace are closed after 94 years.
Apparently because those forces of Christian morality,
the Republicans, accused the Governor of coddling sin.
One thing about politicians, they can never be whores,
they're not honest enough. They screw men in ways that only
satisfy themselves. I sit in this last bastion
of honesty left in the land, this town Lana Turner
came from (I'll always love you, Lan) with the five best reasons
to be shut down: Oasis, Sahara, U. and I., Lux
and Luxette. Gary, I'd like to tie the self-proclaimed forces
of morality in chairs and bring in swinging professors
and good librarians to lecture on real civilization
for at least ten years, and those who cater to plebiscitic
prudes would have to pass an exam before they could eat.
They wonder why no one believes in the system. What system?
The cynical lean with the wind, whatever one's blowing,
if you'll pardon the vulgar expression. No, Gary, I'll
issue a curse out of my half-Irish past on the hyper
respectable everywhere. May the bluebird of happiness
give you a venereal disease so rare the only known cure
is life in the tundra five hundred miles from a voter,
the only known doctor, a mean polar bear. May the eyes of starved
whores burn through your TV screens as you watch Lawrence Welk.
I'm getting far from my purpose. I wanted to tell you
I still love your poems, then got hung up on people
who won't leave people alone. The most beautiful building
in Wallace is the unused railroad station. The lovely
thing is the way the citizens know in the undergrounds
of their hearts that this isn't right, this sudden shutdown
of what men came to expect long ago when they came down
from Lookout Pass and the cold, and the first lights they saw

in the distance warmed them to push on into the waiting
warm arms of release. That's one thing poets best never forget.
May the bluebird of happiness help us remember. Best. Dick.

The Last Stoplight

B ETWEEN THE "BIG DIG" underneath Boston and the "Portal to the Pacific"
through a hillside in Seattle, Interstate 90 curves down through Lookout Pass,
at the western border of Montana, into Wallace, Idaho. There, wedged into
a crevice of mountains, the road once took up only two lanes. It ran atop old Highway
10, a former section of the Mullan Road that curved from Walla Walla, Washington,
to Fort Benton, Montana. Until 1991, the last stoplight on all of Interstate 90 was here,
dangling above the intersection of Sixth and Bank streets. Tractor trailers, sports cars,
dump trucks, and station wagons paused before continuing on, as if kneeling before
the crooked sliver of mountain-blocked sky and evergreens.

I first came through Wallace in 1986. The cars and trucks ahead of me stopped, and
when the light turned green, we accelerated through, one at a time, as if we were passing
through a turnstile, awaiting a nod from a gatekeeper. I was perched in the front seat of
an old Volkswagen Jetta, my feet on the dashboard, while my boyfriend Gary drove. As
we passed through town, I looked at the storefronts—the Elks lodge, the 1313 Club, an old
hotel at the corner, and a few shop windows lined with old mining displays. What I didn't
know as I was slowly moving through town that first time was that the stoplight and these
few businesses weren't the only reasons that people stopped in Wallace. The town offered
another form of release, just a block away from the intersection where we all paused.

The building next to the Silver Corner Café was a working whorehouse, and
everyone in town knew about it. Even in 1986, the Oasis bordello was still functioning,
hosting truckers, who stopped in after a day of hauling, and local young men, led by
their fathers, who traipsed into the first-floor parlor looking for a sophisticated sex-ed
class. Townsfolk cherished the "girls," women who came from as far off as Nevada and
as nearby as Kellogg. Some who lived in Spokane worked for a few weeks and then

brought their wages home to their husbands and children. Other people, now grown, remember selling Girl Scout cookies to the ladies. "They bought all of my boxes," one coffee shop owner told me. "They were the most generous women." And there were other gifts: one year the women of the Oasis purchased a police car for the town, a clever benevolence that protected them from riding in the back seat of it.

Activity at the Oasis was humming and bumping along while Gary and I were pulling up to the light. From my caesura at the intersection, like the pause in a stimulating, cadenced poem, I was oblivious to the inner workings of the town. I was a young woman traveling with her boyfriend, returning from a trip to the Midwest and the East, where we'd told our families that we'd be getting married. We were preoccupied about making our home in the West, and I was speculating about what graduate school would be like at the University of Washington, a place I'd chosen for its location and price, and by the flip of a coin on a motel room bed in Montana. Perhaps at that juncture, we'd said how quaint Wallace seemed, how clear the air and how tall the mountains or how the evergreens were startling—you could smell them. If you'd put a camera to the window of the car as we came through Wallace, you'd probably have seen a book of poems open on my lap, and you'd have glimpsed Gary pointing to the cabins on top of the mountains above town.

What would we have thought of the whorehouse in Wallace? Had I heard about a brothel in the East, one set in a pavement-cracked section of New York or Pittsburgh, I'd have conjured up the image of a tenement house, crumbling stucco covering the building, with bling-laden pimps shouting on the front stoops. I'd assume that the place was dangerous. It would be in a part of the city that I would never visit. If, however, I'd known that the whorehouse existed in Wallace, I'd have thought it quaint, like a good omen from the days of the Wild West. Whoring, here, would be a profession blessed with myths of cleanliness and service, offered with pleasantness and humor out of a storefront wedged between the Silver Corner Café and the bookstore. The rooms upstairs would be wrapped with tasteful velvet curtains folded around the windows. This vision was how a newcomer might imagine the Northwest, as a place where taboo things were nestled into an environment of restorative health.

I had a lot to learn.

In 1973, thirteen years before I went to Wallace that first time, the authorities had closed down the Oasis and the Lux, the U and I, the Luxette, and the Sahara, nearly bringing to an end nearly a century of prostitution in Wallace. Shortly thereafter, the Oasis reopened; despite threats from the Feds, it stayed active until 1988. Though the FBI years of J. Edgar Hoover had just come to an end, an emboldened set of regional directors had embarked on prostitution and gambling crackdowns. Wallace was an easy mark. From the early days of the town, in the 1880s, the whorehouses had established themselves in the civic life of Wallace, and outlawing them dismantled an enterprise sanctioned by its long history there. Since the men who migrated to Wallace were fledgling entrepreneurs (mostly scruffy guys desperate to turn a buck) attracted to the risk, adventure, and potential payoffs of mining that didn't always pan out, they typically arrived alone. Few women followed. Even when the population of the town swelled to around 2,000 in the late 1880s, the ratio of men to women was two hundred to one. From then on, as mining ebbed and flowed between boom times and bust, when the population dropped to lows of 900, the whorehouses stayed in business. During tough times in town, the brothels catered to men on the road.

This was the same era that Richard Hugo came through town. It's 1973 or 1974, I can't tell from the poem, and I can hear the door of his Buick clicking shut. I can see his stocky figure as he heads to the 1313 Club for a drink. Perhaps he's on his way to Spokane, or even to Seattle, to give a poetry reading, or a workshop. But Hugo isn't tweedy; there's no whiff of the academic or the effete poet about him. He's dressed in the clothes any recreational fisherman would wear: old, unpleated khakis, a two-button shirt with a pointy collar, a rumpled canvas jacket. He's walking with a limp from a hip knocked out of sync during football and softball games in years past. Just over fifty, Hugo looks like character actor, a man who might play the local informant in an episode of "Mannix."

At the bar in the 1313 Club, Hugo talks to his fellow drinkers. They tell him about the crackdowns on their card games and about the boarding-up of the whorehouses. The more he hears, the more infuriated Hugo becomes. From the gossip dropped by Wallace insiders, he drafts the poem "Letter to Gildner from Wallace," which will appear, a few years later, in his 1977 collection of poems *31 Letters and 13 Dreams*. As with many of the poems in this book, Hugo addresses this one to a friend, this time to Gary Gildner, a fellow poet and part-time resident of Idaho, and he launches the poem from the town he's passing through—in this case, it's Wallace.

In published form, it's an angry, vitriolic poem in which the speaker, a man closely resembling Hugo, begins: "The houses in Wallace are closed after 94 years." From there, the speaker kicks into a rant, a diatribe that eventually swats local politicians, Lawrence Welk, churchgoers, and "people who won't leave people alone." Hugo proclaims himself the enemy of self-righteousness and insists that erudition and a complexity of historical vision, can cure the morality freaks:

> I'd like to tie the self-proclaimed forces
> of morality in chairs and bring in swinging professors
> and good librarians to lecture on real civilization
> for at least ten years, and those who cater to plebiscitic
> prudes would have to pass an exam before they could eat.

He idealizes the "waiting / warm arms of release" for men who live in the "undergrounds / of their hearts," who are craving female company, at whatever cost. For Hugo, prostitution is clearly more than commerce—it is a promise of succor after coming through the dark pass in the mountains. To him, the transactions are romantic. Their disruption reminds him of the small-town battles between the morality police and the regular folks, between good guys and bad guys—a candid western picture rendered in a fat, robust poem, lines sprawling clear to the edges of the page. As a result, the poem is a Baudelarian margin-to-margin prose poem of curses to the holier-than-thou. Like the nineteenth-century French poet, Hugo too is a romantic, swearing off the "self-proclaimed forces of morality."

The repeated touchstone in "Letter to Gildner" is the "bluebird of happiness," a cliché of the time, often uttered ironically. Once, among indigenous American peoples, the bluebird was a symbol of prosperity and domestic comfort. A bluebird predicted good times ahead—comfort and warmth in one's house. From this lore, Hugo taints the ideal with a curse: "May the bluebird of happiness / give you a venereal disease so rare the only known cure / is life in the tundra five hundred miles from a voter, / the only known doctor, a mean polar bear." The string of insults continues to unravel and pops open the stuffing of the poem.

At first, the poem is a letter addressed, in the first person, to Gary Gildner. Then it veers off to address the hyper-respectable, calling them "you," as in "May the bluebird give you." When Hugo's speaker pivots over to this "you," he issues a preface to Gildner: "No Gary, I'll / issue a curse out of my half-Irish past on the hyper / respectable everywhere." Then he launches into the assault against the righteous. But somehow the "you" also feels like apostrophe, the poet's tool of using direct address to the reader. The poem lashes out. Unsettling accusations are tumbling upon the reader, who is, after all, reading a letter addressed to someone else. It can set her back onto her heels, especially if you are, say, a woman who doesn't approve of prostitution.

Hugo's epistolary form, the letter poem, is both intimate and public. All of the letter poems in the collection *31 Letters and 13 Dreams* have long lines; the rows of words stretch almost as wide as prose does, across the pages. They look like letters he'd actually written and typed. Hugo's colloquialisms—"They screw men in ways that only / satisfy themselves" (the politicians) or "I'll always love you, Lan"—drop the teasing, coy diction into earthy speech, the tone one might find in an intimate correspondence. And there's something else: While a poem typically stages an encounter between reader and speaker of the poem, in Hugo's letter poems there's a triad of relationships: the poet/speaker, the addressee, and the reader. They conjugate a more public access with the privacy of letters, creating a tension of private realms and public ordering—a hunt for authenticity on a theatrical stage. Ultimately, it's personal news in public oratory.

And the poem, finally, forgives. "The lovely / thing," Hugo writes, "is the way the citizens know in the undergrounds / of their hearts that this isn't right." He envisions the "forces of Christian morality" as a separate group from the actual citizenry. And then, at the end, the curse turns into blessing: "May the bluebird of happiness help us remember." He's softening the voice, saying "I still love your poems," turning the "you" back to "Gary" instead of leaving it as a generalized "you," the reader. "I still love your poems" feels very personal.

What I wonder, while I'm reading the poem, is if Gildner and Hugo had visited the houses, or at least had been in Wallace together. Hugo's friend Lois Welch assures me, "If you knew Gildner, if you had known Hugo, you'd never have wondered if they visited the brothels. They wouldn't have." Why, then, had Hugo's rage been so strong? Was he projecting his anger about self-righteous people onto Wallace? When Hugo describes "those forces of Christian morality" and the politicians who could never be as good as the whores because "they're not honest enough," the whorehouses come into focus, and there's Hugo, a man in middle age, heavyset and balding, on the street corner, looking at the places boarded up. He's watching the present seal up the past.

And so am I. One of the things about the West, I realize all these years later, is how gritty and difficult life was in these places. The whorehouses, though charming to Hugo, in actuality were places where the harsh acts of exchanging money for sex wore away at the women who worked there. Hugo's poem pivots from the sentimental assumptions that I might have once had—that these women could light up a poem with Wild West images of flouncing skirts and red lipstick. But they are better left unimagined than fully conjured up: soured girls with money tossed at them after raw and course interactions. Once, I might have thought like Hugo—that there was no real harm to anyone in whoring—and I might have imagined brothels as havens in these isolated places, houses where economies ran on mutual need. I know now that Hugo was wrong about that.

The town of Wallace lies on a cedar swamp at the base of four ore-rich canyons. In the early years, prospectors found their way to Wallace and staked claims throughout the surrounding valleys. Some heard rumors and came west. Others found brochures issued by the Northern Pacific Railroad encouraging precious metal seekers to come to "the celebrated gold fields" of Northern Idaho. The railroad wanted to inspire travel on their new line, and the printed materials worked. Migrants did follow the pamphlets; they arrived and waded into the creeks, stooped over with pans, their boots soaked, shuffling through gravel for gold. But placer mining, a practice of panning in places where tunnels were too difficult to dig, virtually stopped when prospectors spotted veins of quartz in outcroppings of rock near the rivers and creeks. Once they chopped into the cliffs, following the glitter, the quartz led them to threads of silver ore.

By 1888, gold was depleted, and the era of silver and lead mining had begun. From the days of pickaxes, shovels, and draining pans, the equipment of mining quickly evolved into dynamite, hoists, and huge drills. With these came smelters, slag piles, and tailings, as well as cyanide, arsenic, lead, and cadmium, washing a cloudy white, and then red and orange, through the rivers. Above the mines, whole mountains were stripped of timber, the hearts of trees used to prop up the warren of tunnels underground.

In fact, more than ranching or farming, mining generated the transformation of the West—the influx of capital and commerce, and the establishment of property rights settled our geography and established the precedence of land ownership for our legal system.[1] By the end of the 1800s, stamp mills (giant crushers of rock) and smelters (baking systems to amalgamate the precious metals, separating them from ore) were appearing throughout the West. The practices introduced wide-scale pollution and diluted water rights. They also created towns. Not coincidentally, as mining took hold, native peoples were forced onto reservations.

What would Hugo have known of mining? His frustration, planted upon the whorehouse closings, was a righteous anger in favor of working people. But what about the miners? Did he think of them when he wrote about the "undergrounds of their hearts," evoking images of shafts and passageways? Though "Letter to Gildner from Wallace," a poem about being irate in the face of self-righteousness, elitism, and power, doesn't refer to mining or the surrounding mountains, because it is set in Wallace, I can sense tunnels underneath the lines of verse.

Over twenty years after I came through Wallace in 1986, I've learned to read land-scapes as though they were poems. To see through the facade of Wallace, one needs only to fly overhead, or to venture up some side roads. There, the clearings appear: the old wooden mine buildings, the spreads of dirt and flotation ponds, and the clear-cuts. Behind the quaint resides hardship. Extraction industries of timber and mining have hollowed out much of our natural landscapes. More than 500,000 abandoned hard-rock mines remain throughout the West, filling 40 percent of the waterways with acid mine drainage.[2] Around Wallace, I could see wooden shafts from the roads, and they would pull my eye up to the ridges cut into the mountains—to prevent erosion from the timber cutting. They remind me of the byways of the Olympic Peninsula, where thin curtains of trees block a tourist's view of thousands of acres of timber clear-cuts. Mining and logging activities have been well hidden, and it was years before I began to witness their effects, mostly by reading about them. Then I saw them in the rotting wooden shacks and flumes across the mountainsides, in the tumbledown stamp mills and the hills stripped of timber. The more I looked, the more I noticed, as if my actual vision had changed from the time I was that young girl in the car, reading poems and pointing to the mountains, to now—when I'm a middle-aged woman who sees the min-ing leftovers with the attention of a desperate gold-panner, sifting for riches.

And so, though there were larger issues than whoring in Wallace, Hugo had sidestepped them in favor of ranting about the prostitutes being run out of business. In this, our concerns go separate ways. I read the poem again while sitting in my rundown hotel room, up a steep staircase from the street in Wallace, and decide that the whore-houses were merely an indicator species for a much more complex set of problems,

Alley in Wallace, 2007.

dilemmas of strife and hardship in a town of boom and bust, of secrets held and secrets revealed.

A year before the Lux, U and I, Luxette, and Sahara closed, the townsfolk were fighting a far bigger disaster than the FBI's intrusions. They had lost ninety-one miners in the largest mining disaster in the western United States. In 1972, the Sunshine Mine filled with such a high level of carbon monoxide that the men on lunch break actually died sitting up, holding coffee mugs on their knees. One "fell running, his arms and legs in full stride."[3] Over the course of eight days, the townsfolk pulled out body after body, all disfigured; some had some melted into the ground.

Two survivors lasted without food and water for eight days, escaping the poisoned air by moving to a fresh air pocket where they huddled without light. They were 4,800 feet down, clamped into darkness inconceivable to anyone but the blind. Gregg Olsen, a writer who researched and followed the story, named his book after those incalculable lightless depths: *The Deep Dark*. Tracing the events leading up to the leak, and then the chaos of its consequences, Olsen assembled a minute-by-minute chronology. He describes how the media plagued the town for weeks and how insurance personnel and lawyers questioned mine officials and family members: "Carloads of men cloaked in superiority and three piece suits arrived on Sunday in search of motel rooms."[4] The attention of outsiders, including President Nixon, who sent a skimpy telegram, infuriated people in the town. They'd lost husbands, brothers, sons, cousins, nephews, fiancés, boyfriends, and neighbors, and the heaviness of the place wavered between hysteria and an acceptance grimly dispensed.

Day after day, bodies were pulled out and laid into pickup trucks until the corpses stopped coming—and finally the two survivors were lifted out. The men, Tom Wilkinson and Ron Flory, had lasted eight days by sucking clear air through a borehole to the surface. But above ground, shortly after their rescue, they were disdained and taunted. In bars and restaurants and on the streets, relatives of their dead colleagues no longer greeted them; acquaintances mocked them; merchants ignored them. At a Kellogg bar, one of the widows, furious that Ron Flory had survived when her own husband had perished, "slapped him as hard as she could."[5] Both men finally had to leave the area. Eventually, survivor's guilt and anger at the mining companies began to burrow further into the temperament of the town. Wallace had known emotional heaviness and desperation before. It had been hammered into the place from a long history of struggle, survivorship, and hatred. Wallace was the same town where, in 1892, and again in 1899, union and management conflicts had escalated into the murders of union leaders and mine owners alike. This led to the occupation of the town by federal troops: black soldiers who weren't welcome to serve east of the Mississippi. For almost two years, martial law was enforced in Wallace. Union workers, held in a "bullpen" (a prison of wooden planks without insulation), ate poor rations and were forced to continue their long hours with meager wages because they couldn't find other work.[6]

The oscillation between tragedy and anger became the core engine of the town. The place has, in some ways, been the intersection of every kind of disaster. Two fires burned down the town at different times, and floods have torn through the main streets, destroying buildings and furnishings. In 1906, tailings from mining backed up Canyon Creek and the Coeur d'Alene River, washing the streets with sewage and mine drainage. And, during the tragedy at the Sunshine Mine in 1972, there was yet another danger encroaching upon Wallace. On the surface, this one wouldn't be as apocalyptic, but it nonetheless threatened the town's very existence.

As early as 1973, folks in Wallace saw the specter of the highway, Interstate 90, as an enormous, earth-sucking paving machine coming from the east. Since the settlement stretched from one side of the valley to the other—a distance of three or four blocks—there was no room for the road to go off to either side of town. In fact, the entire "Silver Valley," as it's called—a gutter between Coeur d'Alene on the western side of the panhandle and Lookout Pass on the eastern—is a squeeze through the rocks and trees on the steep slopes of the Bitterroot Mountains. There was no choice: the highway would have to pass straight through the town. Wallace residents knew that the highway's expansion would flatten their business district. According to federal highway plans, Wallace would disappear.

Local folks credit Nancy Lee Hanson with organizing against the proposed highway and saving the town. In 1974, her group gathered petitions and, one by one, submitted them to the National Register of Historic Places. By 1976, the group had historic preservation status granted to every building in downtown Wallace. Then, pushing further, the citizen group demanded an environmental impact statement. Suddenly the road was in serious jeopardy. The glossy, huge Interstate 90 might, it seemed, simply stop at the Idaho border.

But there was a long history of the old road funneling necessary transport and supplies through the valley. Before it had been designated to become Interstate 90, the route had been Highway 10, and, before that, it had been "The Mullan Road," a patch of enhanced trail constructed from 1858 to 1862 that connected trading posts and carried mining traffic through the valley and into the cities.[7] Highway 10 traced the Mullan Road like a needle pulling through the fabric of the valley and then departed for Missoula to the east. The plans to transform this segment of highway into Interstate 90 laid out a version of the road that was more than triple the size of Highway 10. And to a road of that ambition, Wallace had defied passage.

The Wallace once slated for demolition, 2007.

There was only one option. The engineers on the project realized that the new freeway had to travel *above* the district, leaving the historic downtown intact. They discarded the old blueprints and reimagined the road as a kind of extended flying buttress, from the outskirts of the historically protected buildings, up and over the environs, and then tilting like a Hot Wheels track off toward the pass. It would be a feat of Richard Serra proportions—a sculpture of engineering. Charles Kuralt, the CBS news reporter, came to town in 1988, spotlighting the freeway plan and the people of Wallace for working to save their town.

The only structure that was moved during the construction was what Richard Hugo called "The most beautiful building / in Wallace." It was the "unused railroad station," and workers moved it near the pilings holding up the new *Star Trek*-like ramp. There, it sat askew from the grid of the streets, underneath the freeway, fronting a little

What the brand new freeway goes by, 2007.

park and commencing its new life as a railroad museum. Overhead, the highway stood, a pillar-lifted cement chute that would run trucks through. In 1991 the road opened and the last section of the unstoppable Interstate 90 was inserted into the narrowest passage of its 3,100-mile span.

Two years after my initial halt at the stoplight in 1986, before the new freeway was under construction, I finished the same program that Richard Hugo had been enrolled in almost forty years earlier—the master's degree in creative writing at the University of Washington (by the time I took my degree, it was an MFA. This was 1988, and Hugo had been dead six years. That same year, while I was wrapping up my manuscript of poems, a little sheaf of lyrics that expressed my own version of longing for a place, the FBI raid closed the Oasis brothel. The women who worked there fled, taking only what they could carry. As the G-men shouldered down the doors and aimed their black semiautomatic guns, they found the rooms abandoned. Bathtubs half full, clothes strewn across the floor, drawers pulled open—the rooms at the Oasis were still warm from the women who had left them in disarray. But the raids turned up few arrests. The FBI had blustered in, and, as the people of Wallace will tell you, the agents made a tempest out of a mild wind. Why didn't they pursue the white militia movement that was becoming so threatening over in Coeur d'Alene instead?

More than the other towns of the Silver Valley, Wallace has always been the town that garners publicity, and it didn't let this latest opportunity slide away. Travelers can wander the rooms of the old Oasis bordello, now a museum ("No Photographs.") and see the condition of the house preserved from the day that the FBI raid happened. Though there aren't visible sex-for-hire parlors any longer, one may still visit the last remaining whorehouse—this time with a reduced entrance fee and a tour of the premises. Wallace is a place that still gets people to stop. The town keeps its carnival version of the past alive, just as the small mining museums and nickel tours of unused tunnels take in the wanderers, steering them toward a version of the town that is washed clean of sweat and dirt. Any reminiscence is an attempt to hold the past still and spit-polishes the days gone by until they look like cartoons of days when things were both exciting and simple. Recently, town activists cajoled a British novelist, Danny Wallace, into writing a young adult novel about Wallace as the "centre of the universe." It's a wholesome and squeaky-clean slant on the town, once home to martial law, murders, whoring, and gambling. In the meantime, the relics grow dusty and the days of brothels feel further and further away.

Now, unlike the Wallace of Hugo's visits, the grid of streets is a hologrammatic mini theme park that art historian Dave Hickey would describe as "authentic" in its typically American fakery of the past. The more we reconfigure long-ago events with new materials to make them look old, the more "real" they feel. It's an American obsession, this insistence on some emaciated version of a historical scenario as a touchstone to inspire commerce. Downstairs from the bordello are six-dollar key chains to remind you of your visit to the Oasis museum. Just below where the stoplight once hung, the same light at which Hugo stopped in his Buick, there is a decorative manhole cover on the street—a Disney-like design reading "Center of the Universe." Because anywhere could be dubbed the center of the universe, as I consider when I stand on the marker, the endlessness of space sprawling outward from

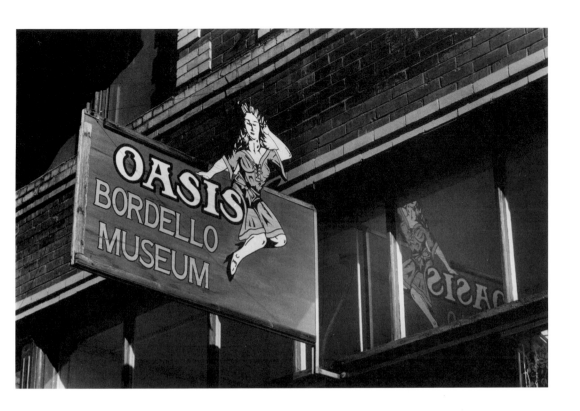

The "Oasis" in Wallace, 2007.

any homely flag stake, this place has as good a claim as any.

Sometimes, tragedies become marketing lures. Fires and floods enshrined in historic photographs line the walls of small-town restaurants. The Oasis Bordello Museum concocts a rendition of chaos to place us in those rooms that the women left so abruptly. That way, we can feel like we're part of something that actually happened; that way we can give some pathetic nod to the authentic in these plucked relics from the oh-so-recent old West. Hugo's poem, on the other hand, memorializes the town in his rage against the willful "improvements" of the haughty. His imaginings travel from "life in the tundra," where he would like to deposit the Republicans, to living rooms where stiff, uptight people are watching Lawrence Welk. It's too bad that the poem isn't a three-dimensional object, a monument that tourists could curve down from the highway to visit.

Wallace is no longer a pass-through; it's a destination. Promotional brochures call it the "Silver Capital of the World" and "our mining camp nestled in the Bitterroot Mountain Range."[8] Wallace projects a quaint workingman's image wrapped in a glossy package. Cheerful advertising celebrates the old brothels. In a sense, Wallace, the town under the freeway ramp, is the Greenwich Village of the valley—especially for second-home-hunting Californians who buy places here for ten cents on the dollar—while the other towns, from the wallowing leftovers of Smelterville to the remnants of Wardner, might be the outcast, poor Bronx.

Mining is what started the place; mining is what sustains it. I can't stop thinking about the "undergrounds" of the hills, the reference that Hugo makes to the hearts of the people of Wallace. So much is buried within them, so much dug up for the wider public to see that the town has mined its own sorrows and celebrated its riches. Traveling through, in search of the places Hugo had visited and memorialized into poems, I wanted to see more about Wallace's past.

Better than bars, better than grocery stores, graveyards are the places where you feel the thrum of heritage, of stories caught forever in a particular slant. Besides, I love the quiet and the lack of interference, an alternative to hours spent with a librarian or a barkeep, trying to learn about a place. On the way from the center of Wallace, I'm following a little fissure of pavement to the north toward Dobson Pass, on to Murray. The road is floss through the wedge of the valley, and just out of town I pass through a smattering of old frame houses and a sawmill or mining spread of some kind. Just beyond, as the route ascends, I see the cemetery.

I look up, turning my head under the windshield. Along the hillsides, the road curves around the graves. They look like haphazard rows of crooked teeth protruding from the ground. Pine needles and cedar leavings fill the rocky openings, and the higher up I drive, the narrower the dirt track becomes. Rocks pitch out and roll downhill. Suddenly, there is sun, still rising across from the hillside. The headstones are turned toward it, facing east. I loop through them, bearing left at another path and following the road back down the hill. As the car bumps over roots and through water seams, I realize that this isn't a place for a car at all. The only motorized transports should be the tractors carrying coffins and headstones. The rest of us, mourners and visitors, should step aside. We should park at the road and walk up.

I close the car door quietly. In front of me are the mountains, ore-dark against the sky. Above: brown grasses, a few pines, and sunshine. If you were on the top of the mountain, I'm imagining, you'd look down over the other side and see the town tucked into the wedge of river floor. The pines, jammed along the hillsides, turn the light a deep spruce blue. It's a kind of luminescent dark, as if the whole scene were outlined by velvet drapes on either side.

At this height, I'm thinking about what it must be like underground—how people took apart these hills for fist-sized rocks of heavy, black, raw silver. Unless you were informed, you wouldn't know that a piece of stone contained a precious metal. From the surface, it's an ordinary rock—dense and dark. You'd have to crush it open to see the metal, and even then, you'd need to know what you were looking for. Likewise, inside those mountains, silver, zinc, and lead are pulled clear of the shafts. Hulks of ore roll out in carts and into the hoists. They'll be stamped, baked, and pushed into flotation pools of cadmium, lead, and arsenic. What precious metals there are will amalgamate, and the leftover fluids will go back into the mountain—and a smaller portion, into the river.

Along the base of the ridge runs the south fork of the Coeur D'Alene. It's been channeled by the Army Corps of Engineers now, but it used to clog up with mine tailings and flood the whole valley. A lot of wood is still used inside the mines: timbers to hold up the tunnels inside the hills. Without the trees on the outside of the mountains, mud slips down the slopes. The furrows along the mountains show that.

I climb back up to the road, looking at old graves—a few of people who died before 1900. Some of the union organizers were probably buried here, and the mine owners must be over in Kellogg. Down in a little valley, between the hills, a few older stones are tumbled, along with some beer cans. I get the feeling that the historical society isn't vigilant about keeping up the place, the way they might be back in southern Ohio or Pennsylvania or New England, where I'm from. Then I see a newer monument, a larger one, set into the back of the clearing. A memorial to the miners who died in 1972. The names of the dead are listed, in the style of the Vietnam Veterans Memorial, along a wall of concrete. Propped against the wind, with the sun coming through the trees, I'm looking out, wondering about the days when the valley huddled under the loss of those men. This, it seems to me, is the real history of the place—the history that Hugo missed.

Years earlier, in 1991, when the stoplight was taken down, the citizens of Wallace held a funeral for the defunct device. They dressed up, as if for Mardi Gras, and paraded through the town, pulling the stoplight in a little hearse. In the end, they buried the thing. The people of Wallace had put something back into the ground, something released from the "undergrounds of their hearts." I'm eating breakfast alongside a grave. I have some leftover tuna salad. It's a meal that Richard Hugo might have eaten, and I'm glad to have it.

Bleachers in Dixon, 2007.

THE ONLY BAR IN DIXON

Home. Home. I knew it entering.
Green cheap plaster and the stores
across the street toward the river
failed. One Indian depressed
on Thunderbird. Another buying
Thunderbird to go. This air
is fat with gangsters I imagine
on the run. If they ran here
they would be running from
imaginary cars. No one cares
about the wanted posters
in the brand new concrete block P.O.

This is home because some people
go to Perma and come back
from Perma saying Perma
is no fun. To revive, you take 382
to Hot Springs, your life savings
ready for a choice of bars, your hotel
glamorous with neon up the hill.
Is home because the Jocko
dies into the Flathead. Home because
the Flathead goes home north northwest.

I want home full of grim permission.
You can go as out of business here
as rivers or the railroad station.
I knew it entering.
                    Five bourbons
and I'm in some other home.

DIXON

Light crawls timid over fields
from some vague source behind the hills,
too gray to be the sun. Any morning
brings the same, a test of stamina,
your capacity to live the long day out
paced by the hesitant river. No chance
you might discover someone dead.
Always you curse the limited goods
in the store and your limited money.
You learn to ignore the wind leak
in your shack. On bad days in the bar
you drink until you are mayor.

On neutral days you hope the school
is adequate though you're no father
and your wife left decades back
when the train still ran. You look
hours down the track. Perhaps a freight.
Only the arrogant wind. You think
the browns are running, hitting bait.
You have waited and waited for mail,
a wedding invitation, a postcard
from New York. You reread the book
about red lovers one more time,
pages torn and the cover gone.

On good days festive cars streak by.
You laugh and wave. Sun on blacktop
whirrs like ancient arrows in the sky.
Cattails flash alive the way they did

when lightning told them, die.
You catch the river in its flowing
never flowing frozen glide.

The small clear river jitters on
to join the giant green one lumbering
a definite west, a lake released.
Your heroes go home green. Bison
on the range are reproducing bears.

ST. IGNATIUS WHERE THE SALISH WAIL
for David and Annick Smith

It's a bad Good Friday, snow and mud
and mongrels in the road. Today's sky said
He'd weigh a ton tonight. A priest
unhooks the hands while Flatheads chant
ninety pounds of spices on the skin.
Another One, not the one they took down from
the cross, is lugged by six old Indians
around the room, five following with songs.

On a real Good Friday, warm and moon,
they'd pack Him outside where bright
fires burn. Here or there, the dialect
burns on their tongues. Elbow joints enflame
and still they crawl
nailed hours to the tomb. For men
who raced young April clouds and won, the pace
of reverence is grim. Their chanting
bangs the door of any man's first cave.

Mongrels have gone home. We slop
toward the car. Every year
a few less live who know the Salish hymns.
The mud is deeper. Snow has turned to rain.
We were renegade when God had gills.
We never change. Still, the raw sound
of their faces and the wailing unpretentious
color of their shawls——

The Flathead Goes Home North Northwest

Three Guys Go into a Bar

THE STORY IS LEGENDARY. It begins like an old joke: "Three guys go into a bar," and people tell it again and again. The three guys were writers Richard Hugo, Jim Welch, and J. D. Reed, on a fishing outing. Afterward, they dropped into the Dixon Bar and during the evening invented a contest—a poet's sort of competition, more collaborative than cutthroat: they each vowed to write a poem about the bar and then try to publish all three poems in the same magazine. As Jim Welch later said, "The title of the poems was 'The Only Bar in Dixon'. . . . Somehow we sent it out to the *New Yorker* on a fluke, and they took them and printed all three in the same issue."[1]

Hugo would later tell people that the Dixon Bar was a beautiful spot with just the kind of interior that inspired him: a long wooden bar with a leather bumper—once red-dyed cowhide but now peeled away into soft suede, running the length of the wooden shaft. Behind it stands a wooden edifice with bumper stickers curling from their tacks, pictures of horses in frames, photos of bar visitors and newspaper articles. One toilet has a sign reading "Pistols," and the other, "Holsters." Dark even in daytime, the Dixon Bar, set near the Flathead River, was a stopover that New Yorkers might imagine as synecdoche for the entire West. In fact, the copy editor who fact-checked Hugo's "The Only Bar in Dixon" tried to impose Eastern notions of geography upon it. The poem came back with the line "the Flathead goes home north northwest" rewritten to "the Flathead goes home north *northeast*." Hugo laughed. "Perhaps that's why it looks so magnificent climbing the Divide," he told his friends.

Imagine the three men: Hugo, a storyteller with a round face, easy laugh, and a rumpled wardrobe; Welch, his plaid shirt tucked into his jeans and his dark hair slicked to the side, wearing large glasses, and J. D. Reed, a huge lantern-jawed man with a warm smile. Reed and Welch were twenty years younger than Hugo; both were his students. The three of them would have left their fishing gear out in the Buick, Hugo's convertible, tugged open the door, and come into the bar, laughing at one of their own jokes.

Inside, they talked and took mental notes and maybe a few people took offense to their poetry banter and loud stories. In the poem "The Only Bar in Dixon," Hugo ("not at all a good drinker," according to his friend John Mitchell) admits to "five bourbons." The owner, Joanne Schmauch, was bartending. She watched over the bar most of the time, and many of the customers became regulars because of her shrewd humor and steady hand. She was the captain of the ship—demanding respect and doling out punishment for any raucous behavior.

The Wager

Over the next two weeks, the three men wrote poems about the bar. Indeed, as Welch said, they sent all three to the *New Yorker* on a whim, and poetry editor Howard Moss accepted all of them. The poems came out in the October 10, 1970, issue of the magazine, a triptych under the same title: "The Only Bar in Dixon."

Hugo had imagined the poems as a kind of homage, a manifesto of camaraderie, for those folks whom they'd met in the sanctuary of Dixon. He envisioned himself as an outsider who'd come into what the poem urgently calls "Home. Home." Once inside, he envisioned belonging there, with the same "people [who] go to Perma and come back / from Perma saying Perma / is no fun." (The bar crowd bonded over their dislike of the next town over, a place with a few feed silos, train tracks, and an old store, a widening in the road with a flagpole just off Highway 200.) Bashing Perma was a way in for Hugo. "I want home full of grim permission," he writes, cautioning, "You can go as out of business here / as rivers or the railroad station."

Though Hugo saw himself as one of the guys while he was in Dixon, the poems separated him, Welch, and Reed from the folks in the bar. Poetry, laid out in free verse rhythms, wasn't the sport of rural places like Dixon, Montana. Gone were the days of Robert Service and Edward Guest; the clanging, full rhymes that schoolchildren once memorized were absent from this more "contemporary" poetry. Locals would find the mere act of writing poems to be an elite gesture, and they would come to see these poems as ironic in their attempts to be down-to-earth. For a person outside the world of slant rhymes and metaphor, a person living in Dixon, perhaps, Hugo's poems might as well have been as alien as Walt Whitman's.

The Fallout

Dixon, it turned out, wasn't ready for irony. The poems didn't go over well at the bar. Schmauch was furious about a line that Welch had written: "You can have the red-headed bartender for a word. . . . " Since Joanne Schmauch *was* a redhead and didn't see herself as that available, she ranted about the poems and the guys who had written them. What right did these professor-types, loose from Missoula, have to come in and mock her bar, her town, her way of joking with her customers? Her affection, appropriated and distorted by the poets, thickened into anger.

After the poems came out in the *New Yorker*, the local paper, the *Missoulian*, published a letter to the editor from Schmauch. Witty, sarcastic, and inflamed by the verses, Schmauch says that she and the mayor of Dixon have been attempting to write "An Ode to Five-Bourbon Hugo," a poem that they "sincerely hope" will cause him to "turn blue over OUR contemporary style."

Hugo takes her on and sends in a response to the *Missoulian*. It's a clever retort, clipped and pedantic at the same time: "Joanne Schmauch finds my poems unflattering to Dixon but my poems are not about Dixon. For Schmauch's edification, poems are works of imagination and are not intended to be factual accounts. . . . If I wanted to write about Dixon, I would write an article." (The line sounds like one he'll write years later in *The Triggering Town*: "If you want to communicate, use the telephone.") Though the letter to the editor is addressed to Joanne Schumach, the instructive tone and abrupt claims feel more like a performance for his friends and colleagues. For me, it presages the letter poems he'll write a few years after this encounter—letters written to individuals but staged for public consumption.

Hugo does express affection for Dixon, and lets on some of his own vulnerability in the letter: "I especially love the Dixon Bar, and if I could still drink, it and Harold's Union Bar in Milltown would get most of my business." Saying that he can't handle alcohol any longer is an anti-macho admission; he can't keep up with the folks in Dixon. However, some phrasing in his *Missoulian* letter is geared more toward an academic crowd: "For Schmauch's edification, poems are works of imagination and are not intended to be factual accounts." This must have seemed a haughty statement to Joanne Schmauch. Couldn't Hugo have written in the plain speak he so admired? Was there a more straightforward way of articulating "I love all places that trigger my imagination and lead me to truth about the human condition that I can reveal . . . ?"

Hugo clipped the two letters from the paper and Xeroxed them, adding a note to Jim and Lois Welch, who were traveling in Greece: "Jim, Lo—Just to say that when the forces of righteousness strike, they strike hard."

When I come across this page in his archives at the University of Washington, I find it remarkable that Hugo has kept a copy in his records, something he rarely does. Several years later, he'll write "Letter to Gildner from Wallace" in which he'll bash "the self-proclaimed forces of morality." His anger toward the high-and-mighty threads through these poems about towns, and he has a particular disdain, it seems, for any sort of politician, even a small-town mayor and bartender from Dixon. The riff traces a classic alignment of liberal/bohemian/academic/effete versus the conservative/"real world"/worker. What Hugo doesn't see is how he represents one end of the polemic, the one with the academics instead of the working folk. Instead, after the poems came out he was irritated and then saddened about the anger flying at him, Welch, and Reed. As his colleague and friend Bill Bevis writes, "He was really hurt when the poems separated him from the people he wished to join, who he believed he *was*."[2] The Dixon poem, meant to pull him in with the people he felt a part of, only isolated him. Hugo was, after all, a university professor from Missoula, the liberal bubble of the state. He was no longer a guy who once shoveled through the slag heap at Boeing; he no longer lived in White Center, the town known for its brawls and poverty.[3] But people at the bar in Dixon didn't know all that.

Writing Is Another Kind of Trade

For Reed and Welch, the poems were artistic speculations. First, they visited the bar. Then they observed details of the people and surroundings and created poems. Welch, encouraged by Hugo, was learning to write about the places and people he knew well—mainly his experiences growing up on the Blackfeet Reservation. Jim Welch had known places like the Dixon Bar, and since it was on the Flathead Indian Reservation, the closest reservation in proximity to the Blackfeet, it was a version of home to him. J. D. Reed, on the other hand, was along for the ride.

For Hugo, there was something else: "Outside of fishing and a few other things, I don't care much for reality. It bores me. I've always had a kind of vivid inner life that's going on all the time, converting things I see. I'll change an old town, for example, into a town the poem can use, then appropriate it."[4] As a poet, Hugo's imaginative trolling feeds off of places that are barely inhabited. He wants to convert real places into made-up ones that "the poem can use." His obsession with small towns led him to bars, establishments where the trade of money for liquor is the most basic reciprocity. "The bar is where the Hugo town has its center," writes Michael Allen.[5] Conversation and camaraderie are unexpected dividends, ones that Hugo didn't have when he was growing up. In the Dixon Bar, he wouldn't have seen himself as a tourist, trading drinks for intimacy, but as one of an itinerant tribe who happened upon the place.

"In all his work you won't find a pleasant bar. Necessary maybe to the dispossessed . . . but not pleasant," Bevis writes.[6] Home, for Hugo, needs to be grim. What he adds, in the poem, is "permission." He wants home to have a "grim permission," allowing the place to bloom into a sanctuary; that's his wish. As Bevis describes, "This is serious drinking beside the beautiful Flathead River, beside the beautiful buffalo range, near the towering Mission Mountains—the land does not redeem. . . . These countryside poems are the cry of a region for something better, not the whine of the privileged to get away."[7] Bevis, who was a friend as well as a fellow professor of Hugo's, reads into the situation a larger political context. In Hugo's drive to find a place that will finally welcome him, he represents the disenfranchised people of the West, hungry for the advantages that Easterners have: wealth, privilege, and the familiar centers of education. "Hugo did not wish to be part of an elite; he would have been happy if everyone had enjoyed his work. But poetry is not easy. His distance from the very audience he identified with sometimes pained Hugo, and his down-and-out poems are not always well received in the communities they so unprogressively describe."[8] The leap of faith, the singular poet representing the isolated westerner who lives without the amenities of the East, can sell his avid readers, but it didn't convince the folks in Dixon.

The newspaper exchange is also compelling in how Hugo sums up the role of towns in his poems: "I love Dixon because a lot of people would not want to live there and many would not even notice it in any detail as they drove through." The act of paying attention to Dixon was the art of paying attention to what most people ignored. Taking a small place and writing it large was Hugo's gift.

Hugo wrote two poems about the Dixon Bar. They appeared on adjacent pages in his 1973 collection *The Lady in Kicking Horse Reservoir.* The first, "The Only Bar in Dixon," uses shorter lines than many of Hugo's other poems—most lingering over six or seven syllables and using more spondaic jolts, stressed syllables set next to one another, than his more iambic poems. Slant rhymes sometimes cement the spondees, as they do in "to Hot Springs, your life savings" and in "Green cheap plaster and the stores." (The *ing* of "Springs" and "savings" and the long *e* sounds within "green" and "cheap" resonate with more alliteration than some of the prosaic lines.) The poem also takes advantage of repetition to carve out louder sounds; some repeated words wind around themselves, spinning locations inside their own referents:

> This is home because some people
> go to Perma and come back
> from Perma saying Perma
> is no fun.

"Perma," in this repetition, sounds like an aversion rather than a destination. Like the first half of the word *permanent,* Perma itself reads as something left undone, something that beckons you, as a traveler or reader, to complete it. The poem also repeats variants of the verb "run." Inside "The Only Bar in Dixon"

> . . . This air
> air is fat with gangsters I imagine
> on the run. If they ran here
> they would be running from
> imaginary cars.

This collection of "run," "ran," and "running" will converge again at the end of *The Lady in Kicking Horse Reservoir* in the poem "Degrees of Gray in Philipsburg," where the idiom will resolve itself in "The car that brought you here still runs."

The Dixon Bar, with Bud Schmauch standing in front, 2007.

Hugo, of course, is desperately staking out a place for himself in Dixon, and around him the landscape does the same: "the Flathead goes home north northwest," where destination and direction are buried within the repetition of "home" and "north." The Dixon Bar, like Harold's Union Bar in Milltown, is a version of "home," and the metaphor's appearance in each stanza underscores the insatiability of the speaker's longing for a place to belong. In fact, the last two lines of "The Only Bar in Dixon" offer a disjointed resolution—the penultimate line of "Five bourbons" indented, sitting below the white space cleared in the line above where there's room for it to fit in, and, ultimately, there's room for the poet/speaker to fit in as well. That line of poetry could slide into the space above it just as Hugo could slide a stool up to the bar at Dixon. "And I'm in some other home," he says. It's a melancholic wish-come-true because the "other home" is an alcoholic haze, a false peace earned through drinking.

Dixon, Again

In fact, Hugo paid attention to the town more than once. The other poem, "Dixon,"
follows "The Only Bar in Dixon" in the collection and has the tone of an epilogue:
"Any morning / brings the same, a test of stamina." Starting out darker than "The Only
Bar . . . ," the second Dixon poem places its speaker, "you," firmly in the role of town
resident: "Always you curse the limited goods / in the store and your limited money."
And things grow worse: "You learn to ignore the wind leak / in your shack. On bad
days in the bar / you drink until you are mayor." The poem rings out as the ulti-
mate, melancholic response to the bartender's letter to the editor, the letter in which
Schmauch and the mayor had been drafting a poem in honor of "Five Bourbon Hugo."
What better response to the townsfolk of Dixon than to write another poem about their
town, this one from a man who wants it to be "home"?

"Dixon" follows a different music, one more prosaic than that in "The Only Bar
in Dixon." (He wrote it sometime afterward.) The "test of stamina" is "your capacity
to live the long day out / paced by the hesitant river." The landscape around the town
can barely support the enterprise of living there. Here, the repetition is not of "home"
or "run" or "north," but the repeated structure of a prepositional phrase, beginning
with "on": "On bad days," "On neutral days," "On good days," and here it's easy to see
the poet's intent to lift the speaker out of the dark bar. Lilting rhythms track the arc
toward renewal: "Sun on blacktop / whirs like ancient arrows in the sky" and the twisting lines: "You catch the river in its flowing / never flowing frozen glide"—a trochaic
emphasis on the first syllables in the metric feet "flowing / never flowing frozen glide."
The music smoothly pushes us out of the poem, away from the scene: "Your heroes go
home," and somehow there's a promise of something better, "a lake released."

Hugo had a lung removed about a year before he died in 1982. Reed died in 2005,
Welch in 2003, both from lung cancer. Before his death, Jim Welch enjoyed a skyrock-
eting career—his books rose to be icons of western literature—*Winter in the Blood, The
Death of Jim Loney, The Indian Lawyer, Fool's Crow,* and *Heartsong of Charging Elk*
were novels that reached a wide readership. His first book, *Riding the Earthboy 40,* was
a collection of poems written under the influence of Hugo, and his nonfiction *Killing
Custer* was based on his experience writing the script for Paul Stekler's 1992 film *Last
Stand at Little Bighorn.* Because of Welch's status, both as a writer and as a Native

American from the area, and because of the following that Hugo inspired, the story of the Dixon Bar lives on. I'm not the only one to come here on a pilgrimage—students from the University of Montana still make the thirty-five-mile drive out from Missoula. The place is a poetry landmark.

Back to the Bar

But the bar is closed now, sort of. I've been there twice, and each time, Bud, Schmauch's son, the current owner, has let me in after I've knocked.

The door is bolted on the day when I come back, this time with Mary Randlett. I know enough to knock, and Bud comes to the door.

"I remember you," he says. "Come on in."

Outside

Across the way, the old train depot, a plain structure, more house than barn, goes unused. The siding is a washed-out grey. Once, a ferry traversed the Flathead. Now the river looks too shallow to accommodate one.

Two hundred and sixteen was the population of Dixon in 2000, including the area south of Charlo. For a while, Dixon was a town of retirees, but now some younger families are moving in, and they are mostly poor. Seventeen thousand dollars is the median household yearly income here, and almost 25 percent of the people are Native Americans. The Flathead Reservation, where Dixon is located, is home to the Salish and Kootenay tribes, and these are a combination of Salish, the Pend d'Oreille, and the Kootenay. The spread of land is quiet, a hush of deerskin-colored hills and some clumps of sage.

Mary and I park near the school, a cheerful building underneath a row of trees, facing a ball field with rickety bleachers about twenty feet long and grey planks six rows high. A few children yell in the playground; only elementary grades are housed here now. The town runs two blocks deep, a string of old storefronts along Highway 200. On the north side, there's an old car repair place, and the more I look around, the more

Dixon train depot, 2007.

I see that there are more cars than people in this town: husks of cars, entrails, shells, and a few intact ones that may be running still. One of the only cars that still runs, I imagine, is the one that brought us here.

Looking back at the two poems about Dixon, I realize that the poet, too, consoles himself with naming the soon-to-be obsolete. The bars that will go out of business, the towns that will go abandoned, even the rivers "slate with crap"—these are the talisman-markers within his poems. Amidst these, he's trying to find a way to fit in, to acknowl-edge the sorrows of the world while also building a respite from them. It's the liquor, ultimately, that does the job.

"Whew!" Mary says. "This place is out there. Where the hell are we?" She laughs and points to the sky, just where it meets the brown mountains in the middle distance.

Mary takes a picture of the depot across from the bar and then turns to follow me in.

Schmauch, Re-dux

After the screen door slams, I pull up a stool and motion Mary over to one next to me. "Beer, please," I say to Bud. "Whatever is good."

He pulls out an MGD from a cooler and serves it up in a Ball jar. He crosses his arms. "For you?" he asks Mary.

"Oh just some water," she says. "You own the place?"

Bud looks at her without changing his expression. "Yup."

"Well this is the real thing," she says. "A real old bar." Mary nods and gets up to look at the stuff on the walls.

"Remember when I was here last?" I say to Bud. "I was talking to you about those poets who came in here and wrote poems about the bar."

"Yeah, I remember that." He spreads his arms wide and, facing me, leans over the surface.

"You're selling the place?"

"Yup. Sure am." He lights a cigarette. Then he goes into sales mode. "Comes with the license. Building next door too."

"Any nibbles yet?" I ask. Behind Bud is a wall of clippings, pictures, bumper stickers, and handwritten signs. One says, "My Montana has a east infection." Another reads, "Save the Northwest, Spay and Neuter Californians." There are pictures of racehorses; Joanne, the former proprietress who was so offended by the poets; Tiger, her husband; and a younger version of Bud.

"Nice picture of your Mom," I say. "She got in a good letter to the paper about the poems that Hugo and those guys wrote." The beer is terrible, but cold.

"Yup. That pissed her off. My Dad too. I remember it."

"I'll bet it did."

"Hugo was an arrogant asshole. That other guy with him too, the Dirty Foot, where's he?"

"Dead," I say. "All of them." I know that he means "Blackfeet" and that he's referring to Jim Welch. But I ignore the slur, even as my stomach washes back some beer into my throat.

"Well, they came in here like they was special. They weren't. They were just assholes like any other assholes." Bud sucks on the cigarette and then pulls on the brim of his baseball cap.

"Made the place famous," I say.

"Some foundation has a hold of the history of it. Before, people didn't know about it being historic. When they catch on, it'll sell." Bud blows the smoke toward the surface of the bar.

I move my beer. "Foundation?"

"Some poetry foundation. They have lots of money. Probably will buy it."

"Oh." I want to laugh, at first. The Poetry Foundation had received a huge donation from Indianapolis heiress Ruth Lilly, who gave about $200,000,000 to the organization in 2002, but the foundation folks apparently were having enough trouble deciding whether to do color plates inside their magazine—a precious little publication that looked humble but was actually a cornerstone of contemporary verse in America—much less venturing into bar ownership. The gift was a big buzz in the poetry world. The foundation wasn't giving any money to institutions, and it had said so. The only money it gave to people was in the form of prizes, like genius grants. In a better world, the Dixon Bar would get a genius grant, I decide.

"How much is it?" I drink a big sip of the beer. "The bar?"

"Seven hundred and fifty thousand for the bar and the other buildings. If you want to buy the core of Dixon, here's your chance."

The core of Dixon, indeed. A concrete stage-set front with a tin-roofed back end, the bar boasts two cement-block chimneys and a couple of boarded-up windows. A dented ice machine sits in front, mounted on a little cement sidewalk that imitated an old boardwalk. A small two-rail metal fence runs along it. "D-i-x-o-n," a neon sign, traces the down-slope above "B-A-R." There is a pay phone sign sticking out from the front of the walkway.

Mary looks over at me and rolls her eyes. She pushes the water glass back onto the bar and then continues pacing around the perimeter of the room, looking at the walls. To Mary, a bar is a cage. She had told me, on one particularly long stretch of road between towns, "I quit drinking when I was forty. Don't ask. You don't want to know." Then, she had grinned and asked, "Where the hell are we, anyway?"

"It's a good place," I say, remembering that Bud's mother claimed that there were only two kinds of people in the world: "Those who live in Dixon and those who wish they did." Process of elimination led me into being the latter kind.

"Take my number and call me if you find a buyer out there in 'poetry land,'" he says.

Finding Rose Bailey

On the way back to the car, Mary sees the senior center. "Hell, I am a senior." She says it like she can't believe it. "So, let's stop in." She smiles. "Senior, what kind of word is that? Maybe they have coffee."

The place is still serving lunch, so I ask a woman who is bringing out the food if she knows of local folks who know the town well, folks who have lived here for a long time. In the meantime, Mary is pulling on the coffee pump, filling her mug to go and stuffing a muffin in her pocket.

"Rose Bailey," the woman says and puts down a bowl of mashed potatoes on the table. "On the road to Charlo."

Ten minutes later, after I've plugged the donation can with quarters and Mary has hurried her coffee out the door, we arrive at Rose Bailey's house. In her crowded kitchen, Rose draws a schematic of the town on the long side of a cigarette carton that she's ripped open and turned inside out. She slowly pulls a line across the cardboard with a pen. Her glasses slip down the bridge of her nose.

"Here was the mercantile," she says. "Had three parts, including a restaurant. Now it's empty." She draws lines very slowly but seems eager to detail the streetscape. "Over there was the hotel. Not there now, though."

As Rose continues to draw, a town plan shows up on the cardboard. It's more crowded than the town is now. Back in Dixon only a few buildings remained. The school and senior center are still open, and the bar, barely so. Outside the window I can see Mary walking the grounds, pointing her camera toward the distant lines of fence.

"Rose," I say, "How old are you?"

"Ninety-four," she says.

"What's the biggest thing that happened in Dixon?'

"Well," she pauses. "It's past lunchtime, isn't it? I think I'll have a little drink. You?"

"No thanks."

She takes a bottle of some kind of syrupy liquor from a cabinet above her. "There was a flatbed car come loose when I was a little girl. The man on top of it went racing through Dixon and out the other side. When he got off, his hair had turned completely white." She emphasizes the mysterious nature of the event by whispering. "It was something," she says. "I was little then, and I saw his hair and I learned the story. I'll always remember it."

I wish Hugo had heard it. I know that the poems he's set in Dixon aren't about Dixon. If Hugo had wanted them to be, he'd have written an article, as he said, or an essay about the place. But the resemblance overwhelms me. There's something back-stage in this town that Hugo has captured on the page. Partly, it's a tendency to repeat things until they feel true, like how Joanne Schmauch had repeated the mythic division of "two kinds of people," the ones who lived in Dixon and the ones who wished they did, or the way small things became lasting metaphors, as the bar had. The twists and turns of the poems, and Hugo's attempts to reside inside them, do map a realistic Dixon, one still visible today. Unlike Hugo's letter poem from Wallace, these verses inspired by Dixon transcribe some of the town's core essence. You can still recognize it even if the bar is closed.

Retroactively, I want to dangle what Rose says from the bottom of the poems. I want to crawl behind the misshapen similarities in the two poems and align them with the bar: the projected despair, the breath of the three men in that winter air, the redhead serving drinks, and the town as it remains when Mary and I come to it—a smattering of old cars, a decaying set of bleachers along the obsolete baseball field, and Rose Bailey's drawing, crude and historically accurate.

On to the Mission

From Rose's place, Mary and I are crossing northeast, still on the Flathead Reservation, toward St. Ignatius. It's only twelve miles, euphemistically a trip down the block in Montana. The road grows narrow and bumpy and then feeds into the mountains.

St. Ignatius sits in the Flathead Valley, against the Mission Ridge, an enormous wall of mountains, less jagged than the Cascades, the range near Seattle. The poem I'm chasing down is "St. Ignatius Where the Salish Wail," dedicated to Annick and Dave Smith, friends of Hugo from both the Seattle days and then the University of Montana. From the road—Highway 93, the narrow north-south highway through the reservation—Mary and I see the town, a sprawling place of ramblers and trailers. Somewhere behind is a looming brick church. There's a sign for the St. Ignatius Mission, a Jesuit landmark in the Northwest, built in the 1890s. In Hugo's day, the 1960s and '70s, the town was so sleepy that dogs lay in the road.

Once off the highway, I'm in a guessing game, winding through town and then onto its edges, trying to get to the mission. Some storefronts are open—a restaurant or two and a thrift store—but most are closed up now. One motel parking lot is full; one is empty.

Finally, I come upon the mission site—what's left are a few small log cabins alongside a giant brick church, much like one you'd find in the Midwest. Fields surround the area, and a few small one-floor ramblers sit across the road. The enormous boarding school that once existed here is gone; so are the printing press, the industrial arts school (containing a blacksmith shop, a sawmill, and a flour mill), and the Jesuit residences and seminary.

The place is so sparse now that it's hard to imagine that it once functioned as its own town. Fewer than 800 people live in the whole area. In 1895, there were almost that many people at the mission alone. Chants in Salish and murmured prayers in English once filled the church, and bright-colored robes adorned the Indians who worshipped there. Today, run-down stores and a shabby school with broken playground equipment outline a place without any color at all.

Inside the Church

Plain and hulking from the outside, the building looks like it would offer varnished pine pews and dark walls on the inside. Instead, when Mary and I open the doors, I immediately think of Easter eggs.

"Holy cow! Just look at this place," Mary says. She walks around with her chin tilted up, and she's pointing to the ceiling and the walls. "These colors are amazing. Aren't they amazing?"

Fifty-eight murals and frescos fill the walls and ceilings. They are the most beautiful paintings I've seen in a long time: an Italian Renaissance look at Judgment Day; the miracle of loaves and fishes; portraits of St. Francis, St. Xavier, St. Joseph, the Blessed Mother, and many others. These murals are completely "other"—like fairy tales in a dry, harsh place of extreme cold and hot. A Jesuit who was cook and handyman for the mission, Joseph Carignano, painted the interior in his spare time. I get the sense that Brother Carignano was homesick for the lavish paintings and altar trimmings of his homeland.

The other high art of St. Ignatius Mission, a place established in 1855 after moving nine miles east from an earlier location, was fine letter press printing. With its release of *Narratives from the Holy Scripture in Kalispel* (a Salish language) and *Dictionary of Kalispel*, both published between 1877 and 1879, the St. Ignatius press had gener-

St. Ignatius Church, 2007.

ated some fine art from the remote mountains of western Montana. Since the Salish
dialects all across the Northwest are disappearing, these books remain substantial con-
tributions to scholarship and the history of our region. "A few less live who know the
Salish hymns," Hugo writes. The dictionary was published in two volumes—English to
Kalispel (456 pages) and Kalispel to English (644 pages).

What Happened to the Natives

The immersion of the Jesuits within Flathead (Salish) cultures, including the Bitterroot Salish, Kootenay, and Pend d'Orielle tribes, deliberately and methodically
changed the Indians' religious views. In doing so, the Catholic missionaries dis-

mantled the indigenous culture of the area. Indian children, forced into assimilation with white culture by the United States government and by the Bureau of Catholic Indian Missions, lived sad lives. They were taken from their families and placed into schools on the mission. The Ursuline Sisters and the Sisters of Providence ran the girls' schools, and the Jesuits governed the boys'. Over the years, financial aid once promised by federal agencies disappeared, as did support from the Catholic Indian bureau. Left in poverty, badly abused, and neglected, many children on the mission suffered. Finally, in 1972 the last of the three schools, the one run by the Ursulines, closed. For almost eighty years, the tribes around St. Ignatius and throughout the Northwest, separated for years from their families because of the schools, struggled to keep their families intact. So many parents and grandparents, raised in boarding schools, had no role models. Today's families on the Flathead are still recovering from this legacy of institutionalization.

Hugo Shows Up with Friends

Hugo arrived with Annick and Dave Smith on a Good Friday, and he imagines the Indians gathering to the church: "Their chanting / bangs the door of any man's first cave." Hugo, Annick, and Dave "slop / toward the car." And the speaker of the poem observes, "Every year . . . the mud is deeper," as if to say that people don't evolve: "We were renegade when God had gills. / We never change." The prehistoric overlay of imagining God with gills sounds like the Jesuits' attempts to bring the highbrow religion of the cathedral into more sanguine surroundings. The priests encouraged the Indians to role-play the whole crucifixion, using a carved, wooden Christ—life size—and carrying him into a "tomb," where he rested until Easter Sunday. To Hugo, it's a sad scene: "Another One, not the one they took down from / the cross, is lugged by six old Indians / around the room, five following with songs." The poem warms a bit when he moves it out of doors, back into the open air: "On a real Good Friday, warm and moon, / they'd pack Him outside where bright fires burn." Hugo is connecting the Indians to their own indigenous practices, where "Here or there, the dialect / burns on their tongues."

The poem closes with a dash, punctuation that Hugo rarely uses at the end of a poem. His work is typically too narrative to depart on such an unfixed gesture. It's part

William Carlos Williams, part e. e. cummings, but the move is laden with sorrow, an ending that is not quite an ending.

And he isn't finished with St. Ignatius. About five years later, in the mid-seventies, he writes "Letter to Hill from St. Ignatius." It's a poem dedicated to a student named Bobbi Hill. He describes the scene at the mission, underneath "the staggering Mission Range just beyond":

> A priest
> Some 80 years back designed a ceremony for Good
> Friday, Indian-Catholic, complete with Flathead chants
> in dialect. It's lovely . . .
> I wept
> the first time I saw it, the beleaguered Indians wailing
> the priest to Stations of the Cross. The pall bearers bearing Christ
> outside around fires and crying the weird tongue stark
> through the night.

It's a personal piece, with an insatiable envy: "I resent you once told me how I'd never know / what being Indian was like," and at the end Hugo pleads: "Let me be Indian." An exaggeration maybe, but Hugo's pain is apparent. "Just as the Indians have suffered," Hugo seems to be saying, "so have I suffered." I have a hard time taking in the whole gesture without feeling helpless, squeezed, queasy.

To the Antlers

On the way out of the mission, back onto Highway 93, Mary and I follow the road south, back toward Dixon and then north again to the National Bison Reserve, a huge bulk of land, where bison roam freely over twenty eight square miles—as opposed to the range of the continent, as in earlier times. Antelope, black bear, elk, and bighorn sheep also live on the reserve. They've been herded here, and people drive through the place, watching the animals from car windows. In the parking lot, as I'm getting out of the car, I notice it: the stack of antlers. They've been hooked within each other and stacked in the shape of a silo. The antlers are as dry as driftwood. In the sunshine, the light gray is silhouetted by dark holes in the stack, and I can't see in. Someone has stacked them here, row by row, until they blur together into one lyric, one song that tells you about the life and death of the place. From Dixon to St. Ignatius, the Flathead sings—and it's one sad, mournful song. In the end, Hugo was right about that.

The Milltown, now "Harold's Club," 2007.

Milltown, Montana

THE MILLTOWN UNION BAR

for Harold Herndon

(Laundromat & Cafe)
You could love here, not the lovely goat
in plexiglass nor the elk shot
in the middle of a joke, but honest drunks,
crossed swords above the bar, three men hung
in the bad painting, others riding off
on the phony green horizon. The owner,
fresh from orphan wars, loves too
but bad as you. He keeps improving things
but can't cut the bodies down.

You need never leave. Money or a story
brings you booze. The elk is grinning
and the goat says go so tenderly
you hear him through the glass. If you weep
deer heads weep. Sing and the orphanage
announces plans for your release. A train
goes by and ditches jump. You were nothing
going in and now you kiss your hand.

When mills shut down, when the worst drunk
says finally I'm stone, three men still hang
painted badly from a leafless tree, you
one of them, brains tied behind your back,
swinging for your sin. Or you swing
with goats and elk. Doors of orphanages
finally swing out and here you open in.

LETTER TO LOGAN FROM MILLTOWN

Dear John: This a Dear John letter from booze.
With you, liver. With me, bleeding ulcer. The results
are the horrific same: as drunks we're done. Christ,
John, what a loss to those underground political
movements that count, the Degradationists,
the Dipsomaniacists, and that force gaining momentum
all over the world, the Deteriorationists. I hope
you know how sad this is. Once I quit drinking it was clear
to others, including our chairman (who incidentally
also had to quit drinking), that less 40 pounds
I look resolute and strong and on the surface appear
efficient. Try this for obscene development: they made me
director of creative writing. Better I'd gone on bleeding
getting whiter and whiter and finally blending
into the snow to be found next spring, a tragedy
that surely would increase my poetic reputation.
POET FOUND IN THAW SNOWS CLAIM MISSOULA BARD
I'm in Milltown. You remember that bar, that beautiful bar
run by Harold Herndon where I pissed five years away
but pleasantly. And now I can't go in for fear
I'll fall sobbing to the floor. God, the ghosts in there.
The poems. Those honest people from the woods and mill.
What a relief that was from school, from that smelly
student-teacher crap and those dreary committees
where people actually say "considering the lateness
of the hour." Bad times too. That depressing summer
of '66 and that woman going—I've talked too often
about that. Now no bourbon to dissolve the tension,
to find self-love in blurred fantasies, to find the charm
to ask a woman home. What happens to us, John?
We are older than our scars. We have outlasted and survived
our wars and it turns out we're not as bad as we thought.

And that's really sad. But as a funny painter said
at a bash in Portland, and I thought of you then,
give Mother Cabrini another Martini. But not ever again
you and me. Piss on sobriety, and take care. Dick.

TO DIE IN MILLTOWN
for Gene Jarvis

is to have an old but firmly painted name
and friends. The Blackfoot stops, funereal
and green, and eagles headed north
for sanctuary wait for our applause
to fly them home. At 6 A.M.
the fast train east divides the town,
one half, grocery store and mill,
the other, gin and bitter loss.

Even the famed drunk has begun to fail.
His face, fat yesterday and warm, went
slack thin color, one more eerie morning
off the river, bones of ugly women
in his bed. The timber train at noon
divides the town an hour into dying cars.
By four, all bears in the protective hills
hum the air alive. And should the girl
all drunks recall, the full one filled with sun
return, her teeth intact and after 40 years
her charm preserved in joke, the aging drunks
will claim they cheated death with mash.
Death, the Blackfoot says, but never snow.

To die in Milltown, die at 6 P.M.
The fast train west rattles your bourbon warm.

The latest joke is on the early drunk:
sing one more chorus and the nun you love
will dance here out of habit. To live
stay put. The Blackfoot, any river
has a million years to lend, and weather's
always wild to look at down the Hellgate—
solid gray forever trailing off white rain.
Our drinks are full of sun. These aging eagles
climb the river on their own.

ELEGY

in memory, Harold Herndon

I expected him to look dead in the casket,
you know, waxy, blue tinge, but he looked
dozing and tanned, and I wanted to poke him
in front of the crowd and say, "Harold, time
to get up. No train to drive today. I brought
you a drink. I heard a new joke. Look. Outside, the sun."

I tried to remember his life. He gave
it to me in pieces over the years: parents
dead early, some orphanage in Belgrade,
Montana, or Manhattan, Montana,
how he came to be a train engineer,
how he came to own the dear bar.
I remember the unobtrusive, tentative
way he introduced himself 17 years ago
and how, my life seemingly a wreck, I wanted him
to be there like a boulder beside the river,
put there by experts to lean on,
to sleep in the shade of.
I used him plenty. I paid him back

what I could, mostly a poem, and now and then
drinking our way right into dawn.

He sold the bar when I was in Scotland.
He went on driving the train, the Helena run,
long leisurely freights. My need of him
had run out and I felt better, felt now
when we met I could give something to him.
I need ask nothing, but this morning I feel
like asking someone a hell of a lot
before the freight pulls out, the freight certain
to be tough going and slow, loaded to the limit
by the heaviest star in the firmament.

Under the Shadow of the Milltown

W HEN RICHARD HUGO said he was going to "the Milltown," he was headed to the Milltown Bar. Hugo frequented the place in the 1960s and '70s, when a laundromat was attached to the building—gone now. "My life was turning to shit," he says of those early days. "My marriage was breaking up. I was drinking, unable to control my outbursts of anger and my fears that I had become too difficult to live with." The bar was the center of town (hardly a town—population a hundred and twenty or so, in a few houses, a market, the old bar, and the heave of a railroad trestle), across Railroad Street from the Milltown Market and a few storefronts.

The glass display windows are sealed over by the time I come, more than forty years after Hugo first laid eyes on the place, but the market, a faded schoolhouse red, still has a bait cooler and some soda fridges inside. The enormous Town Pump gas station just off the highway, the one built since Hugo's time, must be sucking the little grocery's business away. Like so many Montana towns, this one was losing its family-named places, forsaking them for stakes in franchises. If it were a musical composition, Milltown would be all slide guitar, hovering over the same few chords.

It was Hugo's hope that we readers would "hear trumpets when [he] put the name of that bar on the page": the Milltown Union Bar.[1] These days, the bar is called Harold's Club, named after its founding bartender and owner, Harold Herndon, the first man Hugo met in Montana. "Trumpets, too, for Harold Herndon," Hugo writes, "I could not have picked a better bar." The place still stands at the edge of a gravel-dirt lot, over the heave of railroad tracks, a few turns on Milltown's tiny streets, just off Interstate 90. Much of the building's interior is the same as it was in 1964 when Hugo arrived, and he spent many afternoons and evenings there in the years that followed. A goat head, enshrined in Plexiglas, still hangs on the wall over the bar, and I can

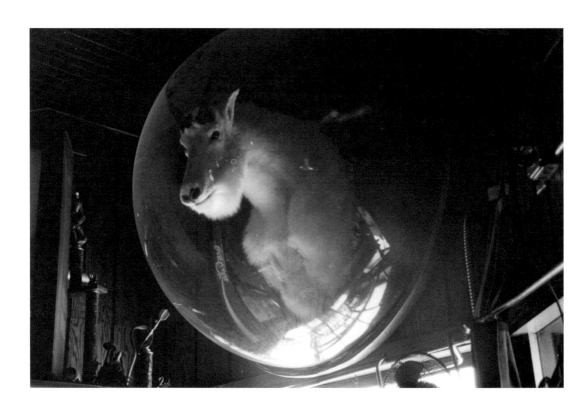

Goat's head under Plexiglas at the Milltown, 2007.

envision Hugo pointing to it from his perch on the stool, cigarette in hand, poking his finger toward the beauty of the bearded, alert-looking visage, and the absurdity of it. I've heard Hugo's smoky laugh on tapes—a throaty set of staccato exhalations—a laugh the goat himself might have uttered before his fate was sealed under plastic. For years, this remarkable piece of taxidermy has lasted through bar smoke and mill soot because it is clamped under the snow-globe dome; the goat's fur is as white as ever.

The bar itself, on the right as you walk in, runs the length of the eastern wall. Behind it, buried in neon beer signs and tacked-up napkins and pictures, the bulwark is a heavy oak frame with a bit of a mirror peeking through the detritus. The windows, '50s sliders, rattle in their frames, and the pool table's felt is red like the worn side of a New England barn. At the back end of the room, darkness is broken up with small tables and wooden chairs. Some people go back there to eat and, later in the evening, to sing karaoke. Someone has cobbled together a smattering of plastic chairs, cyclone-fenced in a little patio outside, and inside there are enough people conversing at the bar that I don't feel completely stared down when I come in, a woman unaccompanied. There's a game, maybe baseball, on the television, and a little bar menu that the cook herself talks me through.

"Go for the burger," she says. "It's the best thing I make." I look at her and smile. I believe her.

Four miles to the east of Missoula, up the Clark Fork, a tributary of the mighty Columbia River, Milltown lies in the valley that begins to spread open after the river's passage through Hellgate Canyon. Both the interstate and a secondary road thread through the crevice now. Fewer than 150 years ago, the Blackfeet regularly ambushed their enemies—Flathead Indians who used the narrow passage as the only trail from the Bitterroot Valley to the rich hunting grounds of the plains—and harassed them at Hellgate. When European trappers arrived in the canyon, they found bones and weapons caught in the brush along the trail. That route, the one that also once passed through Milltown, where it wound around a large reservoir by the Milltown Dam, was the same Indian route that Lewis and Clark's Corps of Discovery took through Hellgate Canyon on their 1806 return east.

If you traveled slowly enough along MT-200, a smaller road that parallels Interstate 90, you might imagine pulling the pavement from its sheath and letting the pines—ponderosas and lodgepoles—fill in the space, opening patches of high grass along the valley floor. Mountain sheep wander a few hundred feet above. If you walked through this passage, you couldn't help but feel that something was askew—as if you were in the shadow of an enormous grave. A grave, after all, is both portal and terminus, depending upon your view of it.

Where these scuffles happened, Hellgate Canyon, is the wedge open to the sky between Mount Jumbo and Mount Sentinel; this was the same fissure Richard Hugo traveled between the University of Montana (then Montana State University) and the Milltown Bar. Milltown itself, tucked around the opposite side of Mount Jumbo from Rattlesnake Creek Street, where Hugo would live for the last nine years of his life, is hidden from Missoula, and from the road it looks like a cluster of railway lines, trestles, and wafts of smoke from the sawmill in Bonner.

Think of Milltown as the back side of Missoula: the darker, almost industrial and definitely working-class settlement under the stocky Mount Jumbo. Milltown was to Missoula what Hugo's hometown of White Center was to Seattle—wood-waste slag heaps and smatterings of shacks and cabins, where a river laced alongside. In Seattle, the river was the Duwamish; in Milltown, it was the Clark Fork and the Blackfoot, converging. Milltown drifted into East Missoula and then around Mount Jumbo into Missoula proper; it resembled the way White Center drifted into West Seattle—the geographic barrier in Montana being the mountains instead of the Duwamish River.

When Hugo moved to Montana, he was forty. Other than his years spent as a bombardier during the Second World War, it was his first move away from Seattle. To teach at the university was one thing—Hugo felt as though he were enough of an imposter taking on that role—but living in the college town of Missoula was quite another. Montana State University was impressive; its old buildings, established in 1893, circled the oval at the campus entrance, and other buildings and sports facilities spread across the valley floor at the base of Mount Sentinel. Though not as big as the University of Washington, where Hugo had gone to school, Montana State was formidable. Academic types and young adults roamed the campus. Perhaps to stay in camouflage, Hugo moved to Milltown instead. Perhaps he couldn't bear to live in the bigger burg, and might have felt most comfortable off to the side in the snug, rubble-strewn town along the tracks.

Hugo and Barbara's apartment was across the gravel driveway from the Milltown Bar. They only lived there for a few weeks before Barbara moved back to Seattle, and Hugo eventually packed his things and rented a house in Missoula. I imagine those early days in that small apartment—the sounds of the clothes dryers from the laundromat during the day and the rowdy bar patrons late at night—and I can see Hugo sitting on a rumpled sofa, waiting for the bar either to open or to close, with his desperate, sad wife sitting on the bed, her head to her knees. "What are we doing here, Dick?" she might have asked, to which he might have said, "What are we doing anywhere?"

And Hugo, not ever ready to concede to being part of the middle class, probably couldn't picture himself taking an apartment in one of the large bungalows near the university. Though he was a professor in the creative writing program, a subchamber of the renowned English department, Hugo saw himself as a working-class guy from White Center—a man who bait-fished and drank beer. He wouldn't have predicted his own central role in a legacy of literary writers who would emerge from the creative writing program; nor would he have guessed that his presence would forever be cited in the history of the place.

For years, The Milltown Union Bar, first a place of convenience for Hugo, became a place of retreat. It was a place where, as the poet Madeline DeFrees tells it, Hugo once received a few comments for wearing a filthy T-shirt. "Alright then," he shouted, slamming his palm on the bar. He went into the bathroom and turned it inside out. When he came back to his drink, he was pointing to the front of his "clean" shirt and smiling.

"Could have used the washer," Harold might have said.

Long before a laundromat attached to a bar became a hipster gimmick (in Seattle during the 1990s there was a trendy music club and bar with washers and dryers called Sit 'N' Spin, which punk rock kids fondly called Shit 'N' Twirl)—the Milltown Union Bar, laundromat, and cafe was built for utility. People from the company cottages near the mill in Bonner and from the railroad—two companies sending trains through—wanted a place to wash their clothes. Drink, too, was essential. Since all you needed was housed at the Milltown, as Hugo put it, "you need never leave." The phone number "was kept on file, along with [his] home phone number, in the English department." Hugo heaved a leg over the barstool, dug in, and made the Milltown Union Bar his own.[2]

Some of the places in which Hugo's main character, his speaker, finds solace and inspiration, remind him of orphanages. The Milltown was one of these: "Doors of orphanages / finally swing out and here you open in." There's release, as if the bar is the next step in a psychological pathway out of abandonment. As a child, Hugo had known what it was like to be left on his own, in the company of people who weren't adequate, and he replayed that scenario with the predictability of a neurotic. Hugo's grandparents were rigid, dogmatic, and fearful adults—"plain, naïve, working class (even peasant class) people, the kind of people who came into that bar."[3] His grandfather manned the parking area at the gas company, while his grandmother tended to the three-room house they lived in. Hugo writes that his grandparents "weren't quite right in the head," and the boy missed his mother, a young woman who had given birth at seventeen and had left soon thereafter. He moved back to the White Center home with his grandparents even after his release from the army. It was as if his mother's example of abandoning her son confounded him, and it became impossible for him to unstick himself from that. For Hugo, the fact that he didn't leave home for so many years displayed "a kind of madness."

Voluntarily, fifteen years later, he makes a home for himself at the Milltown, another venue for outsiders, slipping the shackles of his initial "orphanage" for another self-inflicted one. Even the owner of the bar is "fresh from orphan wars" and "loves too / but as bad as you." There's a comrade in the place, consoling Hugo from drink to drink, trout stream to trout stream, town to town. For Hugo himself, until he marries a second time and finally comes into a family, he's caught in this endless trumping of his outsider status.

During his youthful years with Barbara, they had "haunted" abandoned houses (exploring empty places and imagining what it would be like to live in them or conjuring up the folks who once lived there), drunk regularly, and lived as graduate students might, in a state of transience. A bar, too, became a way of escaping the past. It was a place without tension, a shelter where medicating himself wouldn't involve visits to his grandfather's whiskey still in the garage. At the Milltown, Hugo would discover new folk with whom to commiserate. It also was a place to replay the orphan scenario: a man comes into a place where he's not related to anyone and then bluffs his way through, making it into a kind of tolerable home.

The constant game of creating the orphan/prison and releasing oneself from it resonates in all four of Hugo's poems about the Milltown Bar. First, he writes about the "Laundromat and Cafe" in "The Milltown Union Bar," describing it as a place "you need never leave," where "money or a story brings you booze."

"The Milltown Union Bar" appears in his fourth book of poems, *The Lady in Kicking Horse Reservoir*, and within the same volume of poems, there's another take on the place: "To Die in Milltown." This is the poem in which Hugo decides, self-pityingly, that the bar is a place to wallow, where the "Blackfoot stops, funereal / and green. . . . " He's chasing some delusion of permanence, offering his readers instructions: "To die in Milltown, die at 6 P.M."

Later, in his book *31 Letters and 13 Dreams*, Hugo includes a letter poem to the poet John Logan: "Letter to Logan from Milltown." In this one, he's wrangling with sobriety, passing on a "Dear John letter from Booze." He's afraid of the bar and "can't go in for fear / [he'll] fall sobbing to the floor." Here, desperation replaces the earlier self-pity: "God, the ghosts in there. / The poems. These honest people from the woods and mill." Authenticity, the grail for Hugo, teases him forward through the poem:

> What a relief that was from school, from that smelly
> student-teacher crap and those dreary committees

where people actually say 'considering the lateness
of the hour.'

Hugo's desperation through these poems leads to a crescendo, a poem written
toward the end of Hugo's life, a poem that will be released posthumously: "Elegy." He's
writing it for Harold Herndon, the owner of the Milltown, the man who, like Hugo,
was once an orphan. Hugo wants to "poke him / in front of the crowd and say, 'Harold,
time / to get up.'" Only Harold is in his casket, where he looks "dozing and tanned."
The story of the Milltown, the "dear bar," as Hugo calls it, winds down. While Hugo
was in Scotland on a Guggenheim fellowship, Harold had sold the bar and gone back
to being a train engineer, driving a freight run to Helena. In this final poem about
Milltown, Hugo imagines Harold on those last trips, "tough going and slow." Of Harold's friendship, he realizes, "My need of him / had run out and I felt better, felt now /
when we met I could give something to him."
    The arc of poems about the Milltown traces Hugo's search for the "orphanage" (the
bar), finding it, outgrowing it, and finally mourning it and moving on. Throughout
the poems, one can read a split in the town itself, a fissure that imitates the split of the
orphanage/prison and release from it: "At 6 A.M. / the fast train east divides the town,
/ one half, grocery store and mill, / the other, gin and bitter loss." Sustenance beckons
from the market and the sawmill, while the wall of the speeding train, impenetrable
and loud, blocks the bar folk from crossing over to gather food or go to work.

I used to love going to bars. Like Hugo, I craved a place where people would talk
to each other. Since Hugo had grown up almost in silence—his grandparents were
fatigued and quiet—he was looking for places where conversation gained velocity,
rooms where wit sparked and opinions flared. I too wanted to meet people who would
tell stories; I needed to find my way among strangers. With my roommate from a
boarding school for throw-away kids, I hitchhiked north along Interstate 91 in Mas-
sachusetts, both of us leaning our bodies into the wind-suck of tractor trailers until we
were lifted into the cab of a Mack truck and hauled over the line into Vermont. We
were both seventeen-year-old girls who wanted to "go to a bar." By the time we got to
the Mole's Eye in Brattleboro, it was as if we were kids coming into an amusement park
with free tickets. The drinking age was eighteen then, but the bartender at the Mole's
Eye let us pass—even though the two of us barely looked a day over fourteen. Com-

ing into that place, down the stairs, and into a room centered with a beautiful long beam that we'd pull stools up to, was like coming home. At least for us it was—perhaps because we'd been sent away from our houses, tossed out of other schools, and set loose into the world—we were just kids without any aim or functioning homing devices, so we flung ourselves at whatever looked interesting. Being girls, we weren't like Hugo. We were barely women yet, locked in a situation, a boarding school, that wasn't about poverty exactly, but that still involved a kind of scarcity—a lack of adults who weren't rigid and punitive, or plainly neglectful. The Mole's Eye was a New England version of the Milltown—and though it was a merchant-class tavern in the center of a busy small town rather than a bar at the desolate side of the railroad tracks where sawmill workers came to drink, it was a place that promised you a new take on being yourself. It was our version of Hugo's orphanage. Years later, I would find other bars, and none would stick with me the way the Milltown poems tell you that a place will—but I understood the impulse, and I felt the tingle of being known in run-down taverns between New England and San Francisco. When I came, finally, to the Northwest, there were places almost like the Milltown that I tended to with the attention of a hobbyist, dabbling in making them my own, but none ever stuck.

From 1897 (the founding date claimed by locals) until the 1980s, the Milltown Bar stood as the synecdoche for the town: the row of stools, pool table, and goat head represented the whole of the settlement itself: the insulated, preserved nature of the place, the regularity of the days there, the opportunities for strangers to pass through. The bar was symbolic of the entire sweep of houses and rubble. "The Milltown" meant Milltown.

Like any nostalgist, Hugo wanted to keep the place the way it always had been. He hated the notion of Harold's doing improvements. "I begged Harold for years to leave that beautiful place alone," he insisted.[4] In the end, Hugo probably got his wish. Past Milltown isn't so different from present Milltown. It's a crossroads, always has been, at the confluence of the Blackfoot and the Clark Fork. Then, in the 1990s, came the Town Pump, a Texas-sized gas station with upward of fifty nozzle stands—entire florescent-lit, windy islands just for diesel; a truck stop, market, and casino—where people pull off the highway. Rarely do they come to visit the bar. They can get drinks at the gas station casino. The Town Pump became the newer attraction, a place where the chance to fill up one's car outweighed the impulse of tipping oneself to the local

Old powerhouse at Milltown Dam, now removed, 2007.

trough for a beer. But Milltown has a new prominence. More than for the gas station, more than for the Milltown Bar, the town is recently known for something far more grave, far more consequential, something that is bringing national attention to the small place where Hugo once lived and drank. Milltown is one of the nation's largest Superfund sites, one of the most ecologically devastated places in our country.

Milltown is the town where a dam built in 1906, a river-clogging structure at the convergence of the Blackfoot and Clark Fork rivers, created a catch basin for several million tons of silt containing some of the planet's most hazardous materials: cadmium, arsenic, lead, and other heavy metals. Mine tailings from Butte came downstream in the Clark Fork to Milltown, along the way picking up more waste metals from Anaconda, Drummond, and Deer Lodge, with some squeezing past the dam through town and beyond. To build the dam required flooding 600 acres of the val-

Old black bridge in Milltown, 2007.

ley's rich bottomland, and years later that land would become millions of tons of toxic sediment, the stuff that's being pulled out and shipped to the town of Opportunity, Montana, for burial. ("Opportunity for *whom?*" I wonder.)

In 1908, almost ninety years before ice broke the dam, a flood carried waste from mines at Butte and Anaconda 120 miles downstream to Milltown. Caught by the dam, the tailings from mineral processing sifted into the mud throughout the reservoir. Not until 1981, when someone finally tested for it, was arsenic found in the water. But for more than eighty years, the people living in Milltown, in Riverside, and up the Clark Fork were gathering residue in their bodies. Families of Milltown and Bonner gathered to the "pond" and swam, fished, and hunted. Kids jumped from railroad trestles, and mill houses ran fences along the lapping water. It was the balm to the bruising life of working the mills—a sort of heavy metal Roman bath for the hinterlands.

Ironically, the Milltown Dam was built to generate power, but turned out only a minuscule amount. Washed down from the mines and mills of Butte and Anaconda, tailings held the remains of copper ore after most of the metals had been extracted and were dumped into the pristine Clark Fork. These, along with sulfuric acid generated by pyrite in the ore, kill fish and poison drinking water. During a 1996 break-up of ice floes cracked the dam, and toxins sprang into the river. Only twenty percent of the fish population remained after the surge. "You could drop a fish in the water below the dam," a local man tells me, "and it would be dead in twenty yards."

From the black bridge, now a pedestrian span over the Blackfoot, just north of where it flows into the Clark Fork—or would if there weren't cranes and bulldozers and a dam there—I could imagine seeing trout. What I can't envision is that eating fish from this river, day in and day out, would kill you.

The Environmental Protection Agency has certain specifications for the sites that most need intervention and "cleanup," whatever that ends up being, and the priorities are "Superfund sites." But it doesn't mean that these places will actually receive government funding. In fact, many don't. The federal mandate is to lay the blame for the pollution on whatever companies or remnants of companies it can find; those efforts are fought by corporate legal departments.

The National Priorities List is the chart of worst Superfund sites. The EPA tracks and allocates funds when they are available. There are hundreds of Superfund sites in need of funding, and the budgets have been shrinking over recent years. Some places, such as the Anaconda Copper Mining Company site less than an hour away from Milltown, have also been on the list since 1982. Milltown has too, but the cleanup is moving ahead, across a huge area.

The EPA's cleanup plan covers 120 river miles upstream of Milltown Dam, one of the country's largest Superfund sites. The stretch of the Clark Fork River from Warm Springs to Drummond is contaminated with cadmium, arsenic, lead, copper and zinc. The cleanup will remove 167 acres of polluted soils along the river; treat 700 acres of soil in place; establish a fifty-foot border area on each side; and replant native willows, dogwood, and cottonwood to stabilize fifty-six miles of stream bank and prevent additional heavy toxic metals from entering the river. The entire cleanup will take ten years.[5]

Milltown Superfund site, with mill house in foreground, 2007.

While Richard Hugo sat drinking at the Milltown Bar, a plume advancing down-stream—arsenic, lead, copper, cadmium, and manganese—was running through the groundwater beneath him. Little did he know that his line "where the Blackfoot stops, funereal / and green" was prophetic.

The Milltown Dam was removed in April 2008, shortly after my last visit to the bar. The extensive toxic waste of some 6,600,000 yards will take a few more years to extract.

Outside "Harold's Club," there's no place to walk, no downtown—there's only the hill-ock of road over the trestle, dead-ending at the bar. Milltown is a place that slows a per-son down; the black bridge no longer takes cars, and the roads are narrow. It's a place that makes you feel like walking, even if to clear your head from the activity in the bar. The history that separates Hugo's sojourn from my own tour through Milltown is the

Milltown Superfund site with reservoir drained, 2007.

dam being pulled loose and the public acknowledgement of the extent of the pollution. Back when Hugo wrote these poems, in the 1960s and '70s, it was a sawmill town, a place of work and of people barely carving out a life. Who would guess that they were also being poisoned as they did it? Now it remains another kind of mill town, shifting work from the sawmill to bulldozers that push away sediment, laying temporary gravel roadways and carving out ponds—jobs that are, for the time being, offering more work than the mill at Bonner. The sawmill is closed now, and a developer, I'm told, has a plan to create a little village out of the old cottages.

When I go back into the bar, I avoid the karaoke sessions they've added since Hugo's time. I go at off hours, during the day, and I order beer. While I'm there, a few kids from Missoula come in. They're here for the card game in the back, and they'll probably stay for karaoke. The bartender is a woman who is just working there, holding a job she is not particularly interested in—there is no mystique, no history in it for her. She doesn't, for example, know who Harold is. "I think he died a while back," she says. I can see that his shadow is cast only from his name now—Harold's Club—and even the word "Harold" is disconnected from any actual recollections of his face, his voice.

What of these disconnections? The people who once took pint glasses of beer into their hands and cheered others on; the women who pulled hand-sewn curtains over sticks and mounted them above the windows; the bartender who held a handful of cocktail napkins and spread them under the woes of people gathered to his bar; the bartender who refilled Hugo's own vessels—what happens when the memory of them fades, when the people who knew them go away and die? The passing along is what interests me, and in some tragic way Milltown is a kind of active vanishing. Hugo too, passed along a physical presence and an image—one of a poet who stumbled toward utterance. "To live / stay put," he wrote. "The Blackfoot, any river / has a million years to lend."

In a way, it does. The fishermen will return now that the dam has been removed. The Clark Fork has bike paths and footpaths alongside it, and rafters and kayakers slide downstream. Surely, time flows and bumps along, and just as we get used to it, it fools us. It escalates and slows during times when we'd least expect it. Just when events seem to stretch out forever, they're brought into focus, the middle distance shifting to the tabletop right in front of us.

The bartender points to a row of beer taps. "All of these used to be domestic beers. Now they're filled with microbrews." There used to be a bull elk over the bar, but it wasn't in Plexiglas so it wore out from smoke and dust. Now there's a full-winged turkey, open span. People have just accepted the dam removal, she says. But, says the cook who brings me the burger, "the best swimming and fishing hole in the world is gone."

I leave the bar, the one-beer buzz filling my head beneath flipping clouds and sun. Down the gravel drive, up and over the bump of railroad tracks, I walk past the market, past a smattering of small-framed and aluminum-sided houses with metal window boxes, past a trailer, and down a hill to the old black bridge—a trestle left as a footpath across the bottom of the Blackfoot. To the left, someone has set up sheaves of concrete to slow the river. From the north side of Milltown, you can't see the convergence, and only after passing through several layers of "No Trespassing" signs, walking under a freeway overpass, and kicking along where the dump trucks go, do I see the dam. There it is: a house on top of rapids, a stone cavern lifted onto concrete. Up close, it's like the textile mills that I'd see along the rivers of Vermont, this mill house planted in the river instead of alongside. The dam is brick, and there's a rounded bluff that stops the water from going downstream. A small spillway next to the brick house allows a chute of water to slide through.

I want a view from above, so I go back to the car, heading back toward town until I get to a little turnoff that a woman in town has directed me to. I follow it over the river, up a big hill. When I see a group of ponderosa pines near the crest, I pull over and park. Through the trees, over a barbed-wire fence that is easy to push down with my foot, down a winding trail, I emerge on an enormous shelf of rock layered with dried-out grasses. Ahead of me the bridges across the Blackfoot lie like file dividers as the river disappears into the mountains. Two of the bridges are on Interstate 90, and the third is the black bridge, the one I crossed on foot through Milltown. The river thins as it comes nearer to the cliff. There, it joins the Clark Fork. From this height, the convergence seems contrived—planned in some architect's office.

It probably was. What should be a rough, rocky swell of water and riverbank is a tidy gravel series of waterways and truck paths. The mill house is taken from a Lionel train set in the 1940s, and from up high, the rounded part of the dam is the lid of a rolltop desk. The rest of the scene is coherent from above—you can see the scheme. The whole area, several square miles of construction, is a staging area. Taking out the dam's stone building took a few days, but transport of the contaminants will take years. From the bluff on Deer Creek Road, I'm seeing the construction area travel up the valley floor. Piles of dirt are neatly organized—I can see furrows in between them. Stimson Timber Mill, boarded up now, is in the background. Up the Clark Fork, to my right, are pilings and a burnt patch, ribs of old weirs, and some rectangles of discolored liquid. Red dirt and grasses pop like abstract splashes from the three ponds. Around the perimeter is a road, a raised bed on rocks, pressed down with gravel. That's where the condos will go. That's the word from the bar.

Too high up to fish, the bluff may not be a place that Hugo visited. From here, the rivers are not mighty; they are not powerful. The waterways are shallow and fragile, trickles through sludge, straightened by the intention of environmental planners.

"I tried other bars of course and enjoyed them," Hugo wrote, "but never like the Milltown. That was love, love of home, love of the possibility that even if my life would never again change for the better, at least there, in that unpretentious watering hole that trembled when the Vista Dome North Coast roared by, I could live inside myself warm in fantasies, or chat with honest people who were neither afraid nor ashamed of their responses to life." What Hugo couldn't have known then was that the river would deteriorate and then recover—that the mill would close forever, and little Milltown would become some kind of new American town, a suburb glued to Missoula with small frame houses. What he would see would be "Harold's Club," still aptly named for his hero, the man who would bring us together in a place where wishes and jokes were nailed to the wall.

Mining gallows in Walkerville, 2007.

Walkerville, Montana
(Butte, America)

LETTER TO LEVERTOV FROM BUTTE

Dear Denise: Long way from, long time since Boulder. I hope
you and Mitch are doing OK. I get rumors. You're in Moscow,
Montreal. Whatever place I hear, it's always one of glamor.
I'm not anywhere glamorous. I'm in a town where children
get hurt early. Degraded by drab homes. Beaten by drunken
parents, by other children. Mitch might understand. It's kind
of a microscopic Brooklyn, if you can imagine Brooklyn
with open pit mines, and more Irish than Jewish. I've heard
from many of the students we had that summer. Even seen
a dozen or so since then. They remember the conference fondly.
So do I. Heard from Herb Gold twice and read now and then
about Isaac Bashevis Singer who seems an enduring diamond.
The mines here are not diamond. Nothing is. What endures
is sadness and long memories of labor wars in the early
part of the century. This is the town where you choose sides
to die on, company or man; and both are losers. Because
so many people died in mines and fights, early in history
man said screw it and the fun began. More bars and whores
per capita than any town in America. You live only
for today. Let me go symbolic for a minute: great birds
cross over you anyplace, here they grin and dive. Dashiell
Hammett based *Red Harvest* here though he called it Personville
and "person" he made sure to tell us was "poison" in the slang.

I have ambiguous feelings coming from a place like this
and having clawed my way away, thanks to a few weak gifts
and psychiatry and the luck of living in a country
where enough money floats to the top for the shipwrecked
to hang on. On one hand, no matter what my salary is
or title, I remain a common laborer, stained by the perpetual
dust from loading flour or coal. I stay humble, inadequate
inside. And my way of knowing how people get hurt, make

my (damn this next word) heart go out through the stinking air
into the shacks of Walkerville, to the wife who has turned
forever to the wall, the husband sobbing at the kitchen
table and the unwashed children taking it in and in and in
until they are the wall, the table, even the dog the parents
kill each month when the money's gone. On the other hand,
I know the cruelty of poverty, the embittering ways
love is denied, and food, the mean near-insanity of being
and being deprived, the trivial compensations of each day,
recapturing old years in broadcast tunes you try to recall
in bars, hunched over the beer you can't afford, or bending
to the bad job you're lucky enough to have. How, finally,
hate takes over, hippie, nigger, Indian, anyone you can lump
like garbage in a pit, including women. And I don't want
to be part of it. I want to be what I am, a writer good enough
to teach with you and Gold and Singer, even if only in
some conference leader's imagination. And I want my life
inside to go on long as I do, though I only populate bare
landscape with surrogate suffering, with lame men
crippled by more than disease, and create finally
a simple grief I can deal with, a pain the indigent can find
acceptable. I do go on. Forgive this raving. Give my best
to Mitch and keep plenty for yourself. Your rich friend, Dick.

Where the Poor Look Down Upon the Rich and Some People Dance the Cool-Water Hula

What Denise Levertov Has to Do With It

I T TURNS OUT that Mary Randlett knew Denise Levertov. "At first she kind of brushed me off," Mary tells me. "We were at a party. Denise had just moved to Seattle and she was inundated with people."

Mary is looking over the poem that Hugo wrote for Levertov. We're sitting in a coffee shop in Butte, on our way to take photographs. "You know," Mary says, "I drove Denise around. She didn't have a car. She'd never learned how to drive because she'd lived in London and then in the East."

Mary gets up and goes over to a little shelf, where she takes down a creamer and pours milk into her coffee. "When I read Denise's poems about Mount Rainier, I couldn't believe it," she says. "They were beautiful short poems, like paintings. I offered to drive Denise up Mount Rainier so she could see it up close. 'No thanks,' she'd said. 'I don't want to see how man has touched it.'" Mary shakes her head and sips her coffee. "She was something else, Denise was."

Hearing this reminds me of how strange it would be to imagine Denise Levertov in Butte, Montana. Though she was the same age as Mary Randlett and she loved visual art, I can't see her in this run-down old mining city the way I can see Mary here. Mary just fits into places. She's the photographer who assumes nothing and engages in everything.

Placing Levertov in Butte was an odd choice for Hugo. Clearly he had wanted to dedicate a poem to her, but this town wasn't where any reader would expect to find a poet who was more of a fine art poet than, say, a street poet—a British woman who lived in New York for many years, summered in Maine, who then lived in San Francisco and finally in Seattle—all the while writing exquisite lyrics in which her persona, the first-person "I," was graciously, urbanely, staged. Levertov's prose explained the experiments of her verse, illuminating the poems as if they were delicately laid out by hand, upon velvet, the line breaks twisted together with tiny pliers, the gilded fastener of one pinched into the shimmering link of the next. Envisioning her in the sooty world of Butte, a town littered with mining detritus—old tools discarded along the hillsides, enormous cages that once served as underground elevators and gears the size of small houses and leftover carts from the shafts—is an exercise in juxtaposition.

Hugo must have felt the distance between them—both as writers and as people. He, the shambling "fat man," as he sometimes described himself, from a poor town to the south of Seattle, and she, the scholarly poet whose father was a parson in England. While Hugo was serving as a bombardier over Italy and Yugoslavia during the Second World War, Denise Levertov was working as a nurse in London. Hugo was making one mess and she was cleaning up another. After the war, for the sweep of her career, Levertov committed herself to social causes, to progressive politics, and to bringing literature into places outside the academy.

Levertov and Hugo had met at the University of Colorado, where they both taught briefly at a conference in the summer of 1975. "Dear Denise," he writes after returning West, "Long way from, long time since Boulder." Even a university town in Colorado was upscale for Hugo. For Levertov, it must have been a trip into the hinterlands.

Whatever their acquaintance, clearly, Hugo admires his colleague. "Letter to Levertov . . . " denigrates his whereabouts in comparison to her more glamorous existence:

> You're in Moscow,
> Montreal. Whatever place I hear, it's always one of glamour.
> I'm not anywhere glamorous. I'm in a town where children
> get hurt early. Degraded by drab homes. Beaten by drunken
> parents, by other children.

He's in Butte. And, perhaps more than most towns, this one tells the story of his own past—he could be one of the children who is beaten, degraded, and gets "hurt early." In the poem, perhaps as in life, Hugo aspires to be a "writer good enough / to teach with you . . . " At the end, his parting line after a tour of Butte and of poverty itself is "Your rich friend, Dick." He's richer, the poem indicates, for his experience of being poor.

"My urge to be someone adequate didn't change after the war," Hugo writes in his book of essays *The Triggering Town*. And this urge shows up in "Letter to Levertov from Butte," this poem he called "probably the best of the bunch" from his 1977 book *31 Letters and 13 Dreams*.[1] "That poem," Hugo says in a 1981 interview, "seemed to generate a lot, enabled me to talk about certain things that have been on my mind that I wasn't able to handle in a more conventional form. I imagine I couldn't have done that in a lyric."[2] The poem weaves history of the place with Hugo's self-admitted insecurities ("no matter what my salary is / or title, I remain a common laborer" and "I stay humble, inadequate / inside") and stacks these up against Denise Levertov's globetrotting. His plainspoken, chunky lines stand in juxtaposition to the delicate, hand polished aura of her poems. In hers, the images are figurines, and their proximity to the edges of the shelves (literally the line breaks) set the suspense in the poem. In "St. Peter and the Angel," for example, she writes:

> Delivered out of raw continual pain,
> smell of darkness, groans of those others
> to whom he was chained—
>
> unchained, and led
> past the sleepers,
> door after door silently opening—
> out!
>
> And along a long street's
> majestic emptiness under the moon:
>
> one hand on the angel's shoulder, one
>
> feeling the air before him,
> eyes open but fixed . . .

You feel vulnerable in a completely different way when reading a Levertov poem than you do when reading a Hugo poem. In a Hugo poem, you are walking into the poorest part of town and, having a look, fearing that you might belong there. In a Levertov poem, you are observing the realm of the poem, and you feel unworthy of the scene, because the poet is placing the world above you. You are looking heavenward as you read it.

"Letter to Levertov from Butte" is Hugo's way of connecting both his psyche to a place and his sense of himself as a poet to another poet; that way he'll see himself more clearly. Hugo is trying to cajole Denise Levertov into being a friend—you can feel that—only I'm wondering if it's also some basis for inadvertent competition: the kind men have with women sometimes, while remaining oblivious to it. The chatty greeting ("I hope you and Mitch are doing OK") and the nod to the far-flung places where she travels—these acknowledge her as a colleague. But then Hugo pushes away from her, turning instead to her husband when he describes the hardships of Butte: "Mitch might understand. It's kind / of a microscopic Brooklyn, if you can imagine Brooklyn / with open pit mines, and more Irish than Jewish." The subtext here might read, "You wouldn't understand this kind of poverty, but the man in your life would."

Then, after a creating a litany of the scarcity and desperation in Butte and in Walkerville, the hilltop town above Butte, places where Hugo pictures himself with a pathos that has you on the edge of tears because you can feel the innards of the town and his own sadness, he signs the letter: "Your rich friend, Dick." The line feels triumphant.

It's worth remembering that the year that he taught with Levertov, Hugo was a National Book Award finalist. The near-miss for the prize was a wake-up call, a dash of ammonia under the nose so that he might be aware of his own elite and sanctioned place in American letters, as well as an introduction to the competitions that poetry can find itself in, which all leaves me wondering how self-effacing Hugo really means to be. Is he trumping her in the game of showcasing personal tragedy in American verse? "I only populate bare / landscape with surrogate suffering," he writes at the poem's crescendo, and it rings so true that I can feel Hugo winning out, admitting to his strategy of projecting his own desperate outsider-persona onto the town.

Up High Are the Poor

Lois Welch, one of Hugo's dearest friends, remembers Dick Hugo coming into Butte, looking up, pointing to Walkerville, and saying, "This is the only town I've been to where the poor get to look down on the rich." From a vantage up in Walkerville, the smog that settled below, over Butte, might have made the larger city disappear if it weren't for the steeples and a few ten-story buildings peeking through. Underneath the cloth of gray, the grids of houses and cemeteries crowding the valley floor were a series of enormous props held backstage while the tiny seminal village, Walkerville, insisted its way into the spotlight above the clouds.

There are no cemeteries in Walkerville, by city ordinance, yet down below they sprawl across the flats of Butte. Rumor has it that Butte has the highest number of graves of any town its size. Per capita, matched one-to-one with the living, there were more dead people in Butte than anywhere else. Of course, the dead always outnumber the living, but in this place, it becomes an enormous display of evidence of mining tragedies and the cancer deaths from foul air, tainted water. In the flats of the valley, vacant of rich mineral deposits, the miners didn't dig for ore. Instead, townsfolk sunk bodies into the earth.

On the day I come into the valley, I drive alongside graveyards that stretch for miles.

Along that same hill, Hugo saw in Walkerville and Butte a despair so pervasive that even he cringed under the weight of it. "More bars and whores / per capita than any town in America," Hugo wrote. As in most of his poems triggered by towns, the impoverished places that Hugo had identified and never really come to know, "Letter to Levertov from Butte" sets his own life up against a place he sees as dire. His own life, by comparison, shimmers in the slag.

On October 11, 1904, the Walkerville streetcar slid backward over the hill and started its runaway slide down into Butte. As it picked up speed, the motorman jumped, and the car soared through the curve at Excelsior and Park streets, leaping from the tracks. It crashed into a large telephone pole, a line of fence, and the boardwalks, until it came to rest in front of W. A. Clark's barn.

Clark, one of the "copper barons" of Butte, owned the Moulton Mine, a mining lode he had located in 1875. He was also part owner of the bank and later came into ownership of many more mines. In the construction of his mansion, now a bed and breakfast in Uptown Butte, Clark hired artists who hand-painted frescos in each room. Woodworkers hand carved all of the walls and banisters. The place was magnificent. Like most who made their fortunes on the extraction or processing of natural resources,

Clark was competitive to the point of being sinister and cutthroat. When another investor, Marcus Daly, bought a nearby lode, the Alice Mine, Clark adjusted the water level in Moulton so that it would flood Daly's tunnels. He became a senator even though he had been implicated in a bribery scandal; he later died in his apartment on Fifth Avenue in New York, far from Butte. Like so many who made fortunes in the West, Clark, after extracting what he could, retired to the safety and high-status quarters of the East.

No one was killed when the streetcar slid through the bend. Though onlookers were nearby, only a few people were hurt, and the accident remains a cherished part of Walkerville lore. The streetcar also inspired several holdups. Each time, the same befuddled gripman was in charge. Eventually, in the throes of the Depression, the streetcar closed in 1937. No longer could residents of Walkerville travel down to Butte so easily, and a few shops grew at the top of the hill. By then, though, Walkerville was in its decline. The settlement lost population, sliding downhill to Butte.

Uptown Butte, a crosshatch of streets named for metals—Iron, Aluminum, Silver, Mercury, and Gold—still boasts magnificent dark brick structures and gothic, dark Victorian buildings. It features the kind of historic preservation I feel moved by, one initiated by neglect rather than vanity. Butte, unlike most boom-and-bust mining towns, had "a long heyday, for a mining camp," Fritz Wolff, another writer tells me. In fact, in 1917 Butte had a much bigger population than it does now (some say it had upward of 100,000 people) and was said to be the largest city between Seattle and Minneapolis. Wolff is a former miner who works for the Washington State Department of Natural Resources, where he's cataloguing abandoned mines. He says, "The incomparable high grade underground mines were strong through 1890–1960, World War I, World War II, the Korean War and then they got started on the Berkeley Pit."[3] The pit, opened in 1955, was an enormous open mine, a hole in the earth into which chemicals were poured to leech out precious metals.

As the town's population again plummeted with the shutdown of the Berkeley Pit in 1982, only the hope of attracting tourist dollars and economic block grants would keep Butte going. Uptown Butte is poor to this day, and Walkerville is poorer still.

Settled before Butte and looking out over it from 6,172 feet above sea level, Walkerville first attracted workers to the early copper mines in the area. The houses were spread out—cabins really—with outbuildings and farm animals between them. Who, I wondered, would build a town against the slant of a hill? Walkerville could only expand by pushing down toward the valley. The slope is dramatic, and the view spectacular. At the top fringe of Uptown Butte, you can see Pipestone Pass and the mountains to the south, where the Continental Divide weaves back and forth.

Downshifting into first gear, I coerce my tiny Honda up, past the homes of the copper barons, past the bookstore and a coffee shop. It's a *mountain*, I realize, not some little bump to roll over. Further to the left, up at an elevation of 8,000 feet, is a statue of Mary—Our Lady of the Rockies.

I'm far from the tuck of hills near sea level in Seattle. As the engine on my tiny car spins and whirrs, I'm cresting the top and seeing on the left a "Welcome to Walkerville" sign. It's a metal sheet with a hunk knocked off of the corner. Behind it, a cinderblock building painted white, with faded blue letters: Blaine Center. There's the wheel of a handicapped symbol still visible, another blue swipe against the wall. In front, some bent playground equipment stands crookedly on broken pavement. On the other side of the street, I see the village centerpiece: a large church with the steps coming steeply down to the road. Built by the true working class, the people who could barely scrub themselves clean for Sunday mass, the church was the institution that celebrated the opposite of mining: all the metaphors pointed skyward.

Small streets dip away from this road that I'm still begging my car to climb. The houses look weary in the dirt landscapes beyond them, strung under a wide gray silk sky. The top of Walkerville, like many crests along the ridge, isn't really the top, and I see that I am, instead, on one lift along a little washboard of more hills. Montana, after all, goes on and on. I'd forgotten that for a second. I'm almost 8,000 feet up, and I can feel my ears sealing with air.

The Dark You Can't Imagine

Mining, in Walkerville, was the spark held up to dry grasses. It caught and inflamed the entire area until Butte became known as "the richest hill on earth." The first claims, the Alice and the Lexington and others, were the inaugural ventures. Prospectors came for gold. Placer miners tipped pans in ancient riverbeds because the land seemed, at first, too unstable for tunnels, but they stayed for silver and then, ultimately, for copper. Once these early entrepreneurs hit strings of copper through the rocks in the 1870s, the investors became "copper barons," and the population of Walkerville swelled to 4,000. (Today it is just over 700.) Just before they hit the metal, the men in the mining camp numbered around 50. The Alice Mine stood atop the hill by 1877, and by 1878, frame and log houses and outbuildings dotted the hillside. By 1900, the population of Butte was over 30,000 and the smog and sulfur smoke had become so heavy that dogs and cats couldn't live in the city. When they found their way onto the streets, most died. But Butte kept growing; it reached 60,000, and some say even over 100,000. Today, fewer than 40,000 live in the city, and Walkerville is considered a neighborhood of Butte, just off of Uptown Butte, further up the hill. If you were to look at a scale diorama of the area, then cut a cross section, you'd see a warren of mine shafts like ant tunnels that make a honeycomb of the mountain that Butte is built upon. Like an ornate fossil, the tunnels through the hill are so extensive you might not believe that the city could be supported upright. And Walkerville is the unlikely crown, teetering at the top.

I'm here on a weekday, and the place is silent. No cars pass me as I bump over the holes in the street; on one side, houses are built up, with raised sidewalks and banisters following the shadow of the former boardwalks; on the other, houses are lower than street level and the stairs descend to them.

A mailman stuffs a roll of paper through the slot in one door. He's the only person whom I see. No one stands at the curtains of any of the houses. Some homes have aluminum siding, and Daly Street, the main drag named after one Marcus Daly, of the "Copper Kings," is a set of storefront ghosts. Pisser's Palace is the lone bar, one even Hugo might not have ventured into, and the fake rocks of the façade have me wondering—why not use real stones? There are piles of them all over the vacant lots through town. Early on, the people of Walkerville put up false storefronts, tacked onto the barns. Maybe that's what inspired the use of synthetic rocks on Pisser's.

On the site of the old Walkerville Mercantile, the place I trace back via photos, is the only remaining shop—a state liquor store. It reminds me of a decrepit New England "package store," like one you'd find in Quincy or South Boston. But Walkerville is even poorer—no grocery store, doctor offices, lawyers, or shops—only the liquor store in the washed-out green building and the small houses with the tar paper coming off. A few of them have high cyclone fences and whirligigs spinning out front, pointing to the north— in the direction of Butchertown, where the animals of Butte were slaughtered for meat.

Shaft mining began here when one of the earliest claims, the Lexington Mine, was bought for twenty dollars and a horse. The horse's owner, A. J. Davis, needed a way to

Mercantile in Walkerville, now a state liquor store, 2007.

get into Butte. The town's other major mine, the Alice Mine, was owned and oper-ated by the Walker brothers, for whom the town was named. They were soon joined by miners from Cornwall, England.[4] Between them, the claim owners had, from 1864 to 1867, "located dozens of lode claims, including the Rainbow Lode in present day Walkerville."[5] Both Lexington and Alice established Butte as a "rich silver producer in the late 1870s through the 1880s," and by the end of that run, Alice was the largest silver producer in the country.

Alongside the mine, workers built a cluster of homes and shanties, transforming the prospectors' homes of the 1870s into something that resembled a town. Other mines sprang up; gallows for the hoists—long cables with "cages" for the men to descend in—stood above the town. Dirt pulled out of the shafts mounded up around houses and hoists, and the streets meandered around the heaps. Infrastructure to support the processing of ore began to appear adjacent to the mines: shacks and stacks in the early pictures. By 1889 the cable car was running down the hill, and pipe stacks thrust upward from the mines. Big piles of sand and rock were dug out of the mountain. By the late 1800s, over 300 stamps, enormous crushers to pulverize the ore into gravel or powder, were slamming along, day and night.

Here's how it worked. There were two classes of silver: free and base. Free silver was extracted from a fine powder, and the mercury that clung to it was sloughed off with other wastes into muddy water. The heavier metals sank and were pulled from the settling pans. With base silver, the ore went to the crusher and was reduced to walnut-size pieces. It was dried and mixed with salt. Then it was placed under stamps to crush it. (You can still see ruins of the stamp mills around Montana.) The ore was then roasted with mercury to pull chloride from sulfide and amalgamate. Children called it quicksilver; one longtime resident of Walkerville recalls carrying it in glass beakers around town. Because of the weight of the metal, the bottom would often fall out of the container and the leaden stuff would spill to the ground. Consider this on a grand scale: tons of mercury falling through bins, tossed off into the dirt—a catastrophic amount of pollution.

Until 1893, the Alice Mine was rated as the greatest silver producer in the country. Walkerville was known as a livelier camp than Butte and found its way onto the stock exchanges. Then, when the Silver Bill repeal of 1878 eliminated silver as a precious metal used in U.S. currency, many Montana mining towns went under. As Hugo wrote in "Degrees of Gray in Philipsburg," locals developed a "hatred of the mill, / the Silver Bill repeal, the best liked girls / who leave each year for Butte." But Butte had other metals to rely on—particularly copper. The Alice and Lexington mines, along with the rapid growth of others, attracted investors from the East. Union struggles followed. So did tragedy—in 1917, the Granite Mountain Speculator mine disaster killed 164 men and trapped 400 more. It sparked violence throughout the city. But, as some boosters of Walkerville will tell you, the Alice Mine created a community. Marcus Daly, the more benevolent of the copper kings, encouraged it. There was an Alice Reading Room; a hospital that guaranteed free care to the miners and their families; an Alice Mine and Mill Band; and an exercise room. In some ways, it was a mining camp version of the settlement houses—a rural Hull House on a hill in Montana. These activities were vital in the 1880s, before the town's economy went south.

The Walkerville of today, without working mines of substance, retains the ghosts of the glory days—a few towers and "gallows" frames to the shafts. At a coffee shop, earlier, I'd looked at a photo of the miners early in the century. They're all wearing dark clothes that appear to be made darker by the dirt. Their faces, even when wiped clean, retain the tint of soot. In their pockets are white candles. They light up the photograph, and I think of these candles as a seraph's dynamite—angelic, barely able to hold a flame. The grit of the place greases over everything; even the people resemble aging cast-iron skillets, darkened over time.

From the wide, smoky sky, the miners descended into a darkness unfathomable to walkers upon open ground, a darkness that put their own bodies out of visibility. Imagine knowing that your hand is reaching for your head but you can't see its trajectory, you can only feel it, suddenly, as it makes contact. Think of those spaces below ground: moments when a whoosh through a bore hole would sink the flames of candles—a place where horses, sent vertically down the shafts, lived in a dark unknowable to those at the surface. The dark deprived a man of his senses because his smell and taste and touch and hearing grew so heightened against the lack of sight; the blackness was the sound of trickling water, the humming of nerves. And the squeeze of dampness.

Before the era of motorized wagons on little tracks, before the era of remote-controlled blasts and automated diggers, the men did lower horses into the mines, a fact I can't stop thinking about. The horses never saw daylight again. They were rolled onto their sides, bound in canvas jackets, tied at the legs with ropes, hoisted into the gallows, and lowered into the cage. From the front, if you were watching, you'd see the horse's massive trunk and his penis, the ribs elongated to the bony intersection of his stretched belly, but not his head. You wouldn't see that because it would be covered. Down he'd go, doomed to a life of pulling carts and living in darkness with dynamite blasts shaking the shafts.

Not Diamonds

I've pulled over to the side of a dirt street and am looking at the poem "Letter to Levertov from Butte." Leaning into the dashboard of the little car, I want to rip through the page or slice the thing with a letter opener and see literally what's behind the verse, as if the fat man might appear, Hugo in the flesh, standing right behind the curtain of that poem, finally coming out to his surrogate misery. This inspires me to see the town, the projection, as something whole and clear, something intact with its own pain.

And here, north of Butte, over the top of Butte, "I'm not anywhere glamorous," I think, echoing Hugo. The search for the poem, my desire to meld poem to town as if the amalgamation would yield something precious, the gems of language and the warm rush of intellect and heart merging, settles me beyond the uptown, over the hill from the last coffeehouse, the last sandwich. Here I wonder if "children get hurt early," if they're "degraded by drab homes. Beaten by drunken / parents, by other children?" Aren't they everywhere? Aren't the hygienic suburbs, with their plastic toys and three-car garages, just stage sets for an American mania of distortion and competition twisting children with full bellies into tortured beings, impoverished and distant, into consumers of self-mutilation and crystal meth?

But that's just one slant, one pressed upon me by the dirt and rust of the place. I'm given to bouts of knowing that, simply by living in a particular slice of American culture, children are damaged. And in the poverty that one feels from here, the few houses fallen, trailers pinned to their remaining joists, or the tin hammered over clap-board with drafts rushing through, I can see how a child might feel in such depravity. In fact, though, Walkerville feels like a town in which no one actually lives—a town that Nintendo and Pottery Barn don't reach, a place to which computer keyboards and running shoes will never find their way.

"The mines here are not diamond," Hugo writes, and the tone gives way to a rant against "company or man," the labor wars in which everyone was doomed, no mat-ter which side he was on. In the face of it, the people of Butte began to live in their circumstances, says Hugo's version of history, and they lavished extra coins on bar countertops and whores' bureaus. Though Hugo claims he was a person "coming from a place like this," I know he wasn't, not quite. White Center, though rough and downtrodden, didn't have the physical pollution of Walkerville—the land wasn't ripped open and burnt in smelters. White Center, by contrast, was quiet, and the sea air rolled over it. The desperation of the small houses and truck farms never was this lively, this sopped over with sulfur smoke and rot.

Still, Hugo insists that he is like someone living in Butte:

> I remain a common laborer, stained by the perpetual
> dust from loading flour or coal. I stay humble, inadequate

The back side of Walkerville, 2007.

inside. And my way of knowing how people get hurt, make
my (damn this next word) heart go out through the stinking air
into the shacks of Walkerville . . .

He wasn't the first poet who wrote to console himself through difficult beginnings, but Hugo did devote his poems to retooling the central narrative of his life:
He was an outsider; he'd been abandoned by his mother, neglected and shut out by
his grandparents. His poems replayed the scenario over and over, and if you ask some
critics about Hugo's work, they will tell you that he was writing the same poem again
and again. By admitting that he felt inadequate, he was creating a self in the poems,
and to be trustworthy, Hugo might have felt, was to reiterate his position as a man
not worthy.

Though writing poems was indigenous to Hugo's sensibility, whatever the trigger, the man himself seemed far from the image of a "poet"—often shambling, uncouth, uncool. Hugo emanated an aura of shame. It is the kind of humiliation that comes from a man who never had enough nurturing, who never understood simple affection—unearned and unconditional—and who had, as he put it, "problems with women." Perhaps by dedicating the poem about Butte and Walkerville to Denise Levertov, Hugo was trying to overcome these issues and treat his colleague, a female poet, respectfully and as a peer.

When we were in the coffee shop, Mary Randlett told me that she "had to work on getting to know Denise." It hadn't been easy. "There was a little bit of space there, but we were the same age, and she had a sense of humor that was great. She could really be a human being."

I wondered if Hugo found these same pleasures with his new friend.

A Symbol Becomes an Anecdote Becomes an Open Sore Big Enough to Swim In

While Hugo was flat-panning the background of Butte as if with a camera, sifting through the surface of the place and pinning his heart to the "stinking air . . . the shacks of Walkerville," I was thinking of the horses. Staring at the terrible old photos I'd run across in the bookstore down the hill in Butte, I envisioned the sweaty animals resisting the gags pulled through their mouths and cotton sacks rolled over their heads. I could see the corral where the dust and pebbles flew up under the flick of their hooves. There, they were rolled and bound. That was the image of Walkerville that devastated me. I could see the place as a hinge between Butte and Butchertown, places where animals were tied and shoved into service in a gravelike underground, or sent through the fences to slaughter. The images stick to dusty lots next to the sheds and trailers and houses that I pass.

Hugo, too, illuminating some connection to a place sooty and gone by, imagined his way in through images that led him to abbreviated anecdotes—his method of articulating the pain that lived in that town:

> . . . the wife who has turned
> forever to the wall, the husband sobbing at the kitchen
> table and the unwashed children taking it in and in and in
> until they are the wall, the table, even the dog the parents
> kill each month when the money's gone.

Then, he pivots from the place into his past. "I know the cruelty of poverty," Hugo says, "the embittering ways / love is denied." His narration of the deprivation rings simultaneously true and self-consciously aware, the way a sociologist might integrate himself into a community so that he can authentically observe its comings and goings and then realize that his own participation is displacing what he is narrating.

Down the main drag, Daly Street, I turn at the liquor store. Behind it is a corner of old buildings—a concave darkness that reminds me of a borderland. It feels like a place I couldn't actually go. I've reached some kind of limit. Ahead of me, there are some dumps of earth and ore, perhaps a pile of dust, rock, wood.

I circle back around to see the town again, looking down over the hill toward the Museum of Mines, the Montana Technical College, and, beyond, out toward the interstate. No animals are out. Few cars are parked. I work my way east, doglegging down narrow streets until they tip me out onto Park Street and wrap me around some dirt heaves and closed gates, cyclone fences and abandoned equipment. A wall of dirt is off to my left, increasing in size, and I notice that I'm headed down the hill, out of Walkerville.

Down Park Street, along the hill's barren spots, I see the parking lot on the left and pull in. There are a few tourists—people speaking German, holding cameras—getting out of their cars. I go up to the portable, a trailer that looks like it's made out of cardboard, and there's a guy selling tickets. Across from him is another trailer, wheels removed, with a sign: Gift Shop. The man takes my two dollars and points me through a round tunnel with wooden crossbeams and creosote-wiped planks. At the end is a porthole of light. I walk toward it, under a hill. It's like coming out of a mining shaft, one laid horizontally. Along the way, I'm thinking of Hugo, how his walk was marked with a limp in his later years, how he was out of breath because he'd had a lung removed. His baseball days long behind him, Hugo could hobble perhaps as far as his lawn chair to fish, or make his way from the Buick to the house, or into a bar.

Me? I want to climb the mountains to the south of it all—I want to find some land that is sheltered with trees and look back over to the city and the run-down town above it. I want, almost immediately, to be freed from the chute, through the hill. I want to push back out of it and walk to the parking lot. Instead, I am in the tunnel, walking toward the light ringing from the round circle of the other end. I imagine those dark-clothed miners, their dust-seeped faces, with white, white candles sitting upright in their pockets.

When I push into the light, I am on a viewing deck. There, below, is the biggest quarry I've ever seen: a mile and a half wide, almost a mile deep, ridged along the earth, the colors of sepia and iron around the rim, and the water a green orange—I look at the whole pool as one might regard a steep, high waterfall—taking in the water, section by section, the ridges of earth behind it, and my tiny scale in the face of such an enormous thing. There are even viewing scopes, the kind mounted on cement, that you stick your face into so you can have the effect of cheap binoculars. I take in a breath, staring at the awesome lifelessness of the thing. The scene is an Anselm Kiefer painting, a hulking grace of color—shale and iron and bleached sand. Ridges formed like bathtub rings or the lines inside a tree trunk—the layers are striking, like a painted then sculpted sunset.

The Berkeley Pit, once an open-pit copper mine, is filled with chemicals and water. From end to end, the crater is a mile wide, and the water is more than 900 feet deep. So acidic is the fluid, so rich in heavy metals, that the pit is a greenish tint under certain light, and when the illumination shifts, it's orange. The spectacle is so brilliant, so illuminated and Latin American in color, that I am mesmerized. Then, the shock comes—this is one of the most toxic places on the earth. It's like realizing that the handsome man you've been admiring is really a serial killer.

It's a great big hole in the landscape. Men came in and extracted things from it, leaving behind poisonous materials. Now it's full of heavy metals, and the level is rising each year. Estimates run one foot per month. Eventually, it will overflow and spill into the groundwater, flushing into the nearby Clark Fork River, filling tunnels under Butte until the city comes crashing down.

To offer the landscape a symbolic kind of healing, an artist from Missoula, Kristi Hager, staged a performance art piece at the rim of the Berkeley Pit in 2000. Kristi had lived in Butte for a number of years and knew the land well. She brought together a crowd of people to dance the hula. On the edge of the pit, on a sunny, warm day, they danced, all of them wearing blue sarongs and singing a version of "Cool Water." Here's the way Butte writer George Everett describes it: "The group of men, women, and children clad in cloth sarongs as blue as the sky walked silently to the lip overlooking the Pit, formed ranks and then swayed gracefully to the sounds of the Sons of the Pioneers song, 'Cool Water.' The sound of more than a hundred and fifty dancers singing in harmony to acoustical guitars mixed in the light breeze with the sound of rustling fabric."[6]

For months before the dance, Kristi Hager traveled around the state and encouraged people to form hula groups. In small towns, people gathered. They practiced and learned the music and enlisted friends to learn it too. When the day came, several hundred women and men arrived in Butte, singing and swinging their hips for healing water. It was, as one participant noted, "remarkably outrageous."

The Cool-Water Hula smoothed a gesture of healing over the pit. It was a method much like Hugo's writing poems, bringing Montanans into "creat[ing] finally / a simple grief I can deal with." Along the way, during the realization of the sorrow in the world, "hate takes over," Hugo writes. Leaching precious metals from the earth and leaving poisons behind in an enormous hole is an act mimetic of discarding people through slow poisoning, engulfing "anyone you can lump like garbage in a pit, including women." Even in this despair, when you feel Hugo tossing all hope aside, "Letter to Levertov from Butte" rises from the pollution. It grows beyond his woeful set of projections. This is where I feel released from the sense that Hugo is competing with Levertov, and his insistence upon rivaling her for a trip down the social ladder.

The Cool-Water Hula reminds me of why people write poems in the first place—lyrics are ephemeral, and they mark a moment in time. Poems are ways of keeping track. As I emerge in sunlight on the deck over the Berkeley Pit, I think how unlikely it is that we come to the places we come to, like the doomed snow geese that landed in the orange water of the pit for a rest in their migration, how unlikely our friendships, and how far we have to reach out to secure them.

Traffic light in Philipsburg, 2007.

Philipsburg, Montana

DEGREES OF GRAY IN PHILIPSBURG

You might come here Sunday on a whim.
Say your life broke down. The last good kiss
you had was years ago. You walk these streets
laid out by the insane, past hotels
that didn't last, bars that did, the tortured try
of local drivers to accelerate their lives.
Only churches are kept up. The jail
turned 70 this year. The only prisoner
is always in, not knowing what he's done.

The principal supporting business now
is rage. Hatred of the various grays
the mountain sends, hatred of the mill,
The Silver Bill repeal, the best liked girls
who leave each year for Butte. One good
restaurant and bars can't wipe the boredom out.
The 1907 boom, eight going silver mines,
a dance floor built on springs—
all memory resolves itself in gaze,
in panoramic green you know the cattle eat
or two stacks high above the town,
two dead kilns, the huge mill in collapse
for fifty years that won't fall finally down.

Isn't this your life? That ancient kiss
still burning out your eyes? Isn't this defeat
so accurate, the church bell simply seems
a pure announcement: ring and no one comes?
Don't empty houses ring? Are magnesium
and scorn sufficient to support a town,
not just Philipsburg, but towns

of towering blondes, good jazz and booze
the world will never let you have
until the town you came from dies inside?

Say no to yourself. The old man, twenty
when the jail was built, still laughs
although his lips collapse. Someday soon,
he says, I'll go to sleep and not wake up.
You tell him no. You're talking to yourself.
The car that brought you here still runs.
The money you buy lunch with,
no matter where it's mined, is silver
and the girl who serves your food
is slender and her red hair lights the wall.

Where the Red Hair Lights the Wall

To find the perfect town for his poetry, Hugo had to give up White Center. He had to let go of his claustrophobic childhood in his grandparents' house, his life in the shadow of Boeing, and his failed relationships with women. To take "emotional possession" of towns that presented "towering blondes, good jazz and booze / the world will never let you have" is dependent upon the claim that "the town you came from dies inside." He has to move beyond his origins and find a place in the world, even if his image of it is mythic and a bit sophomoric. Hugo is dreaming of tall women and strong liquor in a haze of good music—all things he's denied— as if he were a young boy describing what he can't have. It reminds me of the same way that Raymond Carver, in his poem "Luck," once described his own self-destructive fantasy:

> What luck, I thought.
> Years later,
> I still wanted to give up
> friends, love, starry skies
> for a house where no one
> was home, no one coming back,
> and all I could drink.

Only the inclusion of jazz in Hugo's version, it seems to me, inspires a depth of feeling and engagement with something substantial. Even if the "towering blondes" conflate skyscrapers with beauty, power and sex—potent imagery, to be sure—their mythic stature feels like a parody.

Though he tries to extinguish the effects his hometown has on him, in every town he goes to Hugo sees some version of White Center. The fatigue of hardworking people is never relieved by the place. Will rage and scorn, Hugo asks, be "sufficient to support a town, not just Philipsburg" but these ideal places of tall blondes and good music? Underneath all towns, Hugo intimates, chugs an engine of madness, of anger. That's what keeps a place alive.

When I come to Philipsburg, Montana, I'm looking for the redheaded waitress who lights up the end of "Degrees of Gray in Philipsburg," even though it's been forty years since the poem was written. She might be dead by now. Or retired, working in her little garden on the hill above town. Naturally, I really want to see the "old mill in collapse that won't fall finally down," but I'm also compelled by the woman who serves Hugo some coffee and then turns away—the girl whose "red hair lights the wall." That image, more than most other closures in Hugo poems, sounds out a jazz riff. It's a glimpse, an improvisation that transports. I feel like I've come up to a door left ajar; I can see some-one inside and I can't quite tell if she is real. Just as in jazz when the listener is never sure which notes will be part of the structure and which are pivots out of the piece, the image of the redhead provides suspense and an odd hint toward reconciliation.

Like some movie junkie who looks for original locations of the shots that appear in the film, I'm following the poem, tracing its origins, the site of its triggering metaphors. When the people live or die or leave town and new folks come in, or when the build-ings and streets change—what do these say about the actual place? What's left when everything, it seems, has been transformed? What do you say about a town you cannot know "until the town you came from dies inside?" Do you have to give up one town before you can love another?

Rather than a strip of roadway or the flinty crooks in a mountain ridge or the beckoning sign of a rustic bar, what pulls me to Philipsburg is that image of the wait-ress, a young woman who still lives in a town where the "best liked girls leave each year for Butte." Imagining a person who was, herself, imagined, but who was at some stage probably an actual person, releases a series of "what ifs" in me: What would she have thought about the poem? What if she remembered Hugo? What if the poem had offended her since she'd been distilled to red hair and a slender figure? This was, after all, the same time frame, the mid to late sixties, when Hugo had also written the Dixon poems in which the use of another redhead for poetic purposes had not come to a happy end. In Philipsburg, I imagine Hugo falling for the girl serving food, an attraction that lasted about thirty seconds, long enough for her to make a cameo at the closure of his poem. She's local, and she transforms his despair into hope. Even when our speaker dreams of leaving ("the car that brought you here still runs"), the waitress represents stasis, stopping him dead in his tracks.

In Hugo's work, women are the harbingers who sound out a world beyond the poem, winding their way back to Hugo and tugging his innards out, tossing them along the margins of the poem. These edges are places that we, as readers, can't quite reach. At first, women emerge through some sort of fog into still-life figures. The fantasy is clear—in "Degrees of Gray in Philipsburg" the waitress doubles as a light source and as a servant who waits on the speaker. Arriving at the very end of the poem, she resembles both angel and devil: her red hair illuminating the café. It's a painter's image—the white wall and the source of light that emanates from her; the juxtaposition ignites the scene.

Poets trade in such distilled "what ifs." They rely on linguistic reductions, for example, like funneling the whole of a town into one character. Or taking a character and using simple traits to condense and replace exposition, that kind of narrative carrying-on that lyric poets find distasteful. That's the impulse Hugo follows when he ends up dropping in the waitress at the end of the poem. The girl is the one person who embodies the story of a whole town, and for me, that red hair, not even the whole person, but the synecdochic hair that stands for the whole of her, for the whole of the town—that hair lights the place as though it were a red lamp. Just like the girl in Hugo's poem "Gooseprairie" who stands alongside a river—"blonde / and sleek with speckles on her back"—this is a woman who is wholesome and almost approachable. She might even have actually existed before she became the myth behind Hugo's poetic invention. She's far from the "towering blondes" he's idealized in the beginning of the poem.

As Hugo admits, women scared him. Hugo's friend Bill Kittredge says that Hugo "was furious at women." Kittredge remembers a time when Hugo and a woman had broken up (she had left to marry someone else). Hugo sobbed and ranted about the loss: "I could never tell the degree to which it was self-indulgent, self-gratifying theater . . . he was carrying on at great lengths."[1] Because "he was uncomfortable being around a lot of women," as Hugo's friend Madeline DeFrees said, he lived in fear of getting his relationships wrong.[2]

"By the time I was a young man I was a mess," he writes. "I had the normal urge to show girls affection and the normal need to receive affection in return. But with my hatred and fears of women, normal relations with them were impossible."[3] The origins of his issues, Hugo writes, were in the "distorted, intense but, by any conventional standards, undemonstrated affection by my grandmother, who I was convinced years later, had not been right in the head" and the fact that he saw his mother "sporadically." The poems convey the urge to display feeling and its accompanying repression. "It is no accident," Hugo insists "that the speaker in many of my poems is alone and that the people he has relations with are usually dead."

His woman in "Duwamish Head," the one based on an actual account, is diced with fishing knives and left for dead in a shack. In Montana, women are also objectified: "The day was a woman who loves you. Open." Even the waitress in Philipsburg is iconic rather than literal, a sconce set on high, complete with gold leaf halo, illuminating the place: "The girl who serves your food / is slender and her red hair lights the wall." There is something simple about placing a woman in the poem, as if Hugo were planting a tree or rock to fill out his invented landscape. However, compared with the woman in "Duwamish Head," the girl in this poem promises something less sinister. She's a healthy, attractive light at the end of the poem.

Still, no woman can be entirely happy with Hugo's choices about the female images in his poems. Either on pedestals, chopped up in riverside shacks, or else the "ghost in any field / of good crops," women appear as victims, Madonnas, or bad omens—a typical formula for the midcentury male poets of Hugo's era. (Adrienne Rich, feminist poet of the same generation, once remarked that Hugo was "more honest" than most of his male contemporaries.[4]) No matter how good his life gets, there's still the darkness of his past lingering in female form.

Perhaps because Hugo had so many friends to whom he told stories, because he gave so many interviews and wrote so clearly about his own "responses to things" in *The Real West Marginal Way*, I start to get a sense of Hugo on the subject of Hugo. The town slides in between the real man and his version of himself. Of course, coming to the real Philipsburg inspires me to look in the diners and bars, hoping for a glimpse of the kind of waitress whom Hugo described. I want to see what's left over from the poem, and since the poem is actually about a person coming into a strange town and having lunch, I come into Philipsburg with the same intentions. I'll find a spot to sit and eat.

I've also been propelled here by an essay by Charles D'Ambrosio, a writer originally from Seattle. D'Ambrosio wrote a line-by-line analysis of "Degrees of Gray" and says that he moved to Philipsburg because of the poem. I think of those lines of "Degrees of Gray" and I can see how they might trigger you into action. You'd just follow the premise "Say your life broke down" and reward yourself with the whim of living in the place. Published in *Orphans*, a collection of nonfiction pieces published by Clear Cut Press, this commentary on "Degrees" begins with a page that flips open to reveal the poem in its entirety, a literary centerfold. From Hugo's work, D'Ambrosio's essay swoops and dives, tracing the poem in and out of his associations with it. There, partly inspired by the town, partly by the poem, partly by the planes hitting the World Trade Center towers and the Pentagon, his essay dives into the wreckage of the hour. It maps what D'Ambrosio calls the "trajectory" of "every Hugo poem": "I'm fucked. You're fucked. Why? Let's have lunch."

Accompanying *Orphans* and Hugo's *Making Certain It Goes On* in my car's passenger seat when I drive into Philipsburg is a worn blue hardback, no jacket or gloss, just the graying edges wearing through the corners. *Small Town Stuff* is a 1932 portrait of a "Mineville," a fictional town that was actually the case-study disguise for Philipsburg.[5] Albert Blumenthal, a graduate student at the University of Chicago, wrote and researched the book, and it reads like a novel. Blumenthal sweeps through chapters, some with compelling titles—"Mineville in Panorama," "Agencies of Social Control," "Churches without Congregations," and "Gossip"—giving pseudonyms to the towns-folk of Philipsburg. It's a version of Winesburg, Ohio, only more factual and recounted by an earnest narrator who is trying to be accurate. Since sociology in the 1930s cowered under the anxiety of proving itself as a science, using a structure that imitated a collage of voices in America was more of a narrative technique than a scientific one. Such a mosaic of impressions would have thrilled John Dewey. I too found *Small Town Stuff*'s arch attempts at disguising the true identity of Philipsburg thrilling, especially in its made up name, Mineville, and its method of burying real towns inside other made-up names. Butte is "Gold," and Granite is "Crystal." The aliases play out syllabi-cally—Gold has one syllable and so does Butte; Crystal has two and so does Granite. "Smelters," though not syllabically in alignment with Anaconda, relies on the visual and olfactory image of the enormous smelters in the actual town. Blumenthal actually went to Philipsburg to live so that he could grapple with the "variety of experiences that make up town life."[6] He is an immersion journalist, an embedded anthropologist, a storyteller. He's a version of Charles D'Ambrosio seventy years earlier.

After reading these three pieces: the poem, the sociological study, and the D'Ambrosio essay, I wanted to see the real Philipsburg. Enough people I met along my way through Montana said that Philipsburg was "really fixed up now" and "a nice town," that it sounded like a place where I could climb up in the old mill sites, have a good cold Moose Drool beer at a bar, and visit the old jail. I'd take pictures, I imagined, of the down-and-out town that had marketed itself as an authentic place. I'd stay, perhaps, at the old hotel, now refurbished by a couple of documentary filmmakers. I'd see whether or not "the principal supporting business now is rage."

Hugo, too, had gone to Philipsburg "on a whim." It was 1966 when Hugo had been reluctant to join his friends Annick and Dave Smith and their boys on the outing. Philipsburg wasn't the kind of Montana place Dick Hugo would be drawn to. He'd be more inclined to end up near a fishing stream, but instead he came to Philipsburg, lured by his friends. Otherwise, he wouldn't have visited. "Too industrial," says Smith when she tells me the story. "Hugo was into flowing things." She laughs and makes an arc over her head—a mimetic fishing cast.

But Hugo did come to Philipsburg, and that accidental adventure led him to a poem that sings in a cadence that resembles the brokenness of the place—the "streets laid out by the insane," and, of course "the huge mill in collapse / for fifty years that won't fall finally down." It also gave him a poem that would change the face of poetry in the American West.

Smith and her husband had convinced Hugo to participate in a little film they were making. They'd document him walking around the area where the old mills stood, in a town that once had a population of several thousand before the Silver Crash of 1893 and only a few hundred by the nineteen sixties. Smith describes the crew who went along that day:

> We visited Philipsburg with Dick and the trip was with Dave Smith, Eric Smith, Steve Smith, Sylvie (our German shepherd—you can see her in the film) and me. We were making the first Hugo film and thought the town and old mill would be a perfect fit with Dick. He balked at going to a mining town ("I'm a poet of rivers and trout") but agreed. We walked the streets and filmed all afternoon, went to our respective homes that evening and it was about 5 am that he called with a draft of the poem.[7]

Early in the morning after visiting Philipsburg, Hugo called Smith and read her a draft of "Degrees of Gray in Philipsburg." She was stunned. "Pretty good work, Dick," she said. "Pretty good." Even now, Smith laughs when she tells it. She knows it is probably Hugo's greatest poem, despite her lackluster, predawn response.

Hugo knew it too. "It was the poem I had been trying to write for twenty years," he said.[8] He wrote it "all within four hours. . . . I had been in Philipsburg only three hours the day before, and that was the only time I'd been there."[9] He'd written through the images he'd encountered in the town, and the poem came out almost intact. After that, Hugo recited it at almost every reading he gave, his fist pounding the air as he delivered the last line.

The film that Smith and her husband created, the black and white sequence that will slide, ten years later, into a color documentary called *Kicking the Loose Gravel Home*, is a visual map of Hugo's poem. Smith says, "The poem matches the film almost image by image—the filming coming BEFORE the poem. When we took Dick there and shot the stuff and ate lunch at the café with the red-haired waitress, we had nothing in mind except visual metaphors for Dick's life and vision."[10] The film, like the poem, pans along the streets "laid out by the insane," captures the "panoramic green high above the town" and takes shots of the jail. The film clips match the order of Hugo's stanzas. It reminds me of Hemingway's advice that a well-constructed fictional scene should order its details in the natural sequence in which the eye would perceive them.

Hugo's friend literary historian Donna Gerstenberger remarks that "Hugo's is not the camera's eye . . . capturing the scene as it exists" but instead "is the poet's eye, catching the scene as it inhabits him."[11] Both the film and the poem documented a place where you'd come "on a whim," and yet both had identically ordered images. It was as if the poem, too, had a camera clipped to it, and Hugo used the camera to wrap words around the imagery.

Kicking the Loose Gravel Home, the polished version of the film, was released in 1976, and it follows Hugo, pronging a cigarette in two fingers and driving his big yellow Buick convertible to his favorite haunts. Along the way, he recites poems. It's the ultimate road movie—say *Two-Lane Blacktop* (a sulky 1970s film) without the lanky, sexy James Taylor but instead with a gruff but lovable hero, the stout Hugo.

Forty years after it was published in the *North American Review*, "Degrees of Gray" still plays a prominent role in American poetry; certainly it is the Hugo poem that people most often remember. Requested by audiences at poetry readings, it was, as Hugo told his friend James Welch, a poem "that left 'em pissing down the chair legs." A surge of interest persists even now, in an era when so much verse has grown cold, when the poet as witness, the narrative "I," has all but disappeared into a fleshy mass of abstraction and associative leaps that deny evidence of hearts beating inside the makers. Perhaps the attraction to "Degrees of Gray" emerges from a collision of themes—the outsider coming into town (an iconic Hugo move) looking for a place to belong, the projection of alienation upon the town itself, and the placement of a woman who lights up the scene. The poem is a convergence of Hugo concerns, all captured in an emotional density, itself as complicated as an actual town. That it transports a visual image of the visitor, a roly-poly version of Gary Cooper, the loner come in from the hinterlands, echoes classic westerns without the shoot 'em ups. Hugo's main character wasn't interested in that kind of confrontation, favoring instead banter with the bartender or a glimpse of a red-headed waitress.

With "the Silver Bill repeal," the seventieth anniversary of the jail, and the "1907 boom, eight going silver mines," Hugo sweeps through a pop version of Philipsburg's history. He's pushing you into the passenger seat alongside him. For the poet, making an entrance is a speculative activity, whether it's in a town or in a poem, and he craves a witness. In this case, he's coming into town and implicating the reader into his sojourn: "You might come here Sunday on a whim," and it sounds, if slurred, like "You might come here *someday* on a whim." No matter where you live you might have the chance, the good luck and inclination, to arrive in Philipsburg, but since you probably won't, Hugo is going to let you ride along with him. It's a daydream gone three-dimensional—built on the faintly possible—"Say your life broke down." "Say" is a "let's pretend" tone, so comic against the gravity of "your life broke down," that it causes you to admit that your own life might be a little shaky too. His life *has* broken down; it's a given, because he's coming into town. And it's probably Sunday, when normal people are in church and most storefronts are shuttered.

Neither nostalgia nor pity is the subject of "Degrees of Gray," nor does a quaintness ever appear in Hugo's descriptions of Philipsburg. Instead, Hugo turns our expectations toward something else: the chilly confines of the town and the "tortured try of local drivers to accelerate their lives." Only the visitor, the storytelling voice of the poem, has the luck of the car that still runs. "The best liked girls leave each year for Butte," he writes, and since Butte itself is a town where working people, mostly miners, struggle for existence, Philipsburg doesn't appear to be a town with a buzzing economy either. It's a place that high school kids would try to escape, and one that leaves us, as readers, with the tension between being a good visitor and desperately wanting to leave. "Degrees of Gray" leaves a reader with an enormous ache. In an interview with Michael Allen, Hugo follows that emptiness to its source:

> . . . of course, it is not the town itself but a way of feeling about oneself. That's what dies inside. I mean that one assumes that one's failure in life is due to some kind of degradation that occurred because of one's circumstances, or one's origins. And the town where one grew up is part of these origins. But what really has to die inside is a way of feeling about the self. . . . It's the town internalized that has to die.[12]

Hugo's version of Philipsburg rings as a testament to the isolated western town: "the church bell simply seems / a pure announcement: ring and no one comes . . . " Michael Allen points out that "the town also represents a human life, a life in which feeling has been lost from defeat 'so accurate'" that the speaker's psyche is imprisoned "in boredom and replays of rage and loss—this is what must die."[13] Though Hugo wouldn't say it the same way, his relentless church bells do conjure up the repetition of a bored psyche and the constant rehearsals of rage and loss. In Hugo's method, he uses the language, the sound, to pivot the poem's imagery—turning from the ring of the steeple bell to "Don't empty houses ring?" Under the shadow of the Rockies, a smattering of houses and businesses in the midst of a long valley with few neighbors, Philipsburg is remote from places that are already remote. You can hear that in Hugo's version of *ring*.

The town that Hugo visited in 1966 with the Smiths was a place long abandoned by mining operations. It was a small place, with one main street that people called "Main Street" instead of "Broadway," its actual name. Home to a few bars, a butcher, and run-down hotel, Philipsburg had passed its prime more than fifty years earlier. With the Silver Bill repeal, the value of ore plummeted, and with that went the jobs in the area. Forty years before Hugo came, Albert Blumenthal came to research *Small Town Stuff* and hiked up to Granite, over four miles of rough, muddy rivulets, up into the Flint Creek Range, and he found the town, once home to 3,000 people, already abandoned. There was only a watchman, who paced along the ruins of the old mills, among mining leftovers and dumped, broken flumes. Townsfolk left in 1905, and when learning of the mill shutdown at 10 A.M., they walked from their homes in Granite four miles down the mountain and got on the 1 P.M. train out of Philipsburg.

With some good luck, I travel to Philipsburg with Hugo's friends. "I'll drive," Annick Smith had said over the phone, and she shows up in her white truck with Bill Kittredge riding shotgun. Charlie D'Ambrosio, the younger writer who never knew Hugo but who wrote so well about "Degrees of Gray," hops in the back, and the two of us end up riding like kids, leaning over the seats to hear what's going on. Through the dry arid hills south of Butte, we listen to stories that Smith and Kittredge tell about Hugo.

In 1969, three years after the trip Hugo took to Philipsburg with Smith and her family, Bill Kittredge came to Missoula. He had been hired as a junior faculty member in the English department's creative writing program, where Richard Hugo was teaching. Kittredge recalls having a few drinks and then going to Hugo's house. When the elder poet opened the door, he said to Kittredge, "I see that you are very drunk." Then he paused and said, "I think I'll join you." And from then on, Hugo and Kittredge were writing, fishing, and drinking buddies.

In person, Kittredge tells funny stories and laughs easily. As a writer, he documents his story of leaving behind the work of cattle ranching for the art of crafting prose. Kittredge moved from short fiction to writing about his life on the ranch that his family owned. *Hole in the Sky*, an account of life there, he describes the unsustainable farming practices that polluted the land, tracing his journey away from that livelihood into one as a writer. His first two collections of stories established him as a gifted storyteller, but it was his nonfiction accounts of his crisis of faith in leaving his family's ranch that told the larger story—what it meant to live a good life in relationship to the land.

"Look," Kittredge says. He points out the window. "The suburbs of Philipsburg." There are a few little shacks along the road and a boy herding cattle while he drives an ATV.

The town looks smaller than I'd imagined. The streets wrinkle in ruts and heaves along the slopes. I can see a brick courthouse on the hill.

"I lived back over in that part," D'Ambrosio says. He's leaning forward. "And the old mills are up there." He nods toward the south of town, beyond the hills where the school is nestled.

Storefronts along Broadway in Philipsburg, 2007.

We drive along Broadway. The hotel is shiny and buffed, ready for guests, and some of the restaurants look upscale.

"It's kind of fancy now," I say. I'd been expecting something more rustic, less touched by the outside world. The four-block string of shops and restaurants reminds me of Wallace, Idaho. Like Wallace, Philipsburg is promoting itself—not any specific attraction or historic obsolescence, but the charming fact of its own image—as being restful and quaint. The Broadway Hotel is a Hollywood fantasy—providing service and modern accommodations while simulating life in "the old West." Re-envisioned to accommodate history as entertainment, both towns draw visitors: they are holograms constructed from marketing to tourists, shellacking over the place's actual history, the soil and blood marking the hardships.

Like a poem, any town is a cobbling together of accident and intention. The streets

Streets laid out by the insane, 2007.

platted after so many horses and carts clomping through the mud; buildings erected from local wood that burned down and was replaced by local stone work; civic leaders instigating parks and regulations—the physical aspects of towns take on this collision of planning and unforeseen events. Ultimately, the citizens of a town affix their hopes and fears onto the town, and both their vision and their absentmindedness shape the place.

We drive through the crosshatch of streets "laid out by the insane," as Hugo describes them, and while I can't see that a mad person designed them, they do wind crookedly over the hills.

Annick Smith takes us up to the mill, or where we thought the mill was, and on the way we see an old man in his yard. We stop for directions, and when I walk over to him, it is as though I am approaching the actual figure in the poem: "the old man, twenty / when the jail was built," his toothless mouth falling in as he recites the route:

Two stacks high above the town, 2007.

"he laughs / although his lips collapse," that striking alliteration of the consonant *ps* sounds, so lippy and collapsed the onomatopoeia imitating the old man's struggle to articulate, that I'm just about living inside the poem. The man might as well have sung, "Someday soon / . . . I'll go to sleep and not wake up."

Instead, he points up the hill. As if in a dream, I climb back into the car.

We round the bend, and there it is: "the huge mill in collapse / for fifty years that won't fall finally down." Kittredge recites it first, and then we all say it: the perfect poetic sentence. The action, Latinate, comes near the end of the phrase: the verb postponed, just before the adverb, then the preposition. It is a lesson on squeezing out the noun and wringing out the action until the end, stimulating our psychological mapping of the place. We take in the features of the site—the stones and wood caught in rubble—and then we walk through it. I say, out loud, "Say your life broke down" to

Old mill at Philipsburg, 2007.

the collection of buildings already collapsed. In the poem, the "fall finally down" line is one of suspense and one of relief. It's the process of becoming historical.

There we are—forty years post-Hugo— Smith, Kittredge, D'Ambrosio, and I, standing in the ruins of the old mill in Philipsburg. For an hour or so, we poke sticks at the big foundation stones; we tap upon fallen roof planks.

Philipsburg crouches below the mountains behind it. Stodgy in the shadows, the two brick smokestacks protrude from the dark shade of the enormous slope. The cylinders, remnants of the old mill, rise over the bumpy hills, their nozzles pointed skyward. Stone by stone, the walls are snug, while the planked roofs have disappeared long ago. To me, it's an altar, one built as much from the eroding forces of wind and air as from the stones pressed together—a hollow where brush finds its way among disintegrating, landlocked driftwood. Visually, it is the "two stacks high above the town" that rips me apart inside, along with the "two dead kilns," a failed history that still roars in some long-gone furnace. And the streets "laid out by the insane," rutted, muddy hatchings that scratch up hills before disappearing into the rustle of grasses.

While I am there with Kittredge, D'Ambrosio, and Smith, I see that what is left is fading; less and less remains. Ruins caught half in rubble and half in glory inspire reverence in me, and perhaps because of my Catholic girlhood partly spent under the spires of a nineteenth-century church, I'm prone to worship things in decay. Tipping my chin so that I can take the whole scene in, I become that child looking up to the pulpit again, the lectern that had a little staircase winding up to it. As the church lost parishioners in the 1960s, fewer visitors came and fewer people wrote checks for upkeep; the wood grew nicked, the limestone stained. Grit filled the corners, and cracks spread through the roof, smearing the ceiling with brown splotches. In the midst of it, I was an altar girl, trained to worship and poised to keep an eye on things. Through the cold aisles, never warmed by enough of a flock on those early days before school when I followed Father Walters over to the altar, I carried the cruets of water, wine, and oil, and made my way while wearing a long robe with a white rope belt. Imagining myself a custodian of the place, I was actually a fourth grader with an eye toward the falling apart. I loved the mustiness, the cold winds that passed through the jambs of those huge doors.

Catching the tumble-down of the hundred-year-old mill gave me an ache to preserve it but also to measure its slow collapse. I was reading the place with crossed desires. I didn't like to think of the scavengers who come in to pull stones and iron spike nails from the foundations.

"We're shipping Montana out of Montana," Kittredge says. "See this stuff? These boards and rocks? These will show up in a law firm down in L.A."

He stands with Smith in the middle of a long shell of a building, pointing to the artifacts of the place.

"Authentically distressed wood," I say. It reminds me of the furnishings in fancy catalogues that accidentally land in my mail slot.

Kittredge nods. "Yup. They'll pay more for the stuff that looks beaten up."

When it comes time for lunch, we walk down Broadway looking for the right spot. One café, according to Kittredge, is "too Missoula," too new and glossy, so we opt for the bar that has a sign out front: "Warm beer and lousy food." Once I see the wood paneling and pull tabs, I figure this is where Hugo would have come for lunch.

As we pass over the tourist spots in favor of the run-down Club Bar, I realize that "Degrees of Gray" turns into a poem about class. It's a riff on scarcity and how being poor at one time, both in money and spirit, impoverishes your vision forever. Hugo, and by implication "you," has to refute the paucity of the past in order to succeed. For Hugo, this was literally true. He'd left behind White Center to enlist in the Army Air Corps, becoming a bombardier over Italy and Eastern Europe, and when he returned he used the GI Bill to attend the University of Washington. Then he worked at Boeing—first in the slag pile and then in a white-collar job—until just after his first book was published, which sprung him into an academic job at Montana. He'd traveled from the bottom of the culture heap to the top (if one considers low-paying professorships to be the top), though his self-image didn't make the journey quite as well as did his artistic production. Hugo's shame lingers in the poem, bearing witness to lives filled by sadness and poverty.

I wonder, sometimes, if Hugo instigated his own competition for higher and higher stakes of martyrdom. It's a sad-sack Hugo, "the last good kiss" Hugo, who is part of the town that goes bust at the same time he's looking at it like a sociologist might, seeing "the tortured try / of local drivers to accelerate their lives." He feels the struggle and the mockery that the locals can't quite rev up their lives and zoom out of town. He can depart Philipsburg anytime, while the townsfolk yearn for an escape. Ironically, only Hugo has the privilege to actually leave: "The car that brought you here still runs." The girl will stay, anchoring the place.

That bar where the four of us have lunch, with its mirrors and veneer-topped tables, with the chipped antlers and fur-worn deer heads with little fur left, with the long stretch of locals drawing on their cigarettes and looking at us over propped elbows, with the glance of the waitress—not a redhead at all—was an establishment both vintage and alive. You could trace the people in there and the stuff, the bric-a-brac nailed to the walls, to some earlier Philipsburg. It reminded me of the pleasures of identifying Mineville as Philipsburg in *Small Town Stuff*.

In fact, Blumenthal's method was a lot like Richard Hugo's. The sociologist, coming to Philipsburg in what feels like an academic's version of a whim, immersed himself in the life of the place and wrote his observations. He tangled his findings into the history and geography of the place, the economics and dispositions of the citizens. He used the techniques of fiction to get to the truth of the locale. Renaming Philipsburg "Mineville," he abandons a "house-to-house canvass" and instead "the main method relied upon was, in short, that of friendly conversation, in which the other person communicates his experiences, feelings, and attitudes much as if he were talking to himself."[14] Hugo's speaker in "Degrees of Gray" responds to the old man by saying, "You tell him no. You're talking to yourself," and the two methods mesh—Hugo's and Blumenthal's—one arcane and deliberate, and one contemporary and poetic. In his belief that through "personal interaction, public opinion is formed," Blumenthal sounds like a poet, one who sees in the small images the entire picture. He's creating composites to represent types of people, building a narrative to surface trends in the community. "Communities, like persons, cannot be understood unless their intimate pasts are known," he writes—unlike Hugo, who projects intimate pasts upon invented strangers.[15]

Hugo's version was shorthand of the sociologist's—he drops into town, looks around, and has lunch. In real life, he's the subject of some filming, landing him as a character in the ruins of the old mill. Then the poet leaves. He goes home and writes a poem.

In the end, Hugo's "Degrees of Gray" is more about the visitor than it is about the town. When I look at the waitress who brings our "porgies" and red beer (tomato juice added), I don't see her as Hugo's slender "girl" whose hair lights up the wall. The bar would have to be cleaner; there would need to be a blank wall; and the waitress would have to be younger, a college girl. Our server is a gruff woman, probably with grandkids at home, working long hours that keep her from them. Nothing glamorous except how she shows up to work and stays in the life she has. For me, that's enough. I can break free of my concerns about Hugo's idealization and sexist flat-screen image of the woman at the end of "Degrees of Gray" because, after all, I'm a woman coming to Philipsburg and idealizing him, Hugo, the poet. I can see that I've locked the real-life Hugo, long dead, into being a fictional character, forever in a position where he represents some kind of lost poet's version of masculinity. I've pinned Hugo as a clumsy fisherman, a good drinking companion, a man uncomfortable in English departments—a Buick-driving, hard-loving character who put his heart out to people he didn't know.

No one in P-burg (as the locals call it) framed the poem and hung it in the bar. Or the library. Or the historical museum. In fact, no one seems to remember the poem at all. "Nope," said the waitress when I asked her. "Not at all," said the librarian. "Doesn't ring a bell."

Hugo never came back to Philipsburg. He'd taken what he needed from the town and moved on. "I had an amazing gift," he said in a 1971 interview, "of being able to walk into a town I'd never been in before and within a few minutes know exactly what that town would mean to someone who had lived there all his life. I cannot do that anymore."[16] There's an illusion in Hugo's work that towns are set up for you to take images from—that's what *The Triggering Town* says—so that in real life the landscapes don't seem to have actual people living behind them. The poet assembles the pieces of what she finds and fashions them into a new creation that simulates something real—a poem that collages together a narrator, a town, and a reader. But the thing is actually a strung-along lattice of words. The slender girl doesn't exist; Philipsburg doesn't really exist.

The summer after I traveled to Philipsburg with Charlie, Annick, and Bill, I went back with Maddy, my daughter, who was eleven then. As we drove into town, she said, "Look at the candy shop, Mama," and I turned to look from the window of the car. I hadn't seen it on my last trip. It was like a shop you'd find in Provincetown or some other tourist place: all red licorice whips and baseball-sized jawbreakers. The colors of the whirling candy stripes stood in contrast to the dusty hills. We stayed in a rented house behind the high school and Maddy befriended a woman growing hydroponics of some kind in her garage next door. Our neighbor left the lights on day and night, farming around the clock. When we left, we went up the mountain around Georgetown Lake, the man-made hole that now hosts a new crop of vacation homes. "Is it all fake?" Maddy asked, her finger pressed to the passenger window.

Then we rolled onto the rib of roadway into Anaconda, the longest stretch of twenty-five miles per hour I've ever seen on the approach to a town. Out the other side of Anaconda, by the enormous pile of leftover black glass that looked like dirt with sparkles, the road pointed south. The route, virtually unmaintained and skunked with frost heaves, passed by areas where plants didn't grow. Nothing seemed to surround the rocks or the loam along the roadway. For miles and miles the road went south, past a few glimpses of old ranches falling down, big fences, a road so long with nothing, no commerce, no intrusions, no signage, just the long parch of narrow pavement, until it ended, quite abruptly at a T. To the left, the sign pointed to Wisdom, a town in the southwestern corner of the state. I wanted to lean into something, get my balance, reach my hand toward a wall. Perhaps a wall lit by a stranger's red, red hair or the sound of a lone jazz note. I needed Wisdom.

Mining gallows
hauled from But[
2007.

SILVER STAR
for Bill Kittredge

This is the final resting place of engines,
farm equipment and that rare, never more
than occasional man. Population:
17. Altitude: unknown. For no
good reason you can guess, the woman
in the local store is kind. Old steam trains
have been rusting here so long, you feel
the urge to oil them, to lay new track, to start
the west again. The Jefferson
drifts by in no great hurry on its way
to wed the Madison, to be a tributary
of the ultimately dirty brown Missouri.
This town supports your need to run alone.

What if you'd lived here young, gone full of fear
to that stark brick school, the cruel teacher
supported by your guardian? Think well
of the day you ran away to Whitehall.
Think evil of the cop who found you starving
and returned you, siren open, to the house
you cannot find today. You question
everyone you see. The answer comes back wrong.
There was no house. They never heard your name.

When you leave here, leave in a flashy car
and wave goodbye. You are a stranger
every day. Let the engines and the farm
equipment die, and know that rivers
end and never end, lose and never lose
their famous names. What if your first girl

ended certain she was animal, barking
at the aides and licking floors? You know
you have no answers. The empty school
burns red in heavy snow.

Short Story in Silver Star

N OT IN WISDOM, but in Silver Star—that's where I end up.

Here, Lloyd Harkins tells me that his dad rode for Buffalo Bill and that his great-uncle died at the Battle of Little Bighorn. We're talking on the porch outside Granny's Country Store in Silver Star, Montana. Ninety miles east of Philipsburg and a forty-minute drive southeast of Butte, I've come to this tiny place after first sweeping through, oblivious that I'd missed it, and then turning around at a gravel lot on the Jefferson River and coming back. I should have known the town because the road is lined with giant wheels. The spokes look like huge hand-drawn stars.

I'm standing outside the store and listening to Lloyd. He's well over six feet tall, and I'm looking up at him while he goes on with the story. "Yup, my great-uncle was killed along with the rest of 'em in the Custer battle," he says. He smiles a little when he tells it. I try to imagine the timeline—Little Big Horn in 1876, Buffalo Bill around 1900, and Lloyd born in the 1920s. Could all be true, I decide.

"My uncle's horse survived, though," Lloyd says. "Someone found it with three arrows in it and nursed it back to health. It lived to be twenty-nine."

"Pretty old for a horse," I say.

"Really old," says Lloyd.

He's wearing a denim farm coat and overalls. Squashed down on his head is an old baseball cap. It has a logo for agricultural equipment wrinkled into it. Lloyd is in his early eighties, the same that Hugo would have been if he were alive.

"This is the final resting place of engines, / farm equipment and that rare, never more / than occasional man," Hugo writes in the poem he wrote in honor of the town. The lines must have been written about Lloyd's yard, because it's what you notice

Lloyd's five-acre Museum, 2007.

when you get out of the car. Lloyd, it turns out, keeps five acres of old ranching and mining equipment he's collected. The poem, too, is furnished with scraps from the "old steam trains" and engines, and the speaker feels "the urge to oil them" and "to lay new track."

"So that's your place," I say. I point to the cyclone fencing and array of equipment in the yard across the road.

"Yup." Lloyd says. He leans over a bit. He must be deaf in his right ear.

"What are those things?" I nod toward the set of star-wheels that are propped up along the side of the road. They are at least twelve feet tall. Set in a line, they look like a fence made by a blacksmith artist. Each wheel stands on a custom-made concrete base that resembles a giant's spoon rest. In miniature, the flywheels would be the spinning parts of gyroscopes.

SILVER STAR, MONTANA   175

Lloyd Harkins's wheeled fence, 2007.

"They spun power for air drills," Lloyd says and pulls down the brim of his cap. "Inside the copper mines up in Butte."

Butte is thirty-six miles away. I imagine the wheels rolling all the way to Silver Star. They're set in a perfect line. There are little paths through the rest of the equipment, and much of it has been freshly painted and set in display poses.

"Some of it comes from the Green Mine and the other ones around here too. Had to haul it here." Lloyd pauses and looks at me. His face is a deep, sunned brown, and his eyes crinkle into a smile.

He leads me across the road and through a large gate in the cyclone fencing. There's a big wooden tower, thirty or forty feet tall, off to the left. At the top, the beams converge into a point.

"The gallows," Lloyd says. "It's what they ran the cables through to hold the cage."

He points to a metal box with corrugated metal netting across the front. The paint, a faded yellow, is chipping off. "Just got that one. Brought it over last week." Lloyd sees the perplexed look on my face. "The cage is what the men took to get down into the mine. It's the elevator." To me, it looks small enough to be a birdcage. I couldn't imagine a group of men wedged into it.

For an hour or so, Lloyd goes off to fix something, and I wander the grounds: acres of machinery parts, large and small. He's collected more of the old mining gallows and cages, mining carts with small wheels and axels for miniature tramways far under the mountains, fire cars, gears and switches for the underground tracks, old air drills, pieces of track and lanterns.

"Collectors' items," Lloyd says when he finds me roaming around a new metal barn. "These are my favorites," he says, pointing to outsized machine parts—giant gears, levers, pulleys, metal boxes, mining carts, and track—which he's painted in cheerful enamel reds, blacks, and greens. As he walks, he limps a little. The machinery glimmers when Lloyd opens the door and lets in the light.

"Is this a museum?" I ask.

"Just my own stuff," he says. "Had it for a long time. Keep getting new pieces. Disneyland France and some Hollywood movie people, they been here and got some things."

The town could have been named for these big flywheels that resemble grounded stars, but Silver Star, the third oldest town in the state, was settled in 1869, before mining had such sophisticated equipment. Thanks to Lloyd, Silver Star now boasts a collection of out-of-scale parts put back into use as souvenirs. What Butte mining engineer would have guessed that the ultimate fate of his giant gears would be to end up as small-town décor?

It's an earthier version of what's been done in Wallace and Philipsburg. In those towns, relics have been rearranged, enshrined, and called "historical." For years, at his own impetus, Lloyd has gathered these pieces into Silver Star, tinkering and repairing them, painting them in high gloss reds, greens, and blacks and then propping them back in the yard and in his barn. He doesn't tag the displays or charge admission; he doesn't insist that the relics mean anything other than what they are. They are as visible and accessible, and as obsolete, as poems are—privately collected from what he can scavenge and publicly showcased on his own acreage.

I'm standing by some of the enormous gears that he's set up in the barn.

"Used those to pull cable for the carts inside the mines," Lloyd says.

"They're huge," I say. "How did they move them around?"

"Horses," says Lloyd.

Hugo's own slice of history, set into three stanzas, is a porthole back to the time when the equipment, "rusting here so long," hadn't come under Lloyd's care. The poem's second-person stance, addressed to "you," brings the reader into his reverie: "You feel the urge / to oil" the decaying machines, the same impulse that Lloyd has acted upon, retooling the old mining gallows and gears, the cars and farm machinery. While Hugo was tinkering with his semi-blank verse, lines flickering around ten syllables in an irregular, iambic shuffle, Lloyd was probably bent over paint cans and rusted metal, sanding and layering on enamels.

The poem instructs, in the last stanza, to "let the engines and the farm / equipment die," as if Hugo's wished-for history would leave the machinery sinking back into the earth. But it doesn't. Instead, it accumulates.

Hugo put the pieces of the town together—the farm equipment, the store, the river, the school—and dedicated "Silver Star" to his friend Bill Kittredge. Together, they'd fished the Jefferson, the river that skims along the back of the store. A fishing access is marked on the road, and as I walk down to the bank, I realize that Hugo's Buick probably knocked over these same stones.

"We were both a little hungover, and Hugo had the yellow convertible," Bill Kittredge told me when I had asked him about the poem. "It wasn't a great fishing day. We didn't threaten to catch fish. We just wandered around in a hapless sort of fashion, dumped lines here and there, and had this great macaroni and cheese lunch and kind of gave it up and came home." Kittredge had laughed when he described it. "A week or so later Hugo showed up with this poem called 'Silver Star,' which is basically about that fishing trip, his feelings about it, the things that he saw, the little town there on the banks of the Jefferson River."

"And," Kittredge added, "his feelings about those isolated towns and the repressed twentieth-century deprivation he saw there . . . human attempts to make a living . . ."

Along the river, I recite the lines:

> The Jefferson
> drifts by in no great hurry on its way

to wed the Madison, to be a tributary
of the ultimately dirty brown Missouri.
This town supports your need to run alone.

I think of Hugo and Kittredge, both with hangovers: slow-motion perceptions, hollowed out and brittle along the skin, that sour wash in the stomach. It might have kept them from an animated exchange, and left them half-heartedly pushing out their fishing casts without much conversation. In fact, the poem feels like a hangover, sensitive to light and sound, prone to depressive utterances: "this town supports your need to run alone," though he's come with a friend to enjoy the place. The only color in this gray landscape arrives at the end of the poem, where "The empty school / burns red in heavy snow." A Hopperesque glimpse of crimson, both realistic and cartoonish, the line echoes "Her red hair lights the wall" at the end of "Degrees of Gray in Philipsburg." There, too, the rouge is luminescent against the tawny landscape, and there's a version of that juxtaposition in "Duwamish," where "madness / means, to Redmen, I am going home." That color sweeps an arc through these poems, from an indication of madness (Duwamish) to a talisman of bad times (Silver Star) to a light of hope (Philipsburg). Traces of the woman killed with fishing knives in a Duwamish shack show up here as well—the girl in Silver Star is also crawling along the floor and barking as she did in "Duwamish Head."

Across the road, I see Lloyd pushing open a tractor hood, a wedge against the horizon. Above the town, a set of rocky, low hills shelter old mines. Lloyd is leaning into the engine and pulling on something. Next to his feet is a big red toolbox.

In 1969, when Hugo and Kittredge met at the University of Montana, the sensation must have been one of old friends reuniting. Though Hugo was ten years older, the two men settled into a camaraderie that brought them together, either drinking or fishing. There's a tenderness between them, palpable in the last interview Hugo gave. In it, he and Kittredge weaved through a conversation about poems, Hugo's health, and what Hugo would write next. I can hear Kittredge's reluctance in pressing Hugo to speak: "I felt very unsure about doing this," he says.[1] Hugo had just had a lung removed and was trying to recover from it. There's an easy affection and you can feel it in that last, formal conversation.

That's why the poem, in contrast, suggests a harshness I hadn't anticipated. It was, I acknowledged, a younger Hugo, one who hadn't yet reached this tender spot in his friendship with Kittredge. I also think that when Hugo dedicates poems, he's not enshrining a shared experience in the place. Rather, it's a masculine epigraph, not intended to slant the reading of the poem toward ruminating on a relationship. Bill Bevis, Hugo's friend, says that the speaker, "'you,' is Hugo/generic, not tied to the dedication and Bill." I agree with Bevis. The poem isn't really about Kittredge at all. It's a gesture from Hugo to let Kittredge know that the poem honors their visit to the town. But it's a lonely poem, almost impenetrable, because even "you" is saddled with harsh imaginings: "This town supports your need to run alone" and "You are a stranger / every day." Part reader, part Hugo, part Kittredge—the "you" locks us all in together. We're stuck in Silver Star, frozen inside the created world where "The empty school / burns red in heavy snow."

Hugo uses rhythm and consonance to emphasize the starkness; he enjambs lines with repeating sounds, driving more bass and treble into the poem. End words are set on edges, where they reverberate—solid long vowels (*no, alone, feel, tributary, Missouri, fear, know, snow*) and humming consonants (*women, population, question, name*; the hard *rrs* of a car pulling out: *car, stranger, farm, rivers, girl, barking*)— gracefully fading into the *oo* of *school* and finally into the long *o*, a terrible harsh *o* in *snow*.

The school, that lonely red-hued place, closed in 1936 and is now used for social events, and when I drive up from Lloyd's place to see it, I can't imagine anyone having a light-hearted wedding or anniversary party there. The place could easily be a jail—a brick, square building. The windows are stingy.

Like Lloyd's yard does for me, the school launches Hugo into an imagined scenario: "What if you'd lived here young, gone full of fear / to that stark brick school, the cruel teacher / supported by your guardian?" Knowing Hugo's past, it's an easy leap to see his own boyhood in this version of "What if?" But there's more to it. When you're standing in Silver Star, at Lloyd's place and then at the school, looking over the big, slow river, in the midst of a town where the population has grown from seventeen to thirty, give or take a birth or death or two, you can see that it isn't just about Hugo. It's about what makes a livelihood in far-flung places. People disappear into the landscape: "There was no house. They never heard your name."

The poem descends into a nightmare of a child running away and then being

Silver Star School, closed in 1936, 2007.

brought back by a policeman, only to find the house missing. "You," the reader, are a person suddenly without history: "You know you have no answers." It's like waking up in a dream that has come true. The house is gone, as Hugo's was when he went back to see it in White Center, and the boy is forgotten. In the end, I believe, the poem is about the fear of erasure: that the boy will disappear, that you will disappear, and that sometimes what remains is what we should fear the most—that school, now empty, bricked in against the snow. The lines are blunt, thumping out the plain subject-verb-object structure, heightening the emotional stakes.

But this won't be Hugo's final resting place. He'll go on for another fifteen years or so. He'll stop drinking for a spell, have a number of years ahead where poems will almost roll out of him, and he'll live out his second chances.

On my way out of town, I stop at the store because I see Lloyd sitting outside. I pull over and get out. I don't want to be the "you" who will "leave in a flashy car / and wave goodbye."

"Your place was beautiful," I say. I walk over to him.

"Old stuff," he says.

"Yes," I say. "But nice." It wasn't like the poem at all. It wasn't farm equipment that was left to die, as Hugo had described. Lloyd had made something out of all those things from the mines. I reach out and shake his hand.

"Nice enough, I guess," says Lloyd. He's leaning up from the chair, halfway standing. "Drive careful."

And I do.

Small house in Pony, 2007.

Pony, Montana

LETTER TO OBERG FROM PONY

Dear Arthur: In a country where a wealthy handful
of people tear down anything you could possibly love,
break your affectionate connections with yourself by whim
for profit, would move, if they could make money moving it,
the national capital to Dubuque, have already
torn down Walt Whitman's home, tried, damn their souls,
to wreck the Pike Place Market, and in their slimy leisure
plot to dismantle Miss Liberty and move her one piece
at a time to Las Vegas where, reassembled, she
will be a giant slot machine (pull the right arm please,
the one with the torch), you'd love to pack your things and move here.
This is lovely. This is too great for a poem. The only
way here is by dream. Call it Xanadu or Shangri-La
or Oz. Lovely old homes stand empty because somewhere
in this floundering world, the owners toil and plan to come
back here to die. I hope I die here. I want to spend my
last years on the porch of the blue house next to the charming
park the town built and no one uses, picnic tables ringed
by willows and the soft creek ringing in the grass. I hope
to sit there drinking my past alive and watching seasons
take over the park. This is only to assure you, Art,
that in a nation that is no longer one but only an
amorphous collection of failed dreams, where we have been told
too often by contractors, corporations and prudes that
our lives don't matter, there still is a place where the soul
doesn't recognize laws like gravity, where boys catch trout
and that's important, where girls come laughing down the dirt road
to the forlorn store for candy. I love Pony like I love
maybe fifty poems, the ones I return to again
and again knowing my attention can't destroy what's there.
Give my best to Barbara and take care. Dick.

Prose Poems in Pony

DIRECTIONS

Follow the whispers of Montanans whom you trust. Listen to Dick Hugo:
"The only / way here is by dream." The road from Whitehall drops
south in a loop—Silver Star, Sheridan, Virginia City, Ennis, Norris,
and Harrison—where the two-lane comes to the last store.
Take your six-mile offshoot to Pony, the town "too great for a poem."
The route long and straight, bumps over heaves and passes a ranch or two.
Breathtaking, that entrance to Tobacco Root Mountains. You can see
the range long before you get there. Pony tucks in at the end of the pavement,
before the road turns gravel then dirt, past a tiny pink house:
"Pony Country" painted in neat, large letters across it.
Maybe the place is a hundred and fifty square feet—
one main room and a little shed roof addition. From the open,
dry grasses, the road will narrow up the slope, through the trees.
Attention can't take away from the place, from the houses
good people buy to come home one day and die in.

TO DIE IN PONY BUT IT DOESN'T WORK OUT THAT WAY

Dick Hugo didn't die in Pony, Montana, but he wanted to.
"I hope I die here," Hugo wrote to his friend Arthur Oberg,
a poet who killed himself not long after. Instead Hugo went

high up in Virginia Mason Hospital, overlooking downtown Seattle,
off of Madison, where he rode the streetcar with John Mitchell
over the ridge to the beach. From his hospital window, if you craned
your neck, you could look south toward White Center. It was 1982,
with Hugo home for leukemia treatment, and, by the end, he'd known.
From that city on the edge of the sound, he dreamed, I hope,
his way back to Pony. Away from the "amorphous collection of failed dreams,"
Pony is the death of what the nation could have been. It's an ode to aging,
a song to life gone by and a melancholic lyric to the rip-it-down
world degrading the West. "In a country where a wealthy handful / of people
tear down anything you could possibly love," he's come across a town
still in the past, a town with a bar and cash store where he can look out
to the Tobacco Root Mountains, a sanctuary from the "whim for profit"
we've all seen. He can have a soul that lifts beyond that gravity.

TRAVEL COMPANIONS

Maddy and I play in the stream where "the soft creek ringing in the grass"
led us through the woods behind "the picnic tables ringed / by willows."
She drags a stick across the stones. The water is ankle deep.
I try to find the blue house where Hugo wanted to sit on the porch.
We come upon the old brick mill office, surrounded with broken
lawn mowers and canopies for pick-up trucks. Trees bend across the walls.
"Look," Maddy says. "Do people live in there?"
"I think so. See? There are curtains, and it looks like there might be furniture."
The place looks like a squatter's, like a place a group of college kids might live,
only the disarray was from actual poverty.
"Well, part of the roof is gone," she says. "Does it snow here?"
"Yes."
We walk up the road, and Maddy keeps pulling me to return to the stream.
"I want to find a place to swim in it," she says.
There is no place deep enough.

Months later, I come back. This time with Mary Randlett. We don't play
in the stream. We look at buildings, more than a hundred years old
and brick. "Geez," she says. "This place must have been booming."
"A long time ago," I say. "Let's drive up and get a view."
The hillsides were dry and the brick office had burned. Maddy saw the place
and Mary saw the ruin. In that span between them, whoever lived inside
used a camper stove and the building caught fire. Out front,
crusts of engines are crisscrossed with yellow crime-scene tape.
We roam along the hillside, up where the old schoolhouse stands,
the brick Victorian houses, the old mercantile and cabins.
A few old stores, dark plank, stand empty. Just past
the Pony Bar, where the Pony Cash Store used to be,
the road turns dirt. The savings bank is a ruin, hillsides overtake.
Burn, burn, sink, and then awake.

NOT NAMED FOR A HORSE

The story goes like this: A lone prospector, Tecumseh Smith, found the spot,
panned gold in the creek. Folks called him Pony (he was slight and small)
and named the town Pony's Gulch and Pony's Creek. His camp disappeared by 1870.
In 1875, a man named George Moreland found a rich gold deposit
under a patch of wild strawberries, up in the hills outside of Tecumseh's place.
Pony became a town. Hard-rock gold mining thrived, and the 100-stamp mill
grew stone by stone, the ruin with the "no trespassing" signs.
"I want to go in there," Maddy said.
"Let's climb over those rocks," said Mary.
Don't get me wrong—any cop from Pony
must be lovely. But I stamped out
words I needed to: "We'd better not,"
and I distracted them with other sights:
Pony's town, Pony's school and bar.

Downtown Pony, 2007.

GHOSTS

On your road map, a little penciled house says Pony. Gray means
ghost town. In 1900, the population was close to a thousand.
Before that, maybe five thousand, some say. Now, just
a few full-timers—185 on the tax rolls.
Town lore: A shadowy man seen behind the Grant House, once a stage station.
Treasure was rumored there. Buried. When people approach, a man
disappears. Even if they watch him, he slides into air. At the crux
of an old spring, his shape spun off a "dancing light" until
the earthquake of 1887. The spring dried up and the ghost went away.[1]

Stamp mill at Pony, 2007.

BLUE HOUSE

Hugo's shape stays on. Not for treasure or to scare,
he's a leftover who hovers over his "last years on the porch"
at the blue house. "I hope to sit there drinking my past alive
and watching seasons / take over the park." Hugo found in Pony
a triggering town wavering between the present and future,
between the living and the dead. He could see himself in it.
He dreamed his way back to Pony. He could be drinking there still.
Acts of imagination are like that. They linger. "I love Pony like I love /
maybe fifty poems, the ones I return to again / and again knowing

Early cabin and the school in Pony, 2007.

my attention can't destroy what's there."
With my companions, we'd all felt exactly the same thing.
Pony. A town that takes hold in the mind, a town that barely isn't.

Fairfield grain bins, 2007.

Fairfield, Montana

FAIRFIELD

"A guy I used to know—he taught me all about the sky."
   —HUMPHREY BOGART *in High Sierra*

I wanted it depressed, one dusty road
and two cafés both with 'help wanted' signs.
Where I ate, the waitress was too in love
with the cook for things I wanted to say.
The canal passed through town ripe green
and grain, I had to admit, grew assured.
A dog slept fat on warm gravel. No trouble foreseen
raising funds to build the new gym.

I'd expected hurt, the small town kind everyone
knows and ignores, a boy who tried and tried
to leave home, sobbing his failure alone
at the mirror back of the bar, still wearing
his '39 letter sweater, still claiming
the girl who moved to Great Falls will return.
I wanted to honor him in this poem,
to have the sky turn dark as I drove off
the town in my rear view mirror
huddled with fear white in black air.

The drunk I saw seemed happy. I drove empty away.
What if Fairfield sent signals to Mars
and signals came back saying all weather is yours
no matter how vulgar? I imagined cruel sky
left every bird orphan. When I passed
Freeze Out Lake I saw herons accepted that refuge
as home, and I knew the water was green with sky,
not poisoned green with resolve.

HIGH GRASS PRAIRIE

Say something warm. Hello. The world
was full of harm until this wind
placated grass and put the fish to rest.
And wave hello. Someone may be out there
riding undulating light our way.
Wherever we live, we sleep here
where cattle sleep beside the full canal.
We slept here young in poems.
The canal runs on without us east
a long flow into Fairfield. The grass flows
ever to us, ever away, the way it did
that war we dreamed this land alive.
The man we hoped was out there
saw our signal and is on the way.
Say something warm. Hello. You can sleep
forever in this grass and not be cold.

Not This Town

PONY FADES. FROM ghost town to pavement, my car moves on, and I'm winding my way north. A few hours later, I'm driving across Rogers Pass with Mary Randlett. We go up and over the Continental Divide—here it's over a mile high—and drop down into a golden prairie of wheat and barley fields, grasses rippling in the wind. "Towns arrive ahead of imagined schedule," Hugo writes, and sure enough the places come into view long before we get to them: lush green islands planted in the midst of an ocean of brown and gold. Rivers trace fluorescent, Miracle-Gro-green ribbons through the plains. This view, the same one the golden eagles see on their migrations, reminds Mary of the area around Walla Walla, Washington, the town where she went to college in the 1940s. Eastern Washington, too, was a natural grassland, now farmed for hay and wheat and primped for expanding wineries. Out here, the farms roll out thousands of acres of wheat and barley, threshing crops for Anheuser-Busch.

Mary watches for the transitions between land and sky.

"Amazing," she says in that voice that pulls you right into her excitement. "These places out here in the middle of nowhere. Look at those clouds!" She rolls down her window and pokes the camera out. Then she looks over at me. "Can we stop?"

I smile and nod. With Mary, I've been constantly pulling off the road so that she can catch just the right angle. I ease the car through a few more curves until I emerge on a straightaway and pull onto the side. I admire how much energy she has to document things. Scene by scene, she isolates a wide terrain into parts and frames them.

"Look out there, Frances. See how the horizon changes?" She's holding the camera with one hand and poking my arm with the other one.

I lean toward the shot and I can see it—the line of horizon quivering on top of a

Downtown Fairfield, Montana, 2007.

butte—sky and earth trading places.

When we get back into the car, we drive on, crossing the Sun River and heading further north into the town of Fairfield, a town that Hugo wrote one of his last published poems about. It was a place that, according to the poem, he tried to insist despair upon. "I wanted it depressed," he writes, opening the poem with a doomed wish for "one dusty road / and two cafés, both with 'help wanted' signs." Instead, what Hugo found when he visited in the 1970s was a place where "a dog slept fat on warm gravel" and there was "no trouble foreseen / raising funds to build the new gym." Fairfield turns out, both for Hugo's visit and my own, thirty-seven years afterward, to be a clean apron of a town, a collection of white houses tidily assembled in a six-block grid with clotheslines strung between garages and porches. Hugo is "unable to turn it into a landscape of failure, as he once might have done," writes critic Jonathan Holden.

"In spite of his wish for his former depressed vision to fictionalize the town, it remains cheerful and healthy-looking."[1]

Not a ghost town with a few living souls or a logging town dark under Spanish moss or a beaten old mining village hunkered down by a river full of tailings, this high plains prairie town boasts a main street that looks scrubbed—clean windows and well-painted signs, a sparkling bakery—the Cozy Corner—where two young Mennonite women greet Mary and me, their hair bun-wrapped and tucked into napkin-sized coverings. They wear white smocks over dresses of petite floral prints.

Outside, we notice more religious influences, adding to the effect of the town being a freshly laundered dreamscape. For a population of 675 souls, the number of churches astounds: three Lutheran ministries (including a hundred-year-old chapel—ancient for out here) and churches for Mennonites; Catholics; and United Church of Christ congregants (with Methodist, Episcopal, and Congregationalist members); as well a Bible church, an Assembly of God church, and the Church of Jesus Christ of Latter-Day Saints.

To my knowledge, after Hugo's own weekly childhood appearances in St. James Lutheran Church in West Seattle, he never set foot into a house of worship again. "Church was a desperate gesture," he writes in "Fort Benton," about another high grass prairie town. "Prayer / was something bitter" to the early white settlers who "faded one at a time alone." No wonder this cheerful, religious place wasn't his kind of town. He couldn't insert his sensibilities into it and "have the sky turn dark" as he drove off.

Instead, it's a sunny here. A water tower with "F-A-I-R-F-I-E-L-D" stenciled across it stands over the collection of buildings, gleaming amid wheat and barley fields, crops spread out to the horizon, where buttes used as buffalo jumps bloom from the prairie. In his poem "Pishkun," Hugo describes a time when the early tribes were hunting through here, some as far back as 500 AD. On horseback, they ran buffalo to the top of the pishkuns and then off the sides, injuring the animals and leaving them at the hands of colleagues who waited at the foot of the rise to finish off the beasts with spears:

> Looking at the model of a pishkun
> in the Russell Memorial Museum
> you have to think converging walls of rock
> back and back ten miles across the plain.
> The rest is clear: blind bison driven down

the cliff by Indians disguised as wolves,
and where the bison land, braves
with arrows finishing the twitch.

From Fairfield, you can look out and see the pishkuns exactly as they were more than two thousand years ago, back when the area was raw grasslands. Gone is the sagebrush those early natives rode through; vanished is the wizened earth of homesteaded prairie.

As long as irrigation has been in the area, since the 1920s, when the Gibson Dam went up on Sun River, Fairfield has thrived as a farming community. Sun River's watershed is vast, encompassing approximately 2,200 square miles. From an elevation of 9,000 feet along the Continental Divide, the river flows almost 100 miles east, down to its confluence with the Missouri River near Great Falls, the closest city. The river traces sandy loams, light clay, and gravelly soil—not at all the kind of land for agriculture, especially at this high an elevation. That's why the dam and the Greenfields Irrigation District were such a boon to the area around Fairfield. They made farming possible, creating 84,000 acres of irrigated lands.

If you think of rivers not as crevices of water flowing from the mountains to the sea but as wires in a system, then in this contemporary network all the conduits would have been rerouted—stopgapped and dammed, and switched again, away from their natural currents. Under these conditions, it's a wonder water flows at all. Today, you can't send a leaf to the sea, and fish have to be carried over cement blockages. The waterways, plugged with shunts, open into flood plains, their boulders surfacing, dry. The rivers don't go where they used to. They're manipulated and worked over—water coming out, water going in, and you wonder how many genetically engineered ingredients, wastes from pesticides, and growth hormones all cycle back into those barley crops that later morph into beer.

Hugo did see indications of the irrigation, in the form of "the canal [that] passed through town ripe green." Wryly, he adds, "Grain, I had to admit, grew assured." The place appears healthier than close inspection of the iridescent fertilizer and waste troughs would indicate. "I'd expected hurt," Hugo writes, "the small town kind everyone / knows and ignores." Instead he finds a drunk who "seemed happy."

"Well, I think he must have had a very bad attitude," Gertrude Weishaar says. She is a retired high school teacher who has lived in Fairfield since 1957. "This poem doesn't even seem to be about our town." She pauses and looks at the open page again. "Now, if it were about Glasgow, Montana, I could understand it. That's a bad town."

We're sitting at a table in the back of Paula's Gifts, a knickknack shop with an espresso machine inserted between displays of figurines, doilies, and brooms with dried flowers tied on the handles. Mary and I have invited Gertrude to have coffee with us, along with her friend Loreva Oakley. Mary met them while she was snapping pictures of downtown Fairfield.

Gertrude and Loreva are looking at Hugo's *Collected Poems*, spread open on the table. Loreva points to one of the lines in "Fairfield."

Gertrude is still shaking her head. "'The boy who never leaves town?' That's pretty sad. A lot of folks do get jobs over in Great Falls. They commute now. And there are some good jobs here in town."

I nod. Reading the poem now, it seems to me, is like trying to map a town that Hugo was hoping to impose on the real town, only we're making the effort on a town he'd never known.

Mary sips her coffee. "Hell, this is a nice place," Mary says. "Pretty windy, though. Lot of wind here?" She puts both hands around her mug and pulls it toward her.

"With the wind, we have something to talk about," says Loreva. "Out here, somebody with nothing to say might say, 'It's a little windy today.'"

The line sounds like vintage Hugo, like "some people / go to Perma and come back / from Perma saying Perma / is no fun."

"Isn't it something?" Mary says. She lifts her voice. "Jesus, it just *rolls* through here." Mary's photographs map the wind's flight through the silver-leaved willows and narrow-leaved cottonwoods.

The night before, I'd awakened to the sound of air charging through the cottonwoods. From my little room, I could hear it rip along the willows as though someone were flicking enormous reams of paper with a board. It blew the grasses flat and rattled the feed bins, a high-pitched whistle and tingle of metal. I was thinking of the lines "This wind / placated grass and put the fish to rest." The prairie replaces the ocean's expanse in Hugo's Montana poems, and this wind is enough to bully everything else into submission. It blows the grasses down and seethes across the silos. The wind takes sand from the streets and rubs it in your eyes. It takes the smell of barley and pushes it into your sinuses.

I want to say to Loreva and Gertrude that I don't think Hugo really is writing about their town. He's imagining what the town might be, what all towns were to him: places to expect hurt, "the small town kind everyone / knows and ignores." He's conjuring up a boy who "tried and tried to leave home." Hugo wants "to honor him in this poem." I don't explain all this—that Hugo had a kind of pathetic and melancholy side, that he was an outsider who was constantly trying to find his way in, and that even though he had a high-class job as a professor of English at the flagship state university, he didn't think himself worthy to take a barstool in a small town. And, come to think of it, I think he was even making some of that up, too, that part where he always imagines himself as not good enough. At this point in my journeys, I'm beginning to wonder if, at this late juncture in his life, Hugo was losing track of where he as a poet ended and where he as a man began. He wrote "Fairfield" for the collection "White Center" at a time when he was achieving the mild fame that most poets can only dream of. Maybe he was getting tired of feeling unworthy. Instead of saying all this, I let the women pick through the poem, looking for what catches their attention.

Gertrude lifts the book closer to her face and then puts it back down on the table. "He says here that we won't have trouble raising money for a new gym. He was right. We did build a new gym. And a swimming pool too. He must have been here while we were fund-raising," she says.

Far from the stingy place Hugo had wished for ("I wanted it depressed, one dusty road / and two cafés both with 'help wanted' signs"), the people of Fairfield passed their dollars through a little economy that sustained itself, a place where the sun sparkled off of the swimming pool at the center of town.

However, it's not the swimming pool that earmarks the town. It's the line of grain bins, eleven of them, standing along Highway 89, the road adjacent to town. The shiny aluminum silos angle into shallow cones—their tops connected to each other with piping. Strung together, they look like heavy flour canisters forming the western barrier between the settlement and the fields, indenting the huge sweep of sky.

They were, as Hugo might have noted, both beautiful and ugly, both imposition and trademark. The poems that he wrote about towns, too, might read the same way, at least on the surface. But there's something else underneath these lines—a despair beyond what he insists upon the towns. It runs like a dark river under the language.

"Say something warm," he'd written as an opening to "High Grass Prairie": "Hello."

The greeting is plain, simple enough. It offers an immediate connection with the reader and then things take a turn: "The world / was full of harm," and then "Wherever we live, we sleep here / where cattle sleep beside the full canal. / We slept here young in poems." Loneliness takes over, and even relief feels impoverished: "You can sleep / forever in this grass and not be cold." Thick and high, that grass was a soft niche that a person could disappear into and take shelter in. The idea that "you can sleep forever" and "not be cold" and that you need someone to "say something warm" is resoundingly sad. I think of that in the warm autumn sunshine of Fairfield, how there's a darkness, a sort of death wish really, that I can't resolve with Hugo's poetic intention to "want it depressed." At the end, the same phrasing returns, "Say something warm. Hello." It reads like a palindrome of a poem, moving backward and forward to reach that center line: "We slept here young in poems."

Past the feed bins, beyond the wheat fields, I can see a slip of clouds coming over the Rocky Mountain front.

"Forest fires," Loreva says when I point to it. "Running bears out of the forests. They spotted one clear over here at the golf course."

"Just when the forest fires end, then the farmers will start burning again," Gertrude says. "They burn off the fields so they can plant. It's not good conservation. The time will come when they can't burn anymore. I don't know what these barley guys will do. It's not good reclamation." I look at Gertrude, wondering if she's a Democrat. That would be rare out here.

"So they can't let the fields rest?" I ask.

"Not when Anheuser-Busch is in charge." Gertrude's hair is pulled back in the wind. Her dress is a pretty plaid print, a dress like the ones coming into fashion in Seattle—a secretarial look, but softer and handmade: Peter Pan collar, matching belt, pleats through the bosom—all beautifully pressed. "They own the bins. Barley. Local farmers sell crops to them, but there's a caveat: they have to buy the seed from the company. Farmers are getting kind of fed up." She pauses. "There's a wonderful price on winter wheat, and some of them are plowing up their barley fields for wheat." As a crop, winter wheat is planted in the fall and has to freeze before its harvest in the spring.

"Winter wheat" is also the title of Mildred Walker's book, a book about a young girl who travels west and becomes a teacher at a one-room schoolhouse in this part of the country. She could have been Gertrude several generations earlier. Ellen, the main character, and Gertrude both possess the same fortitude and poise. The book traced how a winter's hardship can reap revelation.

Walker, the author of thirteen books, and her husband, Dr. Ferdinand Schemm, had raised their children in Great Falls, just under forty miles from Fairfield. Years later, their daughter Ripley Schemm would marry Dick Hugo. Ripley and Hugo would pass through this area on their way to the family's cabin along the south fork of the Teton River. That was the area where the forest fires were now charging through the valleys.

Mary and I bid our farewells to Fairfield and to Gertrude and Loreva. To the north, Route 89 heads up to Browning, the center of the Blackfeet Reservation, and into Glacier National Park. Mary and I follow that route out of Fairfield, driving north toward Choteau, where Ripley and Dick Hugo often traveled on their way to the cabin, on to Bynum and Dupuyer, towns where, according to "Letter to Welch from Browning," Hugo had stopped for drinks.

"Here, Mary, read this last stanza," I say, pointing to the book wedged open between the seats. Then I lean over the steering wheel and I listen.

She reads:

> When I passed
> Freeze Out Lake I saw herons accepted that refuge
> as home, and I knew the water was green with sky,
> not poisoned green with resolve.

"There," she says. "He must have known about the pollution from all this sewage in the canals."

"He also says, 'I imagined cruel sky / left every bird orphan.' He isn't counting on the landscape for any favors."

"Nope," Mary says. "Not at all. Hey, pull over here. I want to get some shots of the lake."

Some farming sludge dumps into Freezeout Lake, a series of shallow, interconnected ponds, while high up Sun River suffers from dewatering, impaired sediment flows, high water temperatures, and more wastewater. Nonetheless, in these alkaline ponds, a succulent red ground covering peeks through the salt; layers of grasses and sage run horizontally next to the water in colors from deep green to fawn brown. The surface of the pools flickers between blue and a muddy tint. The brown buttes stand in the background. As I watch Mary aim her camera toward all of this, I think about how, when the famous pioneer painter Charlie Russell visited here, back when the irrigation district was under construction, he saw some of these colors. As the "first 'Western' artist to live the majority of his life in the West," he might have encountered the same purple and violet that illuminate the Freezeout Lake scene today.[2] In his almost florescent use of color and light, Russell was the Thomas Kinkade of his time, a painter whom Hugo called "fairly good, not really good."

While I'm standing there, grebes, cormorants, and swallows flutter up from the grasses and terns lift through the air like lit bulbs strung over the panorama. Mary takes pictures, and I walk out to the salt-rimmed edges of the lake ponds. Snow geese and swans flutter up from the shallow water, and I tilt my chin to the sky to see whole flocks going overhead. I look south toward Fairfield, that town of cotton linens, fine pastries, and a cold blue swimming pool, wondering if I could be a person who could stay there and learn how to be comfortable with the wind. My fantasy bloomed as the opposite of Hugo's, where the outsider can't find a place and leaves town. Here I was, a woman who came West, away from where I'd started, and found a home in Seattle. Somehow, I'd become a writer who simulated pilgrimages to places as far-flung as Fairfield, believing that road trips would lead me somewhere where literature would come to life, somewhere where I'd come across a version of myself as a narrator, a construct that I hoped I'd be able to tolerate. Just as I'd found Hugo's places in the city, so I'd also find them in the hinterlands. It was another worn-out myth of the West, the easterner who comes and "finds herself"—only in my case, I was stubborn enough to already have a self that I, instead, insisted upon the places I went.

Still, what I consider as I look back over the white salt rims around the miniature lakes, was how Hugo was a regular man with a propensity toward darkness, a man insisting a persona of despair that didn't always stick. Nor could I, as a follower, insist him into all of these towns I was visiting. Where things went out of alignment was exactly the hinge where they got interesting, I decided. "If I went back to the towns in Montana now," Hugo said in his 1978 interview with Michael Allen, "I would get completely different poems out of them, I'm sure."[3] Similarly, I was traveling into Hugo's towns and imagining new versions of the poems, of Hugo, and of my own life in each of them.

I recount Hugo's line "I wanted to honor him in this poem," and what I suddenly realized is that Hugo's persona was wearing out in these poems, and still they revealed a true existential despair behind the constructed one. It was a stark idea: the man who needed the town to be depressed was an actor trying to plant his own depression upon it, except that his melancholy was far worse than that of the character he portrayed. "Fairfield" does capture a feeling of speculation, about imagining things to be worse than they were. About the sad boy who mourns his lost youth, the boy Hugo makes up so that he can write about Fairfield at all, he says:

> I wanted to honor him in this poem,
> to have the sky turn dark as I drove off
> the town in my rear view mirror
> huddled with fear white in black air.

But it didn't turn out like that. The towns, lit underneath clouds as we drive through them, shine with promise. After all, by the time he wrote "Fairfield" and "High Grass Prairie," Hugo's own life was turning out quite well—he was married to Ripley, and together they were parents to Ripley's children, Matthew and Melissa. Most of the time, Hugo's friends tell me, he told stories, watched ball games, and taught classes. Lois Welch remembers that "Hugo could never believe his good fortune as students turned in poems that sent him up and down the hall saying, 'Listen to this, isn't this great?'"[4] He went fishing, toured the country, and gave poetry readings. Like any artist, he made things up, and after a while, Richard Hugo outgrew the things he had to imagine when he was young.

On we go, gliding into Choteau, stopping at the enormous used bookshop that was so famous in these parts, then back in the car for Bynum, a pass-through town with rubble from old cars and trailers strewn across the hillside. There's no market here, though there is a sign for a bar that might open later. Where the road crosses the highway, there's a place with a sign: "Rock Shop." Mary loves it; it's the visual artist's version of the bookstore. "Let's go in," she says. She spends an hour talking to the proprietors while I tour displays of fossils and gems.

Afterward, we drive toward Dupuyer. The road curves and dips up and down, around the buttes. Land becomes less irrigated, more rocky and sandy, though the

Rock shop in Bynum, Montana, 2007.

fields are a bright yellow with canola and errant mustard. Small oil rigs, pumping units, move to and fro like bionic toys, their rods tipping side to side from a pulley.

Across the dip from the little machines, I see a squared-off area at the top of the hill.

"I'll bet that's one of the missile silos," I say.

"Missiles? Are you sure?" asks Mary.

I'd read about the silos in David Quammen's essays, and John Mitchell, Hugo's best friend, had installed some Minuteman missiles out here while he was working for Boeing. I imagine metal doors sliding open in the prairie and huge devices rising up. Those I wanted to see, and I hope Mary can photograph them somehow.

From the road, I can't see a house anywhere in the distance. The silos sit on farmers' land, in exchange for the government keeping the roads maintained, an advantage out here in the winter.

Oil-pumping unit in the high grass prairie, 2007.

"That's we're headed," I say. "I want to have a look."

"Oh, great," says Mary. "We're going to get arrested." I notice that she's grabbing her camera and screwing on a new lens, the biggest one I've seen her use.

I pull the car onto a dirt farm road and park. Ahead of me is a locked cattle fence—six rails of green metal. When I straighten my baseball hat and heave a leg over the gate, Mary is already zooming into the fenced area, taking pictures.

"Hey, better not let George W. Bush see you doing that," she shouts as I walk up the road toward the installation.

The wind picks up, and I button my coat while I walk up the hill to the tall cyclone fences. When I get there, I see a sign: "Warning—Restricted Area—It is unlawful to enter this area without the permission of the Installation Commander." Then, a small citation: "Sec 21 Internal Security Act of 1950." Below that: "While on this installation all personnel and the property under their control are subject to search. Use of deadly force authorized." My companion is standing down by the road, shooting photos. I want to see, up close, if the silos are still in use, as if that might indicate "homeland security."

Inside the fence, there are metal tracks thirty feet long with visible gears that disappear into a round base of new concrete. Around the base are silver pipes, brand new, and off to the side is a square manhole with a crowbar lever. The cover, say fifteen or twenty feet in diameter, has an enormous hydraulic hinge. Surrounding all of the concrete and machinery is a new dump of fist-sized gravel and three telephone poles with sensors in the shape of earmuffs. The whole installation looks brand new.

Down the hill, Mary is zooming her telephoto on me, and I wonder if the box on a pole next to me is a camera that some army man is monitoring from an underground cell nearby. Part of my image of how I'm being watched comes from Quammen's essay about how a group of men, keep an eye on the missiles from over in Conrad, about fifteen or twenty miles from where I stand now. Some low-level military designees sit underground, two at a time, on alert. For a missile to be launched, both would have to turn a key.[5] That way, if one panicked, the other could offset his impulses by preventing the accidental discharge. I figure that they had television monitors far underneath these hills, screens with magnified images of the area, manipulated by the men who attentively studied them for hours at a time. Though I didn't want someone to actually come and interrogate me, I knew that being a white American woman wearing jeans and a baseball hat rather than a dark-skinned man from Iran or Afghanistan would land me a scolding and probably a strong-armed ushering from the property. Maybe I'd get a trespassing ticket, or worse, maybe I'd have to go to a federal court and meet some FBI guys.

But no one comes. I walk back to the car, waving to Mary as I come down the slope. We both get into the car without helicopters landing or sirens engaging.

"They won't come after us," Mary says. "I look like an old lady."

As for Dupuyer, Hugo had misspelled it. I see the sign when we hit the town limits. Not "Depuyer." It's 3:00 P.M. on Monday, and I count the storefronts along the road—eleven of them—and they're all closed. According to the sign, the Ranch House Bar opens at five. We bump along on one of the side streets and find a church. The steeple,

Downtown Dupuyer, 2007.

where the clock should be, is boarded up. Apparently, the town burned three times, and the church outlasted each burn. It was built from 1898 to 1907, the smallest chapel I'd ever seen for such a long period of construction.

People in Dupuyer, according to local chatter in Fairfield and Choteau, sight UFOs and report mysterious cattle mutilations: mysterious, surgical cuts found on dead animals—cows, sheep, even horses. According to local lore, there are never any footprints near the animals, and all the blood from the corpses has been removed. Aliens or cults, locals believe, are responsible. Whether or not Hugo knew of these aspiring astronomers, his poem "Fairfield" points to the sky: "What if Fairfield sent signals to Mars / and signals came back saying all weather is yours . . . ?" In "High Grass Prairie," Hugo's speaker speculates, "Someone may be out there / riding undulating light our way." Underneath that broad sky, the twinkling of satellites and stars, far-off planes sending fog streams and mysterious lights from the air force base inspired all sorts of theories.

Ahead of us, haze from forest fires through the Rockies fills up the skies over the forks of the Teton River and the Rocky Mountain front. Smoke jumpers and firefighters from as far away as Colorado and Wyoming wander back and forth between small motels and their trucks.

We look out the windows of the car, dreaming of the poem—a spectacle, a world we tried to make up and then live in, a world where missiles were kept, unmanned, out in the lonesome prairie and towns were strung along between drinks. The nose of the car pokes north, then west, into the wind.

Gulls off the dock at La Push, 1972.

LA PUSH

Fish swim onto sand in error.
Birds need only the usual wind
to be fanatic, no bright orange
or strange names. Waves fall
from what had been flat water,
and a child sells herring
crudely at your door.

The store has a candy turnover
amazing to the proprietor.
He expected when he came
a Nordic rawness, serrated shore,
a broken moon, artifacts
and silence, large sales of corn.

Smelt are trapped in the river
by a summer habit, limit
of old netting rights ignored.
Who but an officed lawyer
far away has read the treaty,
his sense of rightness rounded
in a bar? The broker's pier
is measuring the day in kings and jacks.

Your land ends at this border,
water and stone, mobile in tide,
diffuse in storm, but here.
The final fist of island rock
does not strike space away. Swim
and you are not in your country.

LETTER TO BLY FROM LA PUSH

Dear Robert
Lots of whales cavort and spout
three hundred yards offshore. The danger
of them there, high waves and cold winds mean
we cannot swim. I'm still not in my country
though fishnets dry and hostile eagles scan
our country's enemy, the empty gray.

It's green here, black green mostly, black
against dark sky—all pines are silhouettes.
Even the sun is solid, and red memories
of better runs, of bigger kings, of jacks
that tore the gill nets in their futile drive.
We have to lie or be dishonest to our tears.
Some days I almost know how tall brown wheat
goes gold against dark sky, the storms
that hate our wheat, the thunder
that will come for wheat, evangelistic anger.

My fish is trout. I hear the long jawed pike
can smile you dead when hooked. My symptoms
never die. I've been away ten years, and spray
has killed four houses I remember and the church.
Birds are still fanatic. The shore is raw.
That last rock fist: the void still makes it stick.
The whales are closer and in colder wind
I send warm regards as always,
Dick

The Last Places

Y ou could say that Hugo predicted his own death. Many poets do—Yeats wrote "Cast a cold eye on life, on death, horseman pass by," and it's etched on his gravestone at Drumcliff, under the hillside of "bare Ben Bulben's head." Similarly, Hugo's cemetery marker reads "Eat Stone and Go On," a line from one of his last poems. A poet, by nature, trades in prophesy and his own death is his simplest, darkest forecast. "You might die anywhere," Hugo writes in "Ayr," though he has already noted, in three other poems, that he wants to die in Pony, burrow under the high grasses of the Montana prairie, and be buried on Skye. In the end, he's laid to rest in Missoula.

Even in the references to his own death and burial, Hugo's language feels mediated with a sensibility of tenderness and wisdom, as it does in "Letter to Garber from Skye," a poem written to Frederick Garber, the literary critic. The form of the letter poem, one he used in the collection, 31 *Letters and 13 Dreams*, returns here as a coda to his work. "Don't laugh but / today I told my wife if I die here here's where I want / to be buried," he writes. Echoing "Letter to Oberg from Pony," where his speaker claims that he wants to die in that town, Hugo is creating a new horizon for the triggering town metaphor.

These poems create venues where Hugo is rehearsing his own mortality and testing out places to suit his imaginings. That's why in his final collections, *White Center* and *The Right Madness on Skye*, both published two years before Hugo died, and the uncollected poems that he wrote between those books and his life's end, there's a heaviness and a reconciliation that is palpable. "We'll be confined and free—a road ends fast," Hugo writes in "A Map of Skye." The awareness of his own death is, at times, acute. His psyche is opening up; he sees that his confines are blessings—perhaps the life inside a family has become a containment that sets him free. Sadly, in the end, his road does end fast.

"If you've got a map," Hugo wrote, "You think I'm skipping about. / Listen. All places are near and far . . . neighbors." Far off, on the Isle of Skye, Hugo was thinking of stone and surf, of cliffs and waves, and of going under. In "Letter in Carloway Broch," his self-prognosis is quite literal: "Given my genes, my medical past and my recent / ability to control bad habits / I expect to reach 83." Sadly, Hugo didn't even reach 1983; he died at fifty-eight, in late 1982.

"Water leads slow ways to open water," and that's where I'm headed. After driving, this time alone, without Mary or Maddy, past the turnoff outside Choteau, the one that leads to Ripley's cabin at the foot of Ear Mountain, moving through the string of towns that Hugo mentions in "Letter to Welch from Browning," I reach Browning itself, on the Highline, Route 2. Turning west, I realize, means I'm going home.

I am leaving Montana. It's always a twinge of loss for me, turning my back to those tawny mountains and hard towns, and facing the long road. Still, I grow restless to get back to Seattle and see my family. Once I'm heading west for a spell, I can envision the Cascades a few hundred miles ahead, and the city on the other side. In "The Braes," a poem from Skye, Hugo writes, "I'll drive this road for the same / old reason, to find a poem." Hugo's process of cruising along, looking for what's familiar and strange, pulling up the language and images to shape his art, inspires me. I have a similar, bracing attention to what I'll find on my way.

This time, for the last stretch of my journey, I'm going back to a beginning of sorts, a place where a much younger Hugo began, a place that comprises the qualities of where he would end. I'm steering straight for the water.

As I imagine the miles I'll cover to reach the far coast, I remember an early pact that Hugo had made. He describes it in *The Real West Marginal Way*: He once said that, as a boy, he drank rainwater from the stump behind his house. When he didn't die from the "poisoned" and "diseased" stuff, it proved to him that he could survive what the world pushed toward him. This was his inner voice for so many years—one that convinced him to test his own mortality, meddling with dark tendencies. It was his "secret shared only with water."

Hugo's late poems show him facing things that in the past have plagued him. "I knew the water was green with sky, / not poisoned green with resolve" closes the last two lines of "Fairfield," and resolve comes up again in Skye when he thinks back to his home country: "Montana wants to be warmer and forget / how many farmed too hard and failed." Then the poem moves on: "Most of all, here we want the self discarded / left unresurrected and wind resolved to move on." Resolve is set into the nature of things, into the land and wind. It's not a resolve of human resistance, one borne on poison or bitterness. In this version of new resolve, he's accepting the way things are.

After years of sad endings, times ruined in alcohol and despair, Hugo finally reaches "that land of slow recovery" where he can "read the water." His ruminations on his own death (a psychologist would call them rehearsals), lie bare across these poems, like stones across the vast and misty landscape of Skye, where "the dead are hidden from the sea." But there's something consoling too; there's a peace in these images. Even the car from Philipsburg, the one that "still runs," is sturdier on Skye: "Our car has never waited for us this long before." Slabs of stones and graves face the open water in these Scotland poems. They're stark. But they are complex and beautiful too: "We can love there well / grateful what is cruel ran out."

Far from the sad, ironic end of "Duwamish," in which Hugo writes "madness, to red-men, means coming home," the Skye poems refer to "the right madness," showing up in the title poem of the collection and in poems like "Semi-lunatics of Kilmuir" and "Villager." It's a settled state of mind, one not riddled with shame and despair. Hugo is blunt: "Now I'm dead, load what's left on the wagon / and have the oxen move on." The instructions to heave his corpse onto a cart and pull away are followed with: "You might note on my stone in small letters: / Here lies one who believed all others his betters. / I didn't really, but what a fun thing to say." It's a lighter sweep than one might find in the poems of *The Lady of Kicking Horse Reservoir.*

Hugo "dream[ed] the sea lanes out." And so did I. After a twelve-hour day across the Highline, I come to its terminus at Everett, Washington. There, I turn south a few miles to the ferry landing at Edmonds. A woman in an orange vest waves me onto the boat. Then I climb the stairs to the deck and look over the rail, back to the city: "I want a last look at Seattle and the way the light / subtracts and adds miles to the journey." On the other side, at Kingston, I'll begin again— this time out to the far end of Washington State.

The Olympic Peninsula, a mitten-shaped outline of land where the back of the hand fends off the sea, takes up one third of our state. Overhead, looking down, you could see the whole of western Washington as a patchwork of gutted land, mountains, and pavement. The Olympic National Park would be a clump of forest in the middle of the peninsula, dirt roads snaking through, and three long lakes would glitter—Quinault, Ozette, and Crescent.

Forks is the town closest to the water, though not actually within sight of it; it's the town with the motels and one big supermarket, the only strip of shops between Port Angeles and Hoquiam to have a chamber of commerce (this one with cheerful volunteers wearing T-shirts outlining "Twilight—a vampire story set in Forks" at the visitor center), the crossroads where timber executives unroll topographical maps in the coffee shop, a place where the Quillayute, Bogachiel, Calawah, and Sol Duc rivers twist around each other and where, from a kayak, you'd be startled by the muck and murk just inland—so different from the green-gray sea. Just off this road and in the mist, always in the mist, I drive west. Toward the far corner of the country, I'm steering to the place where, Hugo says, "the nation quits."

Out of town, at eye level: a tarmac through pine and fir, the chute of road turns into another straightaway. Logging trucks, hauling their stacks of copper-barked rounds, slide past. Signs for "Rayonier," once the pulp and paper company and now a real estate investment trust and manufacturer of rayon, come at intervals, and beyond them I see the Northwest's version of strip mining. The timber people have gone in and raked out the trees. All the other brush and saplings came out too, and the left-overs pile into woody threads, mulch, and twisted brush. Junk timber—alder—pushes in with Scotch broom and salal. Forests are turned upside down, dirt as dark as peat in bundles. Scruffy grow-backs. Joni Mitchell sings on the CD player: "It makes mountains into molehills." Her plaintive, reedy voice sounds in the echo between hills: "We make this earth our funeral pyre." I wheel down the corridor, that *whee* of tires on a spin to the sea.

This is post-spotted-owl terrain, the bird that in 1990 was listed as endangered and that slowed logging in this area. Out-of-work timbermen wore shirts and slapped on bumper stickers that said things like "Save a logger—Shoot an owl." All the roads off this one are dead ends, except the one to the Quillayute Prairie Airport, which rumors say is actually used constantly by military jets—otherwise, why would a far-off Indian reservation need an airport, other than for its proximity to the undefended western border of the county, the one we always thought of as facing Russia but now as facing North Korea? The federal government, either through the auspices of the Olympic

National Park or the reservations, could quickly close off the borderland, even the whole peninsula (Highway 101 is a loop and the only road that goes through) in a time of military confrontation. The other roads, with their single-bar metal gates—most painted yellow—built for logging trucks to gain access, slope upward through the brush. "Harvested 1984," reads one sign. "Planted 1985" and then "Next Harvest 2045." Now and then, on either side of the road, a forest appears, thickening. A small alder rises from a nurse log, a cedar stump. Moss hangs from older trees.

Just when I turn north again, shortly after the new Quileute tribal center, the open Pacific fills the horizon with ottoman-shaped hulks of stone as big as warehouses standing in the surf. La Push, one town I'll be haunted by, lies here, at the mouth of the Hoh River. The Quileute Indians once came through the rain forest and slipped through the muddy river into the ocean. Beyond, the sea laps over the shelf of beach where the water unrolls over and over. New cedar clapboard cottages and two-story motel buildings surround the small cabins that stood alone here fifteen years ago. Now a bulldozer spreads landfill to make room for more.

Richard Hugo first wrote about the town in the 1950s and published the poem "La Push" in his 1961 book, his first volume, *A Run of Jacks.* Hugo had visited the area first with his buddies from childhood and then with friends from Boeing; they fished the Hoh River and camped. When he married Barbara, the two of them traveled often to the coast. In a 1974 interview, Hugo tells of sleeping on Beach #6 near Kalaloch, thirty-five miles south of La Push. The couple stayed four days, their bodies nestling into "sleeping bags on a bed of dry round pebbles rounded from years of sea wash."[1] Hugo left the campsite just a few times—for beer and hot dogs.

In both the real town and the poem, Hugo doesn't write of that simple, unadorned intimacy that he experienced on the beach. The place offers a different kind of muse for his poems, a triggering town that puts aside sentiment in favor of locating the undercurrent of tension that the sea both smoothes over and pushes up in swells. I too can feel resistance in La Push. For many years, the Quileute didn't welcome outsiders to their tribe's core settlement; only grudgingly would they sell goods at the store or turn over the keys to people hoping to rent their cabins. "A child sells herring / crudely at your door," Hugo wrote, and the old store had "a candy turnover / amazing to the proprietor." That place has been closed for years, replaced by a "mercantile" down the hill, at the entrance to town. Things aim to be friendlier, I notice, even as the mist rolls over the shore, and salt water blows in gusts over the town. Everything tastes of the sea and is oppressed by it.

What Hugo saw, and what I see, is a place "at the edge, between the land and sea," where "neither gives a sure sense of home."[2] Hugo's friend Donna Gerstenberger was describing Hugo's hunger for discomfort, tension, and satisfaction that he felt along the water. Standing here, at La Push, I see the trajectory start to falter: the outsider arrives, finds things decaying, sees himself in the dilapidated place, and finally feels he belongs—if only for a few hours, and then he can't align himself fully to the place.

This same realization comes over the poet when he visits Cape Alava, the western-most point of the continental United States, just north of La Push. Overlooking the sea, Hugo writes: "West of here the only west is water." There's a vacancy out there, one he's turning away from. Then a few stanzas later he repeats the line, changing the last word: "west of here the only west is failure," and six stanzas after that: "west of here the only west is future." The progression from a fact—water is what exists to the west—to projections of "failure," and, finally, "future," imitates the course that each town poem takes. Hugo will describe the place, project failure onto them; for years he will even drink himself into that failure. He will try to fit into it. Much later, his existence opens to the warm hope of the "future," and these poems on the Washington seacoast underscore that prophesy. "This was the last name west on charts" Hugo wrote in "Fort Benton," one of his later poems, published in *White Center*, but I can't help moving the reference from high plains Montana to the Washington coast. "West of here the world turned that indefinite white / of blank paper and the settlers faded one at a time alone." In "La Push," that poem written so early in his life, what was west of that town was abstract—undefinable beyond language such as *water, failure,* and *future*. In "Fort Benton," he imagines "that indefinite white / of blank paper" and the settlers dying off. There's a progression of imagination here, reading like Wallace Stevens considering where the mind actually ends. "Your land ends at this border," says the younger Hugo. The elder Hugo says, "This is the town to leave / for the void."

Critic Jonathan Holden says that in Hugo's poems, the "protagonist's landlocked psyche" is "looking for a route to the sea."[3] In poems set far inland, Hugo creates this longing for the edge, the place where the nation finally gives way to water. Just as he's creating a persona who craves the rim of civilization, so Hugo is also working to implicate his readers and himself, the poet, into his dream of isolation. Yet he seems to crave companionship. Holden says that through "you," Hugo "asserts . . . the universality of his protagonist's concerns."[4] The catchall of the apostrophe, the glance out to the reader grows more inclusive as Hugo's work progresses. In *A Run of Jacks*, "La Push" is one of only three poems written in second person. Later, Hugo's poetry will take on the "you" in more and more verses. Holden notes, "We watch the 'you' gradually becoming so carried away with his own creation that he sings himself to the brink of total belief."[5] Sometimes, you realize that Hugo is talking to himself. You are there, as a reader, to overhear his utterances elevated to poetic speech. It's an earmark of his creative method. As Hugo himself said in an interview with Thomas Gardner, "For a long time I was using 'you' poem after poem. The psychology of the person enables you to talk; when you say 'you,' you're able to say certain things that you aren't able to say when you use 'I' and vice versa."[6] To be relegated to three points of view—first, second, and third—isn't enough for Hugo. He creates hybrids, merging the second person with the first, "you" with "I," or the first with the third, "we" with "they." "You" becomes "I," and, eventually, everyone else too—reader, speaker, Hugo, and people who live in the towns.

Even in this early poem, Hugo sees that this place, La Push, is a talisman presaging his end, an end that will come more than twenty years later:

> Your land ends at this border
> water and stone, mobile in tide,
> diffuse in storm, but here.

During the intervening years, Hugo's terrain would expand to Montana, to the Isle of Skye in Scotland, and back to Italy, where he'd flown as a bombardier and had returned to visit, but his poetry ends here, in a place it began, at the edge of the water, where driftwood was heaved upon the beach, as if tossed by some giant's hand roiling up from the sea. A poet's reprieve, this town, a place to consolidate woe.

Where rock meets ocean and the tide wears away solid things, where storms push and erode the land, "here" is a place Hugo sees himself. He knew "the final fist of island rock" from which you "swim / and you are not in your country." Where the land gives out is where his language gives way to silence. Unlike the rivers he follows for trout, the ocean swells limitless, bounded only by the edge you stand upon. Reaching the ocean, for Hugo, is like dropping the subject. Or the subject dropping you.

Long before his health gives in and his poems run out, Hugo dreams of that

La Push, 1972.

edge where the human voices may awaken him while poems drown, where beyond
the fringe of sand and water, language was submerged, irretrievable. Reminiscent of
Stevens' "Palm at the End of the Mind," where the imagination drops "beyond the last
thought," Hugo's coastline hosts no promise of the tropical tree or of any furnishing to
console his through the sojourn. His imagination merely takes us the sea's beginning,
the continent's end. In this prophecy, there is no further place to go; you must retrace
your steps, start the car, follow the one road out.

And so, Hugo leaves La Push, eventually leaves Washington State for Montana,
and leaves his marriage to Barbara. When he returns, years later, he writes "Letter to
Bly from La Push," published in 1978. This time, he's addressing Robert Bly, a poet
long known for his heartfelt poems, often set in the Midwest, and his activism against
the Vietnam War (he distributed his 1968 National Book Award prize money to the war

resistance cause). Bly was only three years younger than Hugo, and shared with Hugo the belief that overlooked people mattered.

"I've been away ten years, and spray / has killed four houses I remember and the church," Hugo writes in this second La Push poem. He sees that the island in the sea is still there, at the mouth of the river: "That last rock fist: the void still makes it stick," echoing the reference back to the first La Push poem's "rock fist." Hugo also echoes another line he wrote in the first poem: "Birds need only the usual wind / to be fanatic." All these years later, he writes, "Birds are still fanatic." Now that his poems can refer back to each other, you wonder if his language has indeed dropped away. You wonder if, there on the edge of the sea, looking out, Hugo's syntax does fall off where the sand disappears, slipping under the water. On land, nets dry in the sun; buoys rest tucked inside crab pots stacked along the docks. The town revives itself, sheathing the old cabins in new roofs, setting new fishing boats into the harbor. You can't help thinking that the edge isn't an edge at all, but a place revised over and over again until the language smoothes into the land.

Epilogue at Taholah, Washington

TAHOLA

Where sea breaks inland, claiming the Quinalt
in a half saltwater lake, canoes turn gray
waiting for the runs. The store makes money
but the two cafés, not open, rot in spray.
Baskets you can buy are rumored Cherokee.
When kings run wild, girls use salmon oil
to stain a doll's face real. The best house
was never envied for its tile. Cars
and philosophic eyes are coated by the sea.

Whites pay well to motor up the river,
harvest blackmouth, humpbacks, silvers,
jacks and sea run cuts. Where rain assaults
the virgin timber and the fish pools boil,
the whites pry stories from the guide
with bourbon. Sunset, and they putt downriver
singing. But the wind, the sea
make all music language, dead as a wet drum.

When whites drive off and the money's gone
a hundred mongrels bark. Indians
should mend the tribal nets in moonlight,
not drink more and hum a white man's tune
they heard upstream. What about the words?
Something about war, translated by the sea
and wind into a song a doll sang
long ago, riding a crude wave in.

ROAD ENDS AT TAHOLA

My nostrils tell me: somewhere mare nostro.
Here the wolf-fish hides his lumpy face in shame.
Pines lean east and groan. Odors of a booze
that's contraband, are smuggled in by storms.
Our booze is legal Irish and our eyes
develop felons in the endless spray.
Mare nostro somewhere, and eternity's
a law, not a felony like here.
That derelict was left for storms to break.

One ship passes denting the horizon,
creeping down the world. Whatever gave us pride
(food en route to Rio) dies. The wake could be
that wave we outrun laughing up the sand.
Night comes on with stars and years of dead fish
lighting foam with phosphorus they left.
All day the boom was protest, sea against
the moon. Mare nostro somewhere and no shame.

Remember once, a scene, a woman naked
clowning in the sea while armies laughed.
Her man, a clown, had courage and he came
and hauled her (both were sobbing) up the stones.
If I were strong, if wolf-fish didn't dive
beyond the range of scorn, you'd be alive.

I can't say mare nostro. Groaning pines
won't harm you, leaning east on galaxies.
I know I'm stone. My voice is ugly.

A kelp bed is a rotten place to hide.
Listen. Hear the booming. See the gleam,
the stars that once were fish and died.
We kiss between the fire and the ocean.
In the morning we will start another stare
across the gray. Nowhere mare nostro.
Don't claim it and the sea belongs to you.

Epilogue

NOT LONG AFTER I return home to Seattle, I decide to take one more trip. My husband Gary and I pack up and head to the town that teeters on the edge of Hugo's imagination, the town most consumed by physical beauty and most immersed in economic woe. Tahola, as Hugo spells it, is really Taholah, a place on the Quinault Indian Reservation, up a spur road from the highway and flush against the open Pacific. The extra *h* in the actual Taholah pulls the name along, a long *ahhh* out of the mouth: a forced whisper. To get there, we follow signs pointing us away from Highway 101 toward Moclips or down through Humptulips. The *m*'s and *p*'s of the town bump our lips along into a hum, and the car pushes north again.

I've been given a little chapbook called "The Road Ends at Tahola," a hand-letterpress collection of a few Hugo poems. It's a small book of beige paper with a red-lettered cover, published in 1978 by my friend Tony (Anthony) Petrosky, of Slow Loris Press in Pittsburgh. "Road Ends at Tahola" originally came out in Hugo's 1965 book *Death of the Kapowsin Tavern*. That collection, centered on the metaphor of an old tavern that burned down, explores "The town that barely is," and that's what I think of when we drive out to Taholah. *Is it a ghost of a place?*

Enough reading of Hugo's poems and a person needs company. I'm bringing my sweetheart, the man whom I drove to Seattle with all those years ago, the one who became my husband. The best cure to this literary melancholy is companionship, I realize, and so I cajole Gary into taking time away from work to drive all the way out to the other end of the Olympic Peninsula. With him, it will be easier to face the gray, open sea in this weather-struck place. Maybe bringing him along is also an act of defiance, pushing back at Richard Hugo by taking my husband, just as Hugo had brought his first wife, Barbara. Their marriage hadn't survived fourteen years. Or perhaps I was considering my own parents, who haven't spoken to each other in forty-three years and whose marriage hadn't lasted two. Whatever preceded us, Gary and I have thrived together for more than twenty years, and it is to him I turn when things get emotional. It always feels good to have him along.

We arrive in town, ten miles from the last evidence of civilization, where the sign reads "Road ends" and the arrow points crossways but there's a bridge straight ahead. The span looks old—the white paint chips off the iron railing. Below, the Quinault River is a broad, graphite murk, chucking up sand and swirling back and forth, gathering into a lagoon at the mouth. The water gleams like airplane metal.

Over the bridge, the road dips and mucks up fast—big holes, slicked-out in mud. An old car torn apart to the axels, with sockets now where headlamps once peered out, hangs over the fringe of the road. From there, the route narrows to a path through the forest. The gazetteer guide shows the bridge as a small red eyelash, barely visible, across the Quinault. Farther up, a gate with keyed access prevents tourism, and the primitive roads are marked as BIA (Bureau of Indian Affairs) tracks. "Okay," says Gary. "Far enough." He knows that I have a predisposition, always, to keep going.

Back to the crosshatch of streets, we come across descendents of the "mongrels" that Hugo writes about, ten or twenty, maybe fifty, generations later—loose dogs roaming the streets. Large brown Samoyed-shepherd mixes, chocolate retriever-husky combos, and ones I can't distinguish. No collars, ungroomed. They amble slowly, some following me to the porch of the store and then sighing, letting their legs give way, and rolling onto their ribs.

Hugo stayed in town and didn't wander much. That's what I gather from the poem. Gary and I walk through the aisles of the store, find something to eat, and then sit at a laminated table and look out toward the beach. While we're unwrapping our sandwiches, I wonder how to translate the poem onto the place. In "Road Ends at Tahola," the poet operates in first person, likening himself to the "wolf-fish" who "hides his lumpy face in shame." Even the landscape pulls away. Quickly, the sea turns dark. "Pines lean east and groan." He's hiding in one of the most hidden places in the world.

Led by his senses to the salty expanse, Hugo finds "mare nostro," *our sea*, a term the fascists used during the Second World War to project their empire onto the Mediterranean. He is "almost superstitious about saying 'mare nostro' about this sea in this place and this time, for to claim possession of it is to lose it."[1] To apply "mare nostro" to Taholah is to release it from its operatic confines and bring European culture to the land of First Peoples, a place where Chief Taholah signed the Olympic Treaty in 1855, creating the Quinault reservation, accommodating the white settlers who were arriving then, homesteading on land with valuable timber. One sense of mare nostro conquest supersedes another.

About extracting the poems' images from the actual place, Hugo says:

> The first four lines of the third stanza are taken from the early flashback sequence in Ingmar Bergman's "The Naked Night." The wolf-fish I saw in an aquarium somewhere, Hoodsport I think . . . I took the title from a highway sign just north of Moclips, about ten miles from Tahola. . . . Barbara and I visited that forlorn rundown village many times. I love it there.[2]

Interestingly, the interviewer asks him about the actual location of the poem. To which Hugo responds:

> In my imagination I suppose I move our camp at Beach Trail 6, north of Kalalock, south about 50 miles or whatever to Tahola. Maybe all beaches are one. Some of the details are about Tahola. For example the pines leaning east and the derelict ship battered by storms. Also the contraband booze. That's a story the tribal chairman Horton Capoeman told us. He runs a café in Tahola. He told Barbara and me about a French ship that ran aground off Tahola many years back. The ship was loaded with booze, brandy, wine, and the Feds put a guard around the ship to keep the Indians from getting the liquor. But the Indians slipped through the cordon in their dugouts and got the booze ashore. "God," Capoeman said, "if you don't think those Indians didn't have a time." Bless them. Bless them all. I think that happened in the early part of the century.[3]

He is, of course, really blessing himself, a man not long home from a war where he'd run bombing missions, destroying whole villages. He'd found another village, this one fragile and isolated, just his kind of place. There, he and his loved one would stare out at the sea, creating fantasies of how to save her. For Jonathan Holden, the poem is about "the speaker reproaching himself for his inability to rescue his mate."[4] This is the fantasy that will play out for Hugo after he and Barbara split up, and it won't be resolved until he marries again and finds a life with a family, intact and consoling.

In the back of the store, seated at the little built-in plastic table, we're looking to the river and out to the hill of sand and rock where the ocean comes in.

"I can see it," Gary says. "I can see Hugo here." He nods toward the broken-down houses.

It's one of the things I love most about him. Gary always sees the beauty in the raw, almost-ruined things.

Our speaker, the sad guy in the poem, is here with someone else too.

Outside, the clouds open into a seam of light, just beyond the driftwood tangle at the water. When "the sea belongs to you," in the poem's closure, it comes at the moment when "we kiss between the fire and the ocean." The transformation from "I" to "we" to "you" is mimetic of the progression from the poem as a theater of witnessing into a place of implication and camaraderie. It's generous, this gesture of inclusiveness, as if he's saying "My life is worth something and so is yours. Let's share it."

Once outside, I'm fumbling for the keys as the dogs lift their heads to see if I've brought them anything. Gary is holding a bag with our leftover sandwiches. Across the road, the river is quiet, reaching its mouth behind the jetty. In the poem, Hugo calls it the "half saltwater lake." There, "canoes turn gray / waiting for the runs." In this sight, there's hope, a poised eagerness to face the ocean and to harvest fish. The mix of native practices ("When kings run wild, girls use salmon oil / to stain a doll's face real") and non-Indian goings-on (" . . . whites drive off and the money's gone") conjure up the town as a haunted, isolated dialogue. Even "the wind, the sea / make all music language, dead as a wet drum."

For Gary and me, there's no place to stay overnight. Taholah is for the people who live there, not for us. It was enough to visit, to be enamored of the setting. We head off, my head leaning on Gary's arm, driving toward Moclips. We are hoping there will be a place for us there, though no poem awaits, no way to know the town ahead of time.

Notes

Setting Out

1 Donna Gerstenberger, video interview with author, July 15, 2003.

2 Ibid.

3 Susan Zwinger, "Remarks by Richard Hugo," *New Letters* 37, no 1 (1971): 11.

4 Dave Smith, "In the Company of a Fisherman," *Slackwater Review* 164, no. 2 (1978): 16.

5 Ibid., 17.

6 Ibid., 18.

7 Richard Howard, "Richard Hugo: Why Track Down Unity When the Diffuse Is So Exacting," *Alone with America: Essays on the Art of Poetry in the United States since 1950* (New York: Atheneum, 1969), 246.

8 Special Collections, University of Montana, Missoula, Montana.

9 Dave Smith, "Getting Right: Richard Hugo's *Selected Poems*," in *A Trout in the Milk: A Composite Portrait of Richard Hugo* (Lewiston, ID: Confluence Press, Lewis-Clark State College, 1982), 277.

10 Donna Gerstenberger, *Richard Hugo,* Western Writers Series (Boise: Boise State University, 1983), 19.

11 Robert Lowell, "Beyond the Alps," in *Life Studies* (New York: Farrar, Straus, and Cudahy, 1959), 14.

12 Michael S. Allen, "'Only the Eternal Nothing of Space': Richard Hugo's West," *Western American Literature* no. 15 (1980): 26.

13 Ibid., 27.

14 David Axelrod, *Troubled Intimacies: Life in the Interior West* (Corvallis: Oregon State University Press, 2004), 16.

15 Frederick Garber, "Fat Man at the Margin: The Poetry of Richard Hugo," *Iowa Review* 3, no. 4 (1972): 61.

16 See Zwinger, "Remarks by Richard Hugo," 16.

17 See Gerstenberger, *Richard Hugo*, 10.

18 Ibid.

19 Gerstenberger, video interview.

20 Annick Smith, video interview with author, December 9, 2004.

21 William Kittredge, video interview with author, December 10, 2004.

White Center, Riverside, and the Duwamish

1   Richard Hugo, *Real West Marginal Way: A Poet's Autobiography* (New York: W. W. Norton & Company, 1986), 164.
2   Ibid., 162.
3   Ibid., 2.
4   Ibid., 3.
5   Ibid., 3.
6   Ibid., 59.
7   See Gerstenberger, *Richard Hugo*, 24.
8   Ibid.
9   See Hugo, *Real West Marginal Way*, 17.
10 "Region 10 Cleanup Report," 2007, U.S. Environmental Protection Agency, Region 10.
11 Coll Thrush, *Native Seattle: Histories from the Crossing-Over Place* (Seattle: University of Washington Press, 2007), 28.
12 Ibid.
13 Ibid.
14 Ibid.
15 See Thrush, quoting Hugo, *Native Seattle*, 155.
16 Ibid., 155.
17 Ibid., 180.

Cataldo, Idaho

1   "The Coeur d'Alene's Old Mission State Park," *State of Idaho Parks and Recreation*, http://parksandrecreation.idaho.gov/parks/oldmission.aspx, accessed September 19, 2007.
2   "CleanupNews," U.S. Environmental Protection Agency report 2003, Office of Site Remediation, issue 14, http://www.epa.gov/Compliance/resources/newsletters/cleanup/cleanup14.pdf, accessed October 20, 2007.
3   Environmental Bulletin, East Mission Flats, June 2007, U.S. Environmental Protection Agency, Region 10.
4   Dennis Farney, "Toxic Tailings: Idaho's Silver Valley, Polluted by Mining, Sparks a Legal Fracas," *Wall Street Journal*, March 5, 1997, eastern edition.
5   Madeline DeFrees, video interview with author, March 12, 2003.

Wallace, Idaho

1   Patricia Nelson Limerick, et al., *Cleaning Up Abandoned Hardrock Mines in the West: Prospecting for a Better Future* (Boulder: Center of the American West, University of Colorado at Boulder, 2005).
2   Ibid., 2.
3   Gregg Olsen, *The Deep Dark: Disaster and Redemption in America's Richest Silver Mine*, (New York: Three Rivers Press, 2005), 3.
4   Ibid., 324.
5   Ibid., 393.
6   Patricia Hart and Ivar Nelson, *Mining Town: The Photographic Record of T. N. Barnard and Nellie Stockbridge from the Coeur d'Alenes*, (Seattle: University of Washington Press, 1984), 74, 90–94.
7   Erick Johnson, "The Evolution of Interstate 90 between Seattle and Missoula," Eastern Washington University, October 1995, Revised 2006, Accessed October 21,

2007. http://nwhighways.amhosting.net/
intersta.html.

8 "Historic Downtown Wallace, Idaho:
Silver Capital of the World," Chamber of
Commerce of Idaho, 4.

Dixon and St. Ignatius, Montana

1 Don Lee, "About James Welch: A
Profile," *Ploughshares* 20, no. 1 (1994).
http://www.pshares.org/issues/article.
cfm?prmarticleID=3676, accessed March
27, 2007.

2 William W. Bevis, *Ten Tough Trips:
Montana Writers and the West* (Seattle:
University of Washington Press, 1990),
152.

3 Jean Malbetch, video interview with
author, 2000. Thanks to fellow Boeing
worker Malbetch, Hugo later received a
better job at Boeing writing persuasive
technical documents to request more
funding from the federal government.

4 Thomas Gardner, "An Interview with
Richard Hugo," *Contemporary Literature*
22, no. 2 (1981): 143.

5 Michael S. Allen, " 'Only the Eternal
Nothing of Space': Richard Hugo's West,"
Western American Literature no. 15 (1980):
28.

6 See Bevis, *Ten Tough Trips*, 151.

7 Ibid., 151.

8 Ibid., 152.

Milltown, Montana

1 See Hugo, *Real West Marginal Way*, 137.

2 Ibid., 138.

3 Ibid., 138.

4 Ibid., 138.

5 "Removing the Dam at Milltown, Montana," Montana River Action, http://
montanariveraction.org/milltown.dam.
html, accessed February 2007–May
2008.

Walkerville, Montana

1 See Gardner, "Interview with Richard
Hugo," 143.

2 Ibid.

3 Fritz Wolff, informal correspondence
with Frances McCue, January 2008.

4 Roberta Carkeek Cheney, *Names on the
Face of Montana: The Story of Montana's
Place Names* (Missoula, MT: Mountain
Press Publishing Company, 1983), 42.

5 "Walkerville," Montana's Gold West
Country, http://goldwest.visitmt.com/
categories/city.asp?CityID=348&SiteID=1,
accessed August 2007.

6 George Everett, "Cool Water Hula by the
Berkeley Pit," 2002, http://www.
butteamerica.com/coolhula.htm,
accessed August 2007.

Philipsburg, Montana

1 William Kittredge, video interview with
author, December 10, 2004.

2 Madeline DeFrees, video interview with
author, March 12, 2003.

3 Ibid.

4 Adrienne Rich, "Caryatid: Rape, War and
Masculine Consciousness," *American
Poetry Review* 2, no. 3 (1973): 11.

5   Ernest Watson Burgess, Papers, Special
    Collections Research Center, University
    of Chicago Library, http://ead.lib.
    uchicago.edu/view-ead.qy?id=ICU.SPCL.
    BURGESS&q=&c=b&sub=&page=,
    accessed January–November 2007.
6   Ibid.
7   Annick Smith, e-mail message to author,
    April 19, 2008.
8   See Gardner, "An Interview with Richard
    Hugo," 2.
9   Ibid.
10 Annick Smith, e-mail message to author,
    APril 19, 2008.
11 See Gerstenberger, *Richard Hugo*, 10.
12 Michael S. Allen, "'Because Poems
    are People': An Interview with Richard
    Hugo," *Ohio Review* 19, no. 1 (Winter
    1978): 77.
13 Michael S. Allen, "'Only the Eternal
    Nothing of Space': Richard Hugo's West,"
    Western American Literature 15 (1980): 29.
14 Albert Blumenthal, *Small Town Stuff*
    (Chicago: University of Chicago, 1932),
    xi.
15 Ibid., 16.
16 See Zwinger, "Remarks by Richard
    Hugo," 13.

Silver Star, Montana

1   See Hugo, *Real West Marginal Way*, 245.

Pony, Montana

1   Norman D. Weiss, *Ghost Towns of the
    Northwest* (Caldwell, ID: Caxton Print-
    ers, 1971), 458.

Fairfield, Montana

1   Jonathan Holden, *The Landscapes of the
    Self: The Development of Richard Hugo's
    Poetry*, Milwood, NY: Associated Faculty
    Press, 1986, 168.
2   See http://www.cmrussell.org/meet.
3   See Allen, "Because Poems are People,"
    83.
4   Lois M. Welch, "Making Certain
    (Once Again) It Goes On," *Cutbank* 40,
    twentieth anniversary issue dedicated to
    Richard Hugo, 1993, 3.
5   David Quammen, *Wild Thoughts from
    Wild Places*. New York: Scribner, 1999,
    145.

La Push, Washington

1   "Interview with Richard Hugo," *New Salt
    Creek Reader* 6 (1974): 86.
2   See Gerstenberger, *Richard Hugo*, 17.
3   See Jonathan Holden, *Landscapes of the
    Self: The Development of Richard Hugo's
    Poetry* (Milwood, NY: Associated Faculty
    Press, 1986), 109.
4   Ibid., 111.
5   Ibid.
6   See Gardner, "Interview with Richard
    Hugo," 151.

Epilogue

1   See Gerstenberger, *Richard Hugo*, 20.
2   Ibid.
3   See "Interview with Richard Hugo," 95.
4   See Holden, *Landscapes of the Self*, 60.

Bibliography

Allen, Michael S. "'Because Poems Are People': An Interview with Richard Hugo." *Ohio Review* 19, no. 1 (Winter 1978): 74–90.

———. *In This We Are Called Human*. Richard Hugo papers and other materials. Special Collections, University of Washington Libraries, Seattle, Washington.

———. "'License for Defeat': Richard Hugo's Turning Point." *Contemporary Poetry* 3, no. 4 (Winter 1978): 59–74.

———. "'Only the Eternal Nothing of Space': Richard Hugo's West." *Western American Literature* 15 (1980): 25–35.

Ashborn, J. K. "A Conversation with Richard Hugo." *Madrona* 3, no. 8 (1974): 45–71.

Autobee, Robert. "The Sun River Project." U.S. Department of the Interior Bureau of Reclamation. http://www.usbr.gov/dataweb/html/sunriverh.html. Accessed May 5, 2007.

Axelrod, David. *Troubled Intimacies: Life in the Interior West*. Corvallis: Oregon State University Press, 2004.

Bevis, William W. *Ten Tough Trips: Montana Writers and the West*. Seattle: University of Washington Press, 1990.

Blodgett, E. D. "Richard F. Hugo: Poet of the Third Dimension." *Modern Poetry Studies* 1 (1970): 268–72.

Blumenthal, Albert. *Small-Town Stuff*. Chicago: University of Chicago Press, 1932.

Bly, Robert. "Notes on Prose vs. Poetry." *Choice* 2 (1962): 62–80.

Brothers, Beverly J. *Sketches of Walkerville: The High and the Mighty*. Butte, MT: Ashton Printing & Engraving Co., 1973.

Broughton, Irving. "An Interview with Richard Hugo." *Mill Mountain Review* 2, no. 2: 30–50.

Burgess, Ernest Watson. Papers. Special Collections Research Center, University of Chicago Library. http://ead.lib.uchicago.edu/view- ead.xqy?id=ICU.SPCL. BURGESS&q=&c=b&sub=&page=. Accessed November 3, 2006.

"A Century of Neglect: Idaho Government and Mining Pollution." *Transitions, in Search of Sustainable Forests and Diversified Economies in America's Northwest* 10, no. 1 (January-March 1997).

Chapman, Ray. *History of Idaho's Silver Valley 1878–2000*. Kellogg, ID: Chapman Publishing, 2000.

Cheney, Roberta Carkeek. *Names on the Face of Montana: The Story of Montana's Place Name*. Missoula, MT: Mountain Press Publishing Company, 1983.

"CleanupNews." U.S. Environmental Protection Agency report 2003. Office of Site Remediation. Issue 14. http://www.epa. gov/Compliance/resources/newsletters/ cleanup/cleanup14.pdf. Accessed May 6, 2007.

"The Coeur d'Alene's Old Mission State Park." State of Idaho Parks and Recreation. http://parksandrecreation.idaho. gov/parks/oldmission.aspx. Accessed September 19, 2007.

Curless, Erica F. "End of an Ugly Era." *Spokesman Review*, December 2, 2007.

D'Ambrosio, Charles. *Orphans*. Astoria, OR: Clear Cut Press, 2004.

Davis, Lloyd. "Semi-Tough: Richard Hugo's 'Degrees of Gray in Philipsburg.'" In *A Book of Rereadings*, edited by Greg Kuzma, 198–204. Crete, NE: Best Cellar Press, 1979.

DeFrees, Madeline. "In Madeline's Kitchen: Dick Talks about Writing." *Slackwater Review* (Autumn 1978): 34–59.

DeFrees, Madeline. Video interview with author, March 12, 2003.

Dillon, David. "Gains Made in Isolation: An Interview with Richard Hugo." *Southwest Review* 62 (1977): 101–15.

"Environmental Bulletin." East Mission Flats. June 2007. U.S. Environmental Protection Agency, Region 10.

Everett, George. "Cool Water Hula by the Berkeley Pit." 2002. http://www.butteamerica.com/coolhula.htm. Accessed August 2007.

Farney, Dennis. "Toxic Tailings: Idaho's Silver Valley, Polluted by Mining, Sparks a Legal Fracas." *Wall Street Journal*, March 5, 1997. Eastern edition.

Friedman, Sanford. "Torn Divinities." *Modern Poetry Studies* 4 (1973): 344–49.

Garber, Frederick. "Fat Man at the Margin: The Poetry of Richard Hugo." *Iowa Review* 3, no. 4 (1972): 58–69.

———. "Large Man in the Mountains: The Recent Work of Richard Hugo." *Western American Literature* 4 (1975): 205–18.

———. "On Richard Hugo and William Stafford." *American Poetry Review* 9, no. 1 (1980): 16–18.

Gardner, Thomas. "An Interview with Richard Hugo." *Contemporary Literature* 22, no. 2 (1981): 139–52.

Gerstenberger, Donna. *Richard Hugo*. Western Writers Series. Boise: Boise State University, 1983.

———. Video interview with author, July 15, 2003.

Haefele, Fred. "Superfund Savior?" *Montana Magazine* (September/October 2007): 48–53.

Hart, Patricia, and Ivar Nelson. *Mining Town: The Photographic Record of T. N. Barnard and Nellie Stockbridge from the Coeur d'Alenes*. Seattle: University of Washington Press, 1984.

Helms, Alan. "Writing Hurt: The Poetry of Richard Hugo." *Modern Poetry Studies* 9 (1978): 106–18.

Hickey, Dave. *Air Guitar: Essays on Art & Democracy*. Los Angeles: Art Issues Press, 1997.

Holden, Jonathan. "Instant Wordsworth." In *The Rhetoric of the Contemporary Lyric*, 112–36. Bloomington: Indiana University Press, 1980.

——. *Landscapes of the Self: The Development of Richard Hugo's Poetry*. Milwood, NY: Associated Faculty Press, 1986.

Howard, Joseph Kinsey. *Montana: High, Wide, and Handsome*. Lincoln: University of Nebraska Press, 1983.

Howard, Joseph Kinsey, ed. *Montana Margins: A State Anthology*. New Haven: Yale University Press, 1946.

Howard, Richard. *Alone with America: Essays on the Art of Poetry in the United States since 1950*, 232–46. New York: Antheneum, 1969.

Hugo, Richard. *31 Letters and 13 Dreams*. New York: W. W. Norton & Company, 1977.

——. *Death of the Kapowsin Tavern*. New York: Harcourt, Brace & World, 1965.

——. *Duwamish Head*. Port Townsend, WA: Copperhead Press, 1976.

——. *Good Luck in Cracked Italian*. New York: World Publishing Company, 1969.

——. *The Lady in Kicking Horse Reservoir*. New York: W. W. Norton & Company, 1973.

——. *Making Certain It Goes On*. New York: W. W. Norton & Company, 1984.

——. *Rain Five Days and I Love It*. Port Townsend, WA: Graywolf Press, 1975.

——. *The Real West Marginal Way: A Poet's Autobiography*. Edited by Ripley S. Hugo, Lois Welch, and James Welch. New York: W. W. Norton & Company, 1986.

——. *The Right Madness on Skye: Poems 1980*. New York: Norton, 1980.

——. *A Run of Jacks*. Minneapolis: University of Minnesota Press, 1961.

——. *Selected Poems*. New York: W. W. Norton & Company, 1980.

——. *The Triggering Town: Lectures and Essays on Poetry and Writing*. New York: W. W. Norton & Company; Reissue edition, 1992.

——. *What Thou Lovest Well, Remains American*. New York: W. W. Norton & Company, 1975.

——. *White Center*. New York: W. W. Norton & Company, 1980.

Hugo, Ripley, James Welch, and Lois Welch. Video interview with author, September 1, 2002.

"Interview with Richard Hugo." *New Salt Creek Reader* 6 (1974): 84–109.

Johnson, Erick. "The Evolution of Interstate 90 between Seattle and Missoula." Eastern Washington University. October 1995, revised 2006. http://nwhighways.amhosting.net/intersta.html. Accessed October 21, 2007.

Kittredge, William. Video interview with

author, December 10, 2004.

Lazer, Hank. "The Letter Poem." *Northwest Review* 19, no. 1–2 (1981): 235–45.

Lee, Don. "About James Welch: A Profile." *Ploughshares.* http://www.pshares.org/issues/article.cfm?prmarticleID=3676. Accessed March 27, 2007.

Limerick, Patricia. *Something in the Soil: Legacies and Reckonings in the New West.* New York: W. W. Norton & Company, 2000.

Limerick, Patricia Nelson, Joseph N. Ryan, Timothy R. Brown, and T. Allan Comp. *Cleaning Up Abandoned Hardrock Mines in the West: Prospecting for a Better Future.* Boulder: Center of the American West, University of Colorado at Boulder, 2005. http://www.centerwest.org. Accessed January 25, 2007.

Lindholt, Paul J. "Richard Hugo's Language: The Poem as 'Obsessive Musical Deed.'" *Contemporary Poetry* 16, no. 2 (Fall 1983): 67–75.

Lowell, Robert. *Life Studies.* New York: Farrar, Straus, and Cudahy, 1959.

Malbetch, Jean. Video interview with author, 2000.

McClure, Robert. "Pollutants Still Flow into River in Stormwater." *Seattle Post-Intelligencer,* November 26, 2007. http://seattlepi.nwsource.com/specials/duwamish/341212_duwamish-stormwater27.html. Accessed December 10, 2007.

———. "Will It Be Safe to Eat Fish from the Duwamish?" *Seattle Post-Intelligencer,* November 27, 2007. http://seattlepi.nwsource.com/specials/duwamish/341220_duwamsih27.html. Accessed December 10, 2007.

"Meet C. M. Russell." C. M Russell Museum. 2006. http://www.cmrussell.org/meet. Accessed April 24, 2007.

Mitchell, John. Video interview with author, Summer 2002.

"Montana's Gold West Country." http://goldwest.visitmt.com/communities/walkerville.htm. Accessed August 2007.

Mooney, James. *Coeur d'Alene Indians.* Vol. 4 of *The Catholic Encyclopedia.* New York: Robert Appleton Company, 1908. http://www.newadvent.org/cathen/04093a.htm. Accessed January 25, 2007.

Nielsen, Peter, and Bruce Farling. "Mining Catastrophe in Clark Fork." *Clementine, the Journal of Responsible Mineral Development* (Autumn 1991): 10–14. Tailings issue.

"The Obsessive Ear: Remarks on the Craft of Poetry." *New Collage* 1, no. 3 (1971).

Olsen, Gregg. *The Deep Dark: Disaster and Redemption in America's Richest Silver Mine.* New York: Three Rivers Press, 2005.

The Pony Homecoming Club and David Zimmerman. *Pony, Montana: A Golden Past, Still a Treasure.* Pony, MT: The Pony Homecoming Club, 2004.

Quammen, David. *Wild Thoughts from Wild Places.* New York: Scribner, 1999.

"Region 10 Cleanup Report." 2007. U. S. Environmental Protection Agency, Region 10.

"Removing the Dam at Milltown, Montana." Montana River Action. http://montanariveraction.org/milltown.dam.html. Accessed February 2007-May 2008.

Rich, Adrienne. "Caryatid: Rape, War and Masculine Consciousness." *American Poetry Review* 2, no. 3 (1973): 11.

Richard Hugo Papers. Acc. 3655. Special Collections, University of Washington Libraries, Seattle, Washington.

Smith, Annick. E-mail message to author, April 19, 2008.

———. Video interview with author, December 9, 2004.

Smith, Dave. "Getting Right: Richard Hugo's *Selected Poems*." In *A Trout in the Milk: A Composite Portrait of Richard Hugo*, 275–90. Lewiston, ID: Confluence Press, Lewis-Clark State College, 1982.

———. "In the Company of a Fisherman." *The Slackwater Review* 164, no. 2 (1978): 16.

Special Collections, University of Montana, Missoula, Montana.

"'The Third Time the World Happens': A Dialogue between William Stafford and Richard Hugo." *Northwest Review* 13, no. 3 (1973): 26–47.

Thrush, Coll. *Native Seattle: Histories from the Crossing-Over Place*. Seattle: University of Washington Press, 2007.

Weiss, Norman D. *Ghost Towns of the Northwest*. Caldwell, ID: Caxton Printers, 1971.

Welch, Lois M. "Making Certain (Once Again) It Goes On." *Cutbank 40—Twentieth Anniversary Issue Dedicated to Richard Hugo* (Spring 1993).

Williams, Norm. "Richard Hugo and the Poetics of Failure." *Yale Literary Magazine* 146: 4–5.

Wolff, Fritz. *A Room for the Summer: Adventure, Misadventure, and Seduction in the Mines of the Coeur d'Alene*. Norman: University of Oklahoma Press, 2004.

——— "Industrial Espionage 1890s Style: Undercover Agents in the Coeur d'Alene Mining District." *Mining History Journal* 9 (2002): 42–53.

——— Informal correspondence with author, January 2008.

Wright, James. "Explorations, Astonishments." *Fresco* 1 (1961): 153–54.

——— "Hugo: Secrets of the Inner Landscape." *American Poetry Review* 2, no. 3 (1973): 13.

Wyckoff, William. *On the Road Again: Montana's Changing Landscape*. Seattle: University of Washington Press, 2006.

Zwinger, Susan. "Remarks by Richard Hugo." *New Letters* 37, no. 1 (1971): 10–16.

Pamphlets/Guides

Dam News. Clark Fork River Technical Assistance Committee, 2007.

Greater Ruby Valley. Chamber of Commerce and Agriculture.

Historic Downtown Wallace, Idaho: Silver Capital of the World. Chamber of Commerce of Idaho.

Obersinner, Rev. Joseph L., S. J., and Judy
    Gritzmacher. *St. Ignatius Mission:*
    National Historic Site. Missoula, MT:
    Gateway Printing & Litho, 1977.
Wallace, Idaho: Silver Capital of the World.
    Historic Wallace Chamber of Commerce,
    2006.

Index

Highway 200, 89, 96, 115

Hill, Bobbi, 105

Hogan, Esther Monk, 13

Hogan, Richard Franklin, 13

Hoh River, 216

Holden, Jonathan, 195, 217, 227

Hole in the Sky (Kittredge), 161

Hoover, J. Edgar, 68

Hoquiam, Washington, 215

Hot Springs, Montana, 84, 93

Howard, Richard, 11

Hugo, Barbara (Williams), 9, 116, 118, 216, 219,
225, 227

Hugo, Richard: Aunt Sarah and Uncle Carleton of, 35; and baseball, 12; biography
of, 20; as bombardier, 116, 133; Buick of,
9, 15, 54, 68, 78, 89, 146, 168; career of,
3; death of, 20; grandparents of, 11–13,
21, 33–34, 36–37, 117, 119, 152, 155; and
leukemia, 186; mother of, 12–13, 117, 144,
155; stepchildren of, 203

Hugo, Ripley Schemm, 54, 201, 203, 213

Hull House, 141

Humptulips, 225

Hurricane Katrina, 40

I

Ida, 17, 33, 43, 45, 46

Idaho Panhandle, 55

Indian Lawyer (Welch), 95

Interstate 90, 53, 66, 75–77, 113, 127

Interstate 91, 119

Isle of Skye, 48, 212–14, 218

Italy, 3, 21, 48, 133, 167, 218

J

James, Clayton, 6

Jarvis, Gene, 110

Jefferson River, 172, 174, 178

Jesuits, 53, 54, 101–4, 172, 174, 178

Jocko River, 84

Justice, Donald, 8

K

Kalaloch, Washington, 216

Kalispel, 103

Kapowsin, Lake, 9

Kapowsin, Washington, 16

Kellogg, Idaho, 52, 60, 66, 74, 81

Kellogg Island, 44, 45

Kicking the Loose Gravel Home, 158

Kiefer, Anselm, 147

Killing Custer (Welch), 95

Kingston, Washington, 214

Kinkade, Thomas, 202

Kittredge, William (Bill), 21, 154, 161, 164–66,
169, 172, 178–80

Kizer, Carolyn, 15

Kootenay tribe, 96, 103

Kuralt, Charles, 76

L

La Push, 4, 9, 209, 216–19

"La Push," 20, 210, 216–19

The Lady in Kicking Horse Reservoir, 93, 118,
214

Lake Crescent, 215

Lake Kapowsin, 9

Lake Meridian, 35

Lake Ozette, 215